W9-CFC-680

SECOND EDITION

Introducing Elixir
Getting Started in Functional Programming

Simon St.Laurent and J. David Eisenberg

Beijing · Boston · Farnham · Sebastopol · Tokyo

Introducing Elixir

by Simon St.Laurent and J. David Eisenberg

Copyright © 2017 Simon St.Laurent and J. David Eisenberg. All rights reserved.

Printed in the United States of America.

Published by O'Reilly Media, Inc., 1005 Gravenstein Highway North, Sebastopol, CA 95472.

O'Reilly books may be purchased for educational, business, or sales promotional use. Online editions are also available for most titles (*http://oreilly.com/safari*). For more information, contact our corporate/institutional sales department: 800-998-9938 or *corporate@oreilly.com*.

Editors: Heather Scherer and Susan Conant
Production Editor: Kristen Brown
Copyeditor: Rachel Head
Proofreader: Amanda Kersey

Indexer: Judy McConville
Interior Designer: David Futato
Cover Designer: Karen Montgomery
Illustrator: Rebecca Demarest

September 2014:   First Edition
January 2017:   Second Edition

Revision History for the Second Edition
2016-12-22:   First Release

See *http://oreilly.com/catalog/errata.csp?isbn=9781491956779* for release details.

The O'Reilly logo is a registered trademark of O'Reilly Media, Inc. *Introducing Elixir*, the cover image, and related trade dress are trademarks of O'Reilly Media, Inc.

While the publisher and the authors have used good faith efforts to ensure that the information and instructions contained in this work are accurate, the publisher and the authors disclaim all responsibility for errors or omissions, including without limitation responsibility for damages resulting from the use of or reliance on this work. Use of the information and instructions contained in this work is at your own risk. If any code samples or other technology this work contains or describes is subject to open source licenses or the intellectual property rights of others, it is your responsibility to ensure that your use thereof complies with such licenses and/or rights.

978-1-491-95677-9

[LSI]

JAN 1 9 2017

Table of Contents

Preface

Elixir offers developers the functional power and concurrent resilience of Erlang, with friendlier syntax, libraries, and metaprogramming. Elixir compiles to Erlang byte code, and you can mix and match it with Erlang and Erlang tools. Despite a shared foundation, however, Elixir feels very different: perhaps more similar to Ruby than to Erlang's ancestor Prolog.

Introducing Elixir will give you a gentle guide to this powerful language.

 This release of *Introducing Elixir* covers version 1.3. We will update it as the language evolves. If you find mistakes or things that have broken, please let us know through the errata system (*http://bit.ly/elixir-2e-errata*).

Who This Book Is For

This book is mostly for people who've been programming in other languages but want to look around. Maybe you're being very practical, and a distributed model, with its resulting scale and resilience advantages, appeals to you. Maybe you want to see what this "functional programming" stuff is all about. Or maybe you're just going for a hike, taking your mind to a new place.

We suspect that functional programming is more approachable before you've learned to program in other paradigms. However, getting started in Elixir—sometimes even just installing it—requires a fair amount of computing skill. If you're a complete newcomer to programming, welcome, but there will be a few challenges along the way.

Who This Book Is Not For

This book is not for people in a hurry to get things done.

If you already know Elixir, you don't likely need this book unless you're looking for a slow brush-up.

If you already know Erlang, this book will give you an opportunity to see how things are different, but odds are good that you understand the key structures.

If you're already familiar with functional languages, you may find the pacing of this gentle introduction hopelessly slow. Definitely feel welcome to jump to another book or online documentation that moves faster if you get bored.

What This Book Will Do For You

You'll learn to write simple Elixir programs. You'll understand why Elixir makes it easier to build resilient programs that can scale up and down with ease. You'll be able to read other Elixir resources that assume a fair amount of experience and make sense of them.

In more theoretical terms, you'll get to know functional programming. You'll learn how to design programs around message passing and recursion, creating process-oriented programs focused more on data flow.

Most importantly, the gates to concurrent application development will be opened. Though this introduction only gets you started using the incredible powers of the Open Telecom Platform (OTP), that foundation can take you to amazing places. Once you've mastered the syntax and learned about Elixir's expectations for structuring programs, your next steps should be creating reliable and scalable applications—with much less effort than you would have needed with other approaches!

How This Book Works

This book tries to tell a story with Elixir. You'll probably get the most out of it if you read it in order at least the first time, though you're always welcome to come back to find whatever bits and pieces you need.

You'll start by getting Elixir installed and running, and looking around its shell, IEx. You'll spend a lot of time in that shell, so get cozy. Next, you'll start loading code into the shell to make it easier to write programs, and you'll learn how to call that code and mix it up.

You'll take a close look at numbers, because they're an easy place to get familiar with Elixir's basic structures. Then you'll learn about atoms, pattern matching, and guards

—the likely foundations of your program structure. After that you'll learn about strings, lists, and the recursion at the heart of much Elixir processing. Once you've gone a few thousand recursions down and back, it'll be time to look at processes, a key part of Elixir that relies on the message-passing model to support concurrency and resilience.

Once you have the foundation set, you can take a closer look at debugging and data storage, and then have a quick look at a toolset that is likely at the heart of your long-term development with Elixir: Erlang's Open Telecom Platform, which is about much much more than telephones.

Finally, you'll learn about Elixir's macro tools, features that give Elixir tremendous flexibility by letting you extend the language.

Some people want to learn programming languages through a dictionary, smashing together a list of operators, control structures, and datatypes. Those lists are here, but they're in Appendix A, not the main flow of the book.

The main point you should get from this book is that you can program in Elixir. If you don't get that, let us know!

Other Resources

This book may not be the best way for you to learn Elixir. It all depends on what you want to learn and why. If you're looking for a faster-flying introduction to the language, *Programming Elixir* (Pragmatic Publishers) jumps in more quickly and emphasizes Elixir's uniqueness more frequently. *Elixir in Action* (Manning) and *The Little Elixir & OTP Guidebook* (Manning) are similarly faster and deeper. *Metaprogramming Elixir* (Pragmatic Publishers) explores a key corner, and *Programming Phoenix* (Pragmatic Publishers) dives into a powerful Elixir-based framework.

If you like the pace of this book and want to try out your new knowledge, you might like *Études for Elixir* (O'Reilly). That book provides descriptions of short programs that you can write in Elixir, and they may ask you to stretch a bit beyond the examples you find here. It is also designed so that its chapters are in parallel with this book's chapters.

The other books in the field all cover Erlang, not Elixir. Hopefully there will be more Elixir-specific work soon. The main Elixir website (*http://www.elixir-lang.org/*) includes a lot of tutorials, documentation, and links to other resources.

If your primary interest in learning Elixir is to break out of a programming rut, you should check out Bruce Tate's wild tour of *Seven Languages in Seven Weeks* (Pragmatic Publishers), which explores Ruby, Io, Prolog, Scala, Erlang, Clojure, and Haskell. Erlang gets only (an excellent) 37 pages, but that might be what you want.

Erlang books can also help you understand what makes Elixir work so well.

For a simple introduction to Erlang that largely parallels this book, *Introducing Erlang* (O'Reilly) will get you started with Erlang and functional programming.

For an online experience (now also in print from No Starch Books) with more snark and funnier illustrations, you should explore *Learn You Some Erlang for Great Good!* (*http://learnyousomeerlang.com/*)

The two classic general books on Erlang are the similarly titled *Programming Erlang* (Pragmatic Publishers) and *Erlang Programming* (O'Reilly). They cover a lot of similar and overlapping terrain, and both may be good places to start if this book moves too slowly or you need more reference material. *Erlang Programming* goes further into what you can do with Erlang, whereas *Programming Erlang* provides a lot of detail on setting up an Erlang programming environment.

On the more advanced side, *Erlang and OTP in Action* (Manning) opens with a high-speed 72-page introduction to Erlang and then spends most of its time applying the Open Telecom Platform, Erlang's framework for building upgradeable and maintainable concurrent applications. *Designing for Scalability with Erlang/OTP* (O'Reilly) explores how OTP and Erlang make things that seem hugely difficult in other environments a normal day's work in Erlang.

You'll also want to visit the main Erlang website (*http://www.erlang.org/*) for updates, downloads, documentation, and more.

Elixir Will Change You

Before you go deeper, you should know that working in Elixir may irrevocably change the way you look at programs. Its combination of functional code, process orientation, and distributed development may seem alien at first. However, once it sinks in, Elixir can transform the way you solve problems (perhaps even beyond the way Erlang does) and potentially make it difficult to return to other languages, environments, and programming cultures.

Conventions Used in This Book

The following typographical conventions are used in this book:

Italic
: Indicates new terms, URLs, email addresses, filenames, and file extensions.

Constant width
: Used for program listings, as well as within paragraphs to refer to program elements such as variable or function names, statements, and keywords.

Constant width bold
> Shows commands or other text that should be typed literally by the user.

Constant width italic
> Shows text that should be replaced with user-supplied values or by values determined by context.

 This icon signifies a tip, suggestion, or general note.

 This icon indicates a warning or caution.

Using Code Examples

The examples in this book are meant to teach basic concepts in small bites, making it easy to see what changed from one example to another. While you may certainly borrow code and reuse it as you see fit, you won't be able to take the code of this book and build a stupendous application instantly (unless perhaps you have an unusual fondness for calculating the speeds of falling objects). You should, however, be able to figure out the steps you need to take to build a great application.

You can download the code from GitHub (*https://github.com/simonstl/introducing-elixir*). (It will also be available from the Examples link on the book's catalog page (*http://bit.ly/introducing_elixir_2e*).)

This book is here to help you get your job done. In general, you may use the code in this book in your programs and documentation. You do not need to contact us for permission unless you are reproducing a significant portion of the code. For example, writing a program that uses several chunks of code from this book does not require permission. Selling or distributing a CD-ROM of examples from O'Reilly books does require permission. Answering a question by citing this book and quoting example code does not require permission. Incorporating a significant amount of example code from this book into your product's documentation does require permission.

We appreciate, but do not require, attribution. An attribution usually includes the title, author, publisher, and ISBN. For example: "*Introducing Elixir*, Second Edition, by Simon St.Laurent and J. David Eisenberg (O'Reilly). Copyright 2017 Simon St.Laurent and J. David Eisenberg, 978-1-491-95677-9."

If you feel your use of code examples falls outside fair use or the permission given above, feel free to contact us at *permissions@oreilly.com*.

Help This Book Grow

While we hope that you will enjoy reading this book and learn from it, we also hope that you can contribute to helping other readers learn Elixir here. You can help your fellow readers in a number of ways:

- If you find specific technical problems, bad explanations, or things that can be improved, please report them through the errata system (*http://bit.ly/elixir-2e-errata*).

- If you like (or don't like) the book, please leave reviews. The most visible places to do so are on Amazon.com (or its international sites) and at the O'Reilly page for the book (*http://bit.ly/introducing_elixir_2e*). Detailed explanations of what worked and what didn't work for you (and the broader target audience of programmers new to Erlang) are helpful to other readers and to me.

- If you find you have much more you want to say about Elixir, please consider sharing it, whether on the web, in a book of your own, in training classes, or in whatever form you find easiest.

We'll update the book for errata and try to address issues raised in reviews. Even once the book is "complete," we may still add some extra pieces to it. If you purchased it as an ebook, you'll receive these updates for free, at least up to the point where it's time for a whole new edition. We don't expect that new edition declaration to come quickly, however, unless the Elixir world changes substantially.

Hopefully this book will engage you enough to make you consider sharing.

Please Use It For Good

We'll let you determine what "good" means, but think about it. Please try to use Elixir's power for projects that make the world a better place, or at least not a worse place.

O'Reilly Safari

 *Safari* (formerly Safari Books Online) is a membership-based training and reference platform for enterprise, government, educators, and individuals.

Members have access to thousands of books, training videos, Learning Paths, interactive tutorials, and curated playlists from over 250 publishers, including O'Reilly

Media, Harvard Business Review, Prentice Hall Professional, Addison-Wesley Professional, Microsoft Press, Sams, Que, Peachpit Press, Adobe, Focal Press, Cisco Press, John Wiley & Sons, Syngress, Morgan Kaufmann, IBM Redbooks, Packt, Adobe Press, FT Press, Apress, Manning, New Riders, McGraw-Hill, Jones & Bartlett, and Course Technology, among others.

For more information, please visit *http://oreilly.com/safari*.

How to Contact Us

Please address comments and questions concerning this book to the publisher:

> O'Reilly Media, Inc.
> 1005 Gravenstein Highway North
> Sebastopol, CA 95472
> 800-998-9938 (in the United States or Canada)
> 707-829-0515 (international or local)
> 707-829-0104 (fax)

We have a web page for this book, where we list errata, examples, and any additional information. You can access this page at *http://bit.ly/introducing_elixir_2e*.

To comment or ask technical questions about this book, send email to *bookquestions@oreilly.com*.

For more information about our books, courses, conferences, and news, see our website at *http://www.oreilly.com*.

Find us on Facebook: *http://facebook.com/oreilly*

Follow us on Twitter: *http://twitter.com/oreillymedia*

Watch us on YouTube: *http://www.youtube.com/oreillymedia*

Acknowledgments

The Elixir community is amazing, open to questions and suggestions from a wide range of perspectives. We've been lucky to be able to ask questions and get them answered, and have enjoyed a rare community that treats "difficult to explain" as a problem worth fixing in code.

José Valim's leadership and explanations have helped us throughout the project. Our competitor Dave Thomas confirmed that yes, Elixir is here and the world is waiting for it. From the Erlang side, Francesco Cesarini encouraged us to pursue this new language sibling. Reviewers Andrea Leopardi, Matt Mills, Bibek Pandey, Alexei

Sholik, David Lorenzetti, Bengt Kleberg, Mistral Contrastin, Augie De Blieck Jr., Arie van Wingerden, Elias Carrillo, and Nicholas helped us find the errors of our ways.

Meghan Blanchette kept the first edition on track, and Maureen Spencer and Heather Scherer kept us honest on the second.

Also, J. David Eisenberg's commitment to the project saved Simon St.Laurent repeatedly!

Thanks also to Simon, who made David's first experience as a coauthor a pleasant one.

## CHAPTER 1

Getting Comfortable

The easiest place to start learning Elixir is in Interactive Elixir, IEx. This command-line interface is a cozy place to get started and a good place to start figuring out what works and what doesn't work in Elixir. Its features will spare you headaches later, so settle in!

Installation

Because Elixir runs on top of Erlang, you'll need to install Erlang on your system first, and then install Elixir.

Installing Erlang

If you're on Windows, installing Erlang (*http://www.erlang.org/download.html*) is easy. Download the Windows binary file, run the installer, and you're set. If you are a brave beginner tackling your first programming language, this is easily your best bet.

On Linux or macOS, you may be able to download the source file and compile it. On macOS you should be able to unzip and untar it and then, from the directory created by the untarring, run `./configure`, `make`, and `sudo make install`. However, that simple sequence works only if you have the right files installed, and it can give you mysterious errors if they aren't. In particular, Apple's shift to the LLVM compiler in newer versions of XCode instead of GCC makes it less likely that GCC will be on newer macOS systems, and Erlang needs GCC.

You can ignore the error about FOP, which Erlang uses to generate PDF documentation you can download elsewhere. Also, on newer Macs, you'll get an error at the end that wxWidgets doesn't work on 64-bit macOS. For now, ignore this too.

If the compilation approach doesn't work or isn't for you, Erlang Solutions (*http://bit.ly/2gPCe6H*) offers a number of installs. Also, many different package managers (Debian, Ubuntu, MacPorts, Homebrew, and so on) include Erlang. It may not be the very latest version, but having Erlang running is much better than not having Erlang running. They do tend to make it run on the latest version of various operating systems, so if you have installation problems, look closely at their requirements.

 Erlang is increasingly part of the default installation on many systems, including Ubuntu, largely thanks to the spread of CouchDB.

Installing Elixir

Once you have Erlang installed, you should be able to download a precompiled version of Elixir (*http://bit.ly/1lbMOnw*) or the GitHub source (*http://bit.ly/elixir-lang*). Some package managers are starting to support Elixir, including Homebrew. The code in this book should work with Elixir 1.3.0.

Then you need to set your path so that it can find *elixir/bin*.

Elixir's instructions for setup are organized into a tutorial (*http://bit.ly/elixir-install*).

Firing It Up

Go to the command line (or shell, or terminal) and type **mix new first_app**. This will invoke Elixir's Mix tool (*http://bit.ly/2gKi01D*), which "provides tasks for creating, compiling, and testing Elixir projects, managing its dependencies, and more." In this case, the command you type creates a new, empty project in a directory named *first_app*:

```
$ mix new first_app
* creating README.md
* creating .gitignore
* creating mix.exs
* creating config
* creating config/config.exs
* creating lib
* creating lib/first_app.ex
* creating test
* creating test/test_helper.exs
* creating test/first_app_test.exs

Your Mix project was created successfully.
You can use "mix" to compile it, test it, and more:

    cd first_app
```

```
    mix test

Run "mix help" for more commands.

$
```

 Make sure that the directory containing the Elixir executable is in your $PATH variable so that Mix can find it.

Rather than compiling and testing the empty project, go into the *first_app* directory and start the IEx shell with these commands:

```
$ cd first_app
$ iex -S mix
```

You'll see something like the following code sample, likely with a cursor next to the iex(1)> prompt. Note that where necessary in the book, some of the longer lines have been reformatted to fit on the page:

```
$ cd first_app
[david@localhost first_app]$ iex -S mix
Erlang/OTP 19 [erts-8.0] [source] [64-bit] [smp:4:4] [async-threads:10] [hipe]
   [kernel-poll:false]

Compiling 1 file (.ex)
Generated first_app app
Interactive Elixir (1.3.1) - press Ctrl+C to exit (type h() ENTER for help)
iex(1)>
```

You're in Elixir! (The first line about Erlang reflects that Elixir runs within Erlang. Don't worry about that part!)

First Steps

Before moving on to the excitement of programming Elixir, it's always worth noting how to quit. The shell suggests Ctrl+C, which will bring you to a menu. If you press "a" in that menu, IEx will stop, and you'll see whatever prompt you had before starting IEx:

```
iex(1)>
BREAK: (a)bort (c)ontinue (p)roc info (i)nfo (l)oaded
       (v)ersion (k)ill (D)b-tables (d)istribution
a
$
```

You can also ask iex (once you start it up again) for help, by entering h() or just h:

```
iex(1)> h()
# IEx.Helpers
```

                              IEx.Helpers

```
Welcome to Interactive Elixir. You are currently seeing the documentation for
the module IEx.Helpers which provides many helpers to make Elixir's shell more
joyful to work with.

This message was triggered by invoking the helper h(), usually referred to as
h/0 (since it expects 0 arguments).

You can use the h function to invoke the documentation for any Elixir module or
function:

  h Enum
  h Enum.map
  h Enum.reverse/1

You can also use the i function to introspect any value you have in the shell:

  i "hello"

There are many other helpers available:
...
:ok
```

So what have you done here? You've issued an iex command, calling a helper function, h(), that provides you with some basic help information. It printed a lot of information to the screen and then ended, returning :ok.

Moving Through Text and History

If you explore the shell, you'll find that many things work the way they do in other shells, or in Emacs. The left and right arrow keys move you backward and forward through the line you're editing. Some of the key bindings echo those of the Emacs text editor. Ctrl+A will take you to the beginning of a line, while Ctrl+E will take you back to the end of the line. If you get two characters in the wrong sequence, pressing Ctrl+T will transpose them.

Also, as you type a closing parenthesis, square bracket, or curly brace, the cursor will highlight the corresponding opening parenthesis, square bracket, or curly brace.

The up and down arrow keys run through the command history, making it easy to reissue commands. You can reference a given result value with $v(N)$, where N is the line number.

Moving Through Files

IEx does understand filesystems to some extent, because you may need to move through them to reach the files that will become part of your program. The commands have the same names as Unix commands but are expressed as functions. IEx starts wherever you opened the shell, and you can figure out where that is with pwd():

```
iex(1)> pwd()
/Users/elixir/code/first_app
:ok
```

To change directories, use the cd() function, but you'll need to wrap the argument in double quotes:

```
iex(2)> cd ".."
/Users/elixir/code
:ok
iex(3)> cd "first_app"
/Users/elixir/code/first_app
:ok
```

You can look around with the ls() command, which will list files in the current directory if you give it no arguments, and list files in the specified directory if you give it an argument.

Doing Something

One of the easiest ways to get started playing with Elixir is to use the shell as a calculator. Unlike with your typical command line, you can enter mathematical expressions and get useful results:

```
iex(1)> 2 + 2
4
iex(2)> 27 - 14
13
iex(3)> 35 * 42023943
1470838005
iex(4)> 4 * (3 + 5)
32
iex(5)> 200 / 15
13.333333333333334
```

The first three operators are addition (+), subtraction (-), and multiplication (*), which work the same way whether you're working with integer values or floating points. Parentheses let you modify the order in which operators are processed, as shown on line 4. (The normal order of operations is listed in Appendix A.) The fourth operator, /, supports division where you expect a floating-point result (a number with a decimal part), as shown on line 5. You don't have to put spaces around operators, but it can make your code more readable.

Calling Functions

Functions are bits of logic that accept arguments and return a value. Mathematical functions are an easy place to start. For example, if you want an integer result (and have integer arguments), use the div() function instead of the / operator, with rem() to get the remainder, as shown on lines 6 and 7:

```
iex(6)> div(200,15)
13
iex(7)> rem(200, 15)
5
iex(8)> rem 200, 15
5
```

Line 8 demonstrates a feature of Elixir syntax: parentheses around the arguments to a function are optional. If you think they make your code clearer, use them. If you think they are just extra typing, don't.

Elixir will interpret a space after the function name as the equivalent of the opening of a set of parentheses, with the parentheses assumed to close at the end of the line. When this produces unexpected results, Elixir may ask in an error message that you "do not insert spaces in between the function name and the opening parentheses."

Elixir will accept integers in place of floats, but floats are not always welcome where integers are used. If you need to convert a floating-point number to an integer, you can use the round() built-in function:

```
iex(9)> round 200/15
13
```

The round() function drops the decimal part of the number. If the decimal part was greater than or equal to .5, it increases the integer part by 1, rounding up. If you'd rather just drop the decimal part completely to get the integer part, use the trunc() function.

You can also refer to a previous result by its line number using v(). For example:

```
iex(10)> 4*v(9)
52
```

The result on line 9 was 13, and 4*13 is 52.

If you're feeling adventurous, you can use negative numbers to reference prior results. v(-1) is the previous result, v(-2) is the result before that, and so on.

If you want to do more powerful calculations, Elixir lets you use Erlang's math module, which offers pretty much the classic set of functions supported by a scientific calculator. These functions return floating-point values. The constant pi is available as a function, :math.pi(). Trigonometric, logarithmic, exponential, square root, and (except on Windows) even the Gauss error functions are readily available. (The trigonometric functions take their arguments in radians, not degrees, so be ready to convert if necessary.) Using these functions is a little verbose because of the need to prefix them with :math., but it's still reasonably sane.

For example, to get the sine of zero radians, you could write:

```
iex(11)> :math.sin(0)
0.0
```

Note that the result is 0.0, not just 0, indicating that the number is floating point. (And yes, you could have written :math.sin 0 without the parentheses.)

To calculate the cosine of pi and 2pi radians, you'd write:

```
iex(12)> :math.cos(:math.pi())
-1.0
iex(13)> :math.cos(2 * :math.pi())
1.0
```

To calculate 2 taken to the 16th power, you'd use:

```
iex(14)> :math.pow(2,16)
65536.0
```

The full set of mathematical functions supported by Erlang's math module and accessible through Elixir is listed in Appendix A.

Numbers in Elixir

Elixir recognizes two kinds of numbers: integers and floating-point numbers (often called floats). It's easy to think of integers as "whole numbers," with no decimal point, and floats as "decimal numbers," with a decimal point and some value to the right of the decimal. 1 is an integer, while 1.0 is a floating-point number.

However, it's a little trickier than that. Elixir stores integers and floats in a very different way. Elixir lets you store massive integers, but whether they're big or small, they are always precise. You don't need to worry about their values being off by just a little.

Floats, on the other hand, cover a wide range of numbers but with limited precision. Elixir uses the 64-bit IEEE 754-1985 "double precision" representation. This means that it keeps track of about 15 decimal digits, plus an exponent. It can also represent some large numbers—powers up to positive or negative 308 are available—but because it tracks only a limited number of digits, results will vary a little more than may seem convenient, especially when you want to do comparisons:

```
iex(1)> 3487598347598347598437583475893475843749245.0
3.4875983475983474e42
iex(2)> 2343243.3454358938502345433339545
2343243.3454358936
iex(3)> 0.000000000000000000000000000000002343243243243223423232324
2.3432432432432235e-30
```

As you can see, some digits get left behind, and the overall magnitude of the number is represented with an exponent.

When you enter floating-point numbers, you must always also have at least one number to the left of the decimal point, even if it's zero. Otherwise, Elixir reports a syntax error—it doesn't understand what you're doing:

```
iex(4)> .000000000000000000000000000000002343243243243223423232324
** (SyntaxError) iex:4: syntax error before: '.'
```

You can also write floats using the digits-plus-exponent notation:

```
iex(4)> 2.923e127
2.923e127
iex(5)> 7.6345435e-231
7.6345435e-231
```

Floats' lack of precision can cause anomalous results. For example, the sine of zero is zero, and the sine of pi is also zero. However, if you calculate this in Elixir, you won't quite get to zero with the float approximation Elixir provides for pi:

```
iex(6)> :math.sin(0)
0.0
iex(7)> :math.sin(:math.pi())
1.2246467991473532e-16
```

If Elixir's representation of pi went further, and its calculations of pi went further, the result for line 7 would be closer to zero.

If you need to keep track of money, integers are going to be a better bet. Use the smallest available unit—cents for US dollars, for instance—and remember that those cents are 1/100 of a dollar. (Financial transactions can go to much smaller fractions, but you'll still want to represent them as integers with a known multiplier.) For more complex calculations, though, you'll want to use floats, and just be aware that results will be imprecise.

Elixir supports integers in a few bases other than 10. For example, if you wanted to specify the binary value of 1010111, you could write:

```
iex(8)> 0b01010111
87
```

Elixir reports back with the base-10 value of the number. Similarly, you can specify hexadecimal (base-16) numbers by using x instead of b:

```
iex(9)> 0xcafe
51966
```

To make any of these numbers negative, just put a minus sign (-) in front of them. This works with integers, numbers in hex or binary, and floats:

```
iex(10)> -1234
-1234
iex(11)> -0xcafe
-51966
iex(12)> -2.045234324e6
-2045234.324
```

Working with Variables in the Shell

The v() function lets you refer to the results of previous expressions, but it's not exactly convenient to keep track of result numbers, and the v() function works only in the shell. It isn't a general-purpose mechanism. A more reasonable solution stores values with textual names, creating variables.

Elixir variable names begin with a lowercase letter or an underscore. Normal variables start with a lowercase letter, whereas "don't care" variables start with an underscore (see "Underscoring That You Don't Care" on page 33). For now, stick with normal variables. You assign a value to a variable using a syntax that should be familiar from algebra or other programming languages, here with n as the variable:

```
iex(1)> n=1
1
```

To see the value of a variable, just type its name:

```
iex(2)> n
1
```

Elixir, unlike many other functional programming languages (including Erlang), will let you assign n a new value:

```
iex(3)> n=2
2
iex(4)> n=n+1
3
```

Elixir makes the righthand side of an expression, after the =, match the lefthand side. It will assign a new value to n if you ask it to do so, and will even use the old value of n on the righthand side to calculate a new value for n. n=n+1 means "assign the value n+1, which is 3, to n."

When you assign a value to a variable, you should make sure that all the calculations are on the right side of the equals sign. Even though we know that m should be 6 when 2*m = 3*4, Elixir doesn't:

```
iex(5)> 2*m=3*4
** (CompileError) iex:12: illegal pattern
```

IEx will remember your variables until you quit or tell it to forget them.

You can also put multiple statements on a line with a semicolon (;). Syntactically, it acts just like a line break:

```
iex(6)> distance = 20; gravity = 9.8
9.8
iex(7)> distance
20
iex(8)> gravity
9.8
```

IEx will only report the value of the last statement, but as you can see on lines 19 and 20, all the values were assigned.

If it's all getting too messy, call clear. It will just clear the screen for you.

Before moving on to the next chapter, which will introduce modules and functions, spend some time playing in IEx. The experience, even at this simple level, will help you move forward. Use variables, and see what happens with large integers. Elixir supports large numbers very well. Try mixing numbers with decimal values (floats) and integers in calculations, and see what happens. Nothing should be difficult yet.

## CHAPTER 2

Functions and Modules

Like most programming languages, Elixir lets you define functions to help you represent repeated calculations. While Elixir functions can become complicated, they start out reasonably simple.

Fun with fn

You can create functions in IEx using the keyword `fn`. For example, to create a function that calculates the velocity of a falling object based on the distance it drops in meters, you could do the following:

```
iex(1)> fall_velocity = fn (distance) -> :math.sqrt(2 * 9.8 * distance) end
#Function<6.6.111823515/1 in :erl_eval.expr/5>
```

That binds the variable `fall_velocity` to a function that takes an argument of `distance`. (Parentheses are optional around the argument.) The function returns (we like to read the `->` as "yields") the square root of 2 times a gravitational constant for Earth of 9.8 m/s^2, times distance (in meters). Then the function comes to an end.

The return value in the shell, `#Function<6.6.111823515/1 in :erl_eval.expr/5>`, isn't especially meaningful by itself, but it tells you that you've created a function and didn't just get an error. (The exact format of that return value changes with Elixir versions, so it may look a bit different.)

Conveniently, binding the function to the variable `fall_velocity` lets you use that variable to calculate the velocity of objects falling to Earth:

```
iex(2)> fall_velocity.(20)
19.79898987322333
iex(3)> fall_velocity.(200)
62.609903369994115
```

```
iex(4)> fall_velocity.(2000)
197.9898987322333
```

If you need to do something more complex, you can separate pieces of your function with newlines. IEx will keep the line *open* until you type end, as in this more verbose version:

```
iex(5)> f = fn (distance) ->
...(5)> :math.sqrt(2 * 9.8 * distance)
...(5)> end
#Function<6.54118792/1 in :erl_eval.expr/5>
iex(6)> f.(20)
19.79898987322333
```

This can be useful when you want to include multiple statements in a function.

You need the period between the variable name and the argument when you call a function that is stored in a variable. You won't need it for functions declared in modules, coming later in this chapter.

If you want those meters per second in miles per hour, just create another function. You can copy and paste the earlier results into it (as we did here), or pick shorter numbers:

```
iex(7)> mps_to_mph = fn mps -> 2.23693629 * mps end
#Function<6.54118792/1 in :erl_eval.expr/5>
iex(8)> mps_to_mph.(19.79898987322333)
44.289078952755766
iex(9)> mps_to_mph.(62.609903369994115)
140.05436496173314
iex(10)> mps_to_mph.(197.9898987322333)
442.89078952755773
```

Probably best to stay away from 2,000-meter drops.

Prefer the fall speed in kilometers per hour?

```
iex(11)> mps_to_kph = fn(mps) -> 3.6 * mps end
#Function<6.54118792/1 in :erl_eval.expr/5>
iex(12)> mps_to_kph.(19.79898987322333)
71.27636354360399
iex(13)> mps_to_kph.(62.60990336999411)
225.39565213197878
iex(14)> mps_to_kph.(197.9898987322333)
712.76363543604
```

You can also go straight to your preferred measurement by nesting the following calls:

```
iex(15)> mps_to_kph.(fall_velocity.(2000))
712.76363543604
```

However you represent it, that's really fast, though air resistance will in reality slow the objects down a lot.

This is handy for repeated calculations, but you probably don't want to push this kind of function use too far in IEx, as quitting the shell session makes your functions vanish. This style of function is called an *anonymous function* because the function itself doesn't have a name. (The variable name isn't a function name.) Anonymous functions are useful for passing functions as arguments to other functions, and for returning functions as results. Within modules, though, you can define named functions that are accessible from anywhere.

And the &

Elixir offers a shortcut style for defining anonymous functions using &, the *capture operator*. Instead of fn, you'll use &; and instead of naming the parameters, you'll use numbers, like &1 and &2.

Previously, you defined `fall_velocity` as:

```
iex(1)> fall_velocity= fn (distance) -> :math.sqrt(2 * 9.8 * distance) end
#Fun<erl_eval.6.111823515>
```

If that is too verbose for you, you could use the &:

```
iex(2)> fall_velocity= &(:math.sqrt(2 * 9.8 * &1))
#Function<6.17052888/1 in :erl_eval.expr/5>
iex(3)> fall_velocity.(20)
19.79898987322333
```

When getting started, it's probably easier to use parameter names, but as impatience sets in, the capture operator is there. Its value will become clearer when you do more complex things with functions, as shown in Chapter 8.

Defining Modules

Most Elixir programs, except things like the preceding simple calculations, define their functions in compiled modules rather than in the shell. Modules are a more formal place to put programs, and they give you the ability to store, encapsulate, share, and manage your code more effectively.

Each module should go in its own file, with an extension of *.ex*. (You can put more than one module in a file, but keep it simple while getting started.) You should use *name_of_module.ex*, where *name_of_module* is the lowercase version of the module name you specify inside of the module file. The Mix tool will help you with this. We created Example 2-1, which you can find in the examples archive (*https://github.com/simonstl/introducing-elixir/tree/master/code*) at *ch02/ex1-drop*, by typing this at the command line:

```
$ mix new ch02/ex1-drop --app drop
```

ch02/ex1-drop is the pathname of the directory to create. Mix took the application name drop and created a *lib* subdirectory with a file named *drop.ex*. That file looked like this when it was created:

```
defmodule Drop do
end
```

We then inserted the previously defined functions, with the result seen in Example 2-1.

Example 2-1. Module for calculating and converting fall velocities

```
defmodule Drop do
  def fall_velocity(distance) do
    :math.sqrt(2 * 9.8 * distance)
  end

  def mps_to_mph(mps) do
    2.23693629 * mps
  end

  def mps_to_kph(mps) do
    3.6 * mps
  end
end
```

defmodule contains the functions that the module will export. It takes the name of the module—this time starting with a capital letter—and contains function definitions. These begin with def, using a slightly different structure than you used when defining functions with fn, and you don't need to assign the functions to variables.

 Function definitions inside of a module must use the longer do...end syntax rather than the shortcut -> syntax. If your function definition is very short, you may put it all on one line like this:

```
def mps_to_mph(mps), do: 2.23693629 * mps
```

You may see this "one-liner" version in other people's code, but for consistency and readability, we recommend that you use the full do...end syntax for all your functions.

Any functions you declare with def will be visible outside of the module and can be called by other code. If you want keep some functions accessible only within the module, you can use defp instead of def, and they will be private.

Usually the code inside of the module will be contained in functions.

But how do you make your module actually do something?

It's time to start compiling Elixir code. The shell will let you compile modules and then use them immediately. If you are using a Mix project (as we are doing here), you start IEx from the same directory as your project:

```
$ iex -S mix
Erlang/OTP 19 [erts-8.0] [source] [64-bit] [smp:4:4] [async-threads:10] [hipe]
 [kernel-poll:false]

Compiling 1 file (.ex)
Generated drop app
Interactive Elixir (1.3.1) - press Ctrl+C to exit (type h() ENTER for help)
iex(1)>
```

Mix will create a _build directory; if you were to look in _build/dev/lib/drop/ebin, you would find a file named Elixir.Drop.beam.

If you make a change to a source file in a text editor and want to recompile without exiting and reentering IEx, you can use the recompile command. In the following example, we added a blank line to the drop.ex file to show a recompile in action:

```
iex(2)> recompile
Compiling 1 file (.ex)
:ok
```

If everything is up to date, you will see a response of :noop (no operation) instead of :ok.

If you are not using Mix, which we do not recommend, you need to start IEx from the same directory as the file you want to compile, and then use the c command with the filename:

```
iex(1)> c("drop.ex")
[Drop]
```

If you were to look at the directory where your drop.ex file is, you would now see a new file named Elixir.Drop.beam.

Once compiled, you can use the functions in your module:

```
iex(2)> Drop.fall_velocity(20)
19.79898987322333
iex(3)> Drop.mps_to_mph(Drop.fall_velocity(20))
44.289078952755766
```

They work the same way as the functions you defined earlier, but now you can quit the shell, return, and still use the compiled functions:

```
iex(4)>
BREAK: (a)bort (c)ontinue (p)roc info (i)nfo (l)oaded
       (v)ersion (k)ill (D)b-tables (d)istribution
a
$ iex -S mix
Erlang/OTP 19 [erts-8.0] [source] [64-bit] [smp:4:4] [async-threads:10] [hipe]
```

```
[kernel-poll:false]

Interactive Elixir (1.3.1) - press Ctrl+C to exit (type h() ENTER for help)
iex(1)> Drop.mps_to_mph(Drop.fall_velocity(20))
44.289078952755766
```

Most Elixir programming involves creating functions in modules and connecting them into larger programs.

If you aren't sure which directory you are in, you can use the pwd() shell command to find out. If you need to change to a different directory, use cd(*pathname*). In the following example, the cd("..") returns you to the directory you started from:

```
iex(1)> pwd()
/Users/elixir/code/ch02/ex1-drop
iex(2)> cd("lib")
/Users/elixir/code/ch02/ex1-drop/lib
iex(3)> pwd()
/Users/elixir/code/ch02/ex1-drop/lib
iex(4)> cd("..")
/Users/elixir/code/ch02/ex1-drop
iex(5)>
```

If you find yourself repeating yourself all the time in IEx, you can also use c to "compile" a series of IEx commands. Instead of defining a module in an *.ex* file, you put a series of commands for IEx in an *.exs* (for Elixir script) file. When you call the c function with that file as its argument, Elixir will execute all of the commands in it.

Elixir Compilation and the Erlang Runtime System

When you write Elixir in the shell, it has to interpret every command, whether or not you've written it before. When you tell Elixir to compile a file, it converts your text into something it can process without having to reinterpret all of it, tremendously improving efficiency when you run the code.

That "something it can process," in Elixir's case, is an Erlang BEAM file. It contains code that the BEAM processor, a key piece of the Erlang Runtime System (ERTS), can run. BEAM is Bogdan's Erlang Abstract Machine, a virtual machine that interprets optimized BEAM code. This may sound slightly less efficient than the traditional compilation to machine code that runs directly on the computer, but it resembles other virtual machines. (Oracle's Java Virtual Machine, or JVM, and Microsoft's .NET Framework are the two most common virtual machines.)

Erlang's virtual machine optimizes some key things, making it easier to build applications that scale reliably. Its process scheduler simplifies distributing work across

---

multiple processors in a single computer. You don't have to think about how many processors your application might get to use—you just write independent processes, and Erlang spreads them out. Erlang also manages input and output in its own way, avoiding connection styles that block other processing. And the virtual machine uses a garbage collection strategy that fits its style of processing, allowing for briefer pauses in program execution. (Garbage collection releases memory that processes needed at one point but are no longer using.)

When you create and deliver Elixir programs, you will be distributing them as a set of compiled BEAM files. You don't need to compile each one from the shell as we're doing here, though. `elixirc` will let you compile Elixir files directly and combine that compilation into make tasks and similar things, and calling `elixir` on *.exs* files will let you run Elixir code as scripts outside of the IEx environment.

From Module to Free-Floating Function

If you like the style of code that `fn` allows but also want your code stored more reliably in modules where it's easier to debug, you can get the best of both worlds by using &, the capture operator, to refer to a function you've already defined. You can specify the function to retrieve with a single argument in the form *Module_name.function_name/arity*. *Arity* is the number of arguments a function takes—1 in the case of `Drop.fall_velocity`:

```
iex(1)> fun=&Drop.fall_velocity/1
&Drop.fall_velocity/1
iex(2)> fun.(20)
19.79898987322333
```

You can also do this within code in a module. If you're referring to code in the same module, you can leave off the module name preface. In this case, that would mean leaving off `Drop.` and just using `&fall_velocity/1`.

Splitting Code Across Modules

The `Drop` module mixes two different kinds of functions. The function `fall_velocity()` fits the name of the module, `Drop`, very well, providing a calculation based on the height from which an object falls. The `mps_to_mph` and `mps_to_kph` functions, however, aren't about dropping. They are generic measurement-conversion functions that are useful in other contexts and really belong in their own module. Examples 2-2 and 2-3, both in *ch02/ex2-split*, show how this might be done.

Example 2-2. Module for calculating fall velocities

```
defmodule Drop do
  def fall_velocity(distance) do
    :math.sqrt(2 * 9.8 * distance)
  end
end
```

Example 2-3. Module for converting fall velocities

```
defmodule Convert do
 def mps_to_mph(mps) do
   2.23693629 * mps
  end

  def mps_to_kph(mps) do
   3.6 * mps
  end
end
```

Next you can compile them, and then the separated functions will be available for use:

```
$ iex -S mix
Erlang/OTP 19 [erts-8.0] [source] [64-bit] [smp:4:4] [async-threads:10] [hipe]
 [kernel-poll:false]

Compiling 2 files (.ex)
Generated drop app
Interactive Elixir (1.3.1) - press Ctrl+C to exit (type h() ENTER for help)
iex(1)> Drop.fall_velocity(20)
19.79898987322333
iex(2)> Convert.mps_to_mph(Drop.fall_velocity(20))
44.289078952755766
```

That reads more neatly, but how might this code work if a third module needed to call those functions? Modules that call code from other modules need to specify that explicitly. Example 2-4, in *ch02/ex3-combined*, shows a module that uses functions from both the drop and convert modules.

Example 2-4. Module for combining drop and convert logic

```
defmodule Combined do
  def height_to_mph(meters) do
    Convert.mps_to_mph(Drop.fall_velocity(meters))
  end
end
```

This will only work if the Combined module has access to the Convert and Drop modules, typically by being in the same directory, but it's quite similar to what worked directly in IEx.

The combined function lets you do much less typing:

```
$iex -S mix
Erlang/OTP 19 [erts-8.0] [source] [64-bit] [smp:4:4] [async-threads:10] [hipe]
[kernel-poll:false]

Compiling 3 files (.ex)
Generated combined app
Interactive Elixir (1.3.1) - press Ctrl+C to exit (type h() ENTER for help)
iex(1)> Combined.height_to_mph(20)
44.289078952755766
```

If you're coming from Erlang, you're probably used to the discipline of thick module walls and functions that only become accessible through explicit -export and -import directives. Elixir goes the opposite route, making everything accessible from the outside except for functions explicitly declared private with defp.

Combining Functions with the Pipe Operator

There's another way to combine functions: using Elixir's |> operator, called the *pipe operator*. The pipe operator, sometimes called *pipe forward*, lets you pass an expression into the first argument of the next function. Example 2-5, in *ch02/ex4-pipe*, shows the operator in use.

Example 2-5. Using the pipe operator

```
defmodule Combined do
  def height_to_mph(meters) do
    Drop.fall_velocity(meters) |> Convert.mps_to_mph
  end
end
```

Note that the order is reversed from Example 2-4, with Drop.fall_velocity (meters) appearing before Convert.mps_to_mph. If you read |> as "goes into," the logic may be clearer. You can have several of these in a row, converting functions that used to be deeply nested into (hopefully) clearer sequences.

The pipe operator only passes one result into the next function, as its first parameter. If you need to use a function that takes multiple parameters, just specify the additional parameters as if the first one weren't there.

Importing Functions

As long as you fully specify the name of the function, Elixir does a great job of seeking out the code. However, if you're working with code that constantly relies on code in a particular module, it may be appealing to reduce your typing by formally importing it.

Example 2-6, in *ch02/ex5-import*, shows a simple use of `import` to bring in all the functions (and macros, though there aren't any yet) in the `Convert` module.

Example 2-6. Module for combining drop and convert logic, with imported Convert

```
defmodule Combined do
  import Convert

  def height_to_mph(meters) do
    mps_to_mph(Drop.fall_velocity(meters))
  end
end
```

The `import Convert` line tells Elixir that all of the functions and macros (except those starting with underscore) in the `Convert` module should be available without prefixes in this module.

Importing an Erlang module, as shown in Example 2-7, is much the same, except that you prefix the module name with a colon and don't start the name with an uppercase letter.

Example 2-7. Importing the Erlang math module

```
defmodule Drop do
  import :math

  def fall_velocity(distance) do
    sqrt(2 * 9.8 * distance)
  end
end
```

Importing entire modules might create conflicts with function names you are already using in your own module, so Elixir lets you specify which functions you want with the `only` argument. For example, to get just the `sqrt` function with an arity of 1, you could use:

```
defmodule Drop do
  import :math, only: [sqrt: 1]
  def fall_velocity(distance) do
    sqrt(2 * 9.8 * distance)
```

```
    end
  end
```

If you just need to import a module for one function, you can place the `import` directive inside of the `def` or `defp` for that function. It won't apply beyond that function's scope:

```
defmodule Drop do
  def fall_velocity(distance) do
    import :math, only: [sqrt: 1]
    sqrt(2 * 9.8 * distance)
  end
end
```

> If you want all of the functions except for some specific functions, you can use the except argument:
>
> ```
> import :math, except: [sin: 1, cos: 1]
> ```

Use `import` with caution. It certainly spares you typing, but it can also make it harder to figure out where functions came from.

Default Values for Arguments

If you wanted to deal with astronomical bodies other than Earth (and you'll be doing a lot of that in subsequent chapters), you might want to create a `fall_velocity/2` function that accepts both a distance and a gravity constant:

```
defmodule Drop do
  def fall_velocity(distance, gravity) do
    :math.sqrt(2 * gravity * distance)
  end
end
```

You can then calculate velocities from Earth, where the gravity constant is 9.8, and the moon, where the gravity constant is 1.6:

```
$ iex -S mix
Erlang/OTP 19 [erts-8.0] [source] [64-bit] [smp:4:4] [async-threads:10] [hipe]
 [kernel-poll:false]

Compiling 1 file (.ex)
Generated drop app
Interactive Elixir (1.3.1) - press Ctrl+C to exit (type h() ENTER for help)
iex(1)> Drop.fall_velocity(20, 9.8)
19.79898987322333
iex(2)> Drop.fall_velocity(20, 1.6)
8.0
```

If you anticipate dropping objects primarily on Earth, Elixir lets you specify a default value for the `gravity` parameter by putting the default value after a pair of back-slashes, as in Example 2-8, which you can find in *ch02/ex6-defaults*.

Example 2-8. Function with a default value

```
defmodule Drop do
  def fall_velocity(distance, gravity \\ 9.8) do
    :math.sqrt(2 * gravity * distance)
  end
end
```

Now you can specify only the first argument for Earth, and both arguments for other astronomical bodies:

```
iex(3)> recompile
Compiling 1 file (.ex)
:ok
iex(4)> Drop.fall_velocity(20)
19.79898987322333
iex(5)> Drop.fall_velocity(20, 1.6)
8.0
```

Documenting Code

Your programs can run perfectly well without documentation. Your projects, however, will have a much harder time.

While programmers like to think they write code that anyone can look at and sort out, the painful reality is that code even a little more complicated than that shown in the previous examples can prove mystifying to other developers. If you step away from code for a while, the understanding you developed while programming it may fade, and even your own code can seem incomprehensible.

Elixir's creators are well aware of these headaches and emphasize treating documentation "as a first-class citizen" (*http://elixir-lang.org/docs/stable/elixir/writing-documentation*).

The simplest way to add more explicit explanations to your code is to insert comments. You can start a comment with #, and it runs to the end of the line. Some comments take up an entire line, while others are short snippets at the end of a line. Example 2-9 shows both varieties of comments.

Example 2-9. Comments in action

```
# convenience functions!
defmodule Combined do

  def height_to_mph(meters) do # takes meters, returns miles per hour
    Convert.mps_to_mph(Drop.fall_velocity(meters))
  end
end
```

The Elixir compiler will ignore all text between the # sign and the end of the line, but humans exploring the code will be able to read it.

Informal comments like these are useful, but developers have a habit of including comments that help them keep track of what they're doing while they're writing the code. Those comments may or may not be what other developers need to understand the code, or even what you need when you return to your own code after a long time away. More formal comment structures may be more work than you want to take on in the heat of a programming session, but they also force you to ask yourself who might be looking at your code in the future and what they might want to know.

Elixir's documentation support goes way beyond basic comments, offering a set of tools for creating documentation you can explore through IEx or separately through a web browser.

Documenting Functions

The `Drop` module contains one function: `fall_velocity/1`. You probably know that it takes a distance in meters and returns a velocity in meters per second for an object dropped in a vacuum on Earth, but the code doesn't actually say that. Example 2-10 shows how to fix that with the @doc tag.

Example 2-10. Documented function for calculating fall velocities

```
defmodule Drop do
  @doc """
  Calculates the velocity of an object falling on Earth
  as if it were in a vacuum (no air resistance).  The distance is
  the height from which the object falls, specified in meters,
  and the function returns a velocity in meters per second.
  """

  def fall_velocity(distance) do
    import :math, only: [sqrt: 1]

    sqrt(2 * 9.8 * distance)
```

```
      end
end
```

After you compile that, the h() function in IEx will now tell you useful information about the function:

```
iex(1)> recompile
Compiling 1 file (.ex)
:ok
iex(2)> h Drop.fall_velocity
        def fall_velocity(distance)

Calculates the velocity of an object falling on Earth
as if it were in a vacuum (no air resistance).  The distance is
the height from which the object falls, specified in meters,
and the function returns a velocity in meters per second.
```

That's a major improvement, but what if a user specifies "twenty" meters instead of "20" meters? Because Elixir doesn't worry much about types, the code doesn't say that the value for distance has to be a number or the function will return an error.

You can add a tag, @spec, to add that information. It's a little strange, as in some ways it feels like a duplicate of the method declaration. In this case, it's simple, as shown in Example 2-11.

Example 2-11. Documented function for calculating fall velocities

```
defmodule Drop do

@doc """
Calculates the velocity of an object falling on Earth
as if it were in a vacuum (no air resistance).  The distance is
the height from which the object falls, specified in meters,
and the function returns a velocity in meters per second.
"""

  @spec fall_velocity(number()) :: float()

  def fall_velocity(distance) do
    import :math, only: [sqrt: 1]

    sqrt(2 * 9.8 * distance)
  end
end
```

This specification says that the function can take any kind of number() as input (either integer or floating point), but the result will always be a float() (floating-point) value.

Now you can use the s() function to see type information about your function from IEx:

```
iex(1)> s(Drop.fall_velocity)
@spec fall_velocity(number()) :: float()
```

You can also use s(Drop) to see all the specs defined in the Drop module.

 This chapter has demonstrated only the float() type and the number() type, which combines the integer() and float() types. Appendix A includes a full list of types.

Documenting Modules

The modules in this chapter have been very simple so far, but there is enough there to start documenting, as shown in the files at *ch02/ex7-docs*. Example 2-12 presents the Drop module with more information about what version it is (@vsn), who created it, and why.

Example 2-12. Documented module for calculating fall velocities

```
defmodule Drop do
  @moduledoc """
  Functions calculating velocities achieved by objects dropped in a vacuum.

  from *Introducing Elixir*, Second Edition, O'Reilly Media, Inc., 2017.
  Copyright 2017 by Simon St.Laurent and J. David Eisenberg.
  """

  @vsn 0.1

  @doc """
  Calculates the velocity of an object falling on Earth
  as if it were in a vacuum (no air resistance).  The distance is
  the height from which the object falls, specified in meters,
  and the function returns a velocity in meters per second.
  """

  @spec fall_velocity(number()) :: number()

  def fall_velocity(distance) do
    import :math, only: [sqrt: 1]

    sqrt(2 * 9.8 * distance)
  end
end
```

You can now use h to learn more about the module:

```
iex(1)> h Drop

                              Drop

Functions calculating velocities achieved by objects dropped in a vacuum.

from *Introducing Elixir*, Second Edition, O'Reilly Media, Inc., 2017.
Copyright 2017 by
Simon St.Laurent and J. David Eisenberg.
```

Having good documentation is useful for anyone else who is reading your code (and if you are away from your code for a few months, when you return, *you* will be that "anyone else"). You can also use this documentation to create web pages that summarize your modules and functions. To do this, you need the ExDoc tool. ExDoc recognizes Markdown (*http://bit.ly/df-markdown*) formatting in your documentation, so your documentation can include emphasized text, lists, and links, among other things. For more details on using ExDoc, see Appendix B.

## CHAPTER 3

Atoms, Tuples, and Pattern Matching

Elixir programs are at heart a set of message requests and tools for processing them. Elixir provides tools that simplify the efficient handling of those messages, letting you create code that is readable (to programmers at least) while still running efficiently when you need speed.

Atoms

Atoms are a key component of Elixir. Technically they're just another type of data, but it's hard to overstate their impact on Elixir programming style.

Usually, atoms are bits of text that start with a colon, like :ok or :earth or :Today. They can also contain underscores (_) and at symbols (@), like :this_is_a_ short_sentence or :me@home. If you want more freedom to use spaces, you can start with the colon and then put them in single or double quotes, like :'Today is a good day'. Generally, the one-word lowercase form is easier to read.

Atoms have a value—it's the same as their text:

```
iex(1)> :test
:test
```

That's not very exciting in itself. What makes atoms exciting is the way that they can combine with other types and Elixir's pattern-matching techniques to build simple but powerful logical structures.

Pattern Matching with Atoms

Elixir used pattern matching to make the examples in Chapter 2 work, but it was very simple. The name of the function was the one key piece that varied, and as long as you provided a numeric argument, Elixir knew what you meant. Elixir's pattern matching offers much more sophisticated possibilities, however, allowing you to match on arguments as well as on function names.

For example, suppose you want to calculate the velocity of falling objects not just on Earth, where the gravitational constant is 9.8 meters per second squared, but on Earth's moon, where it is 1.6 meters per second squared, and on Mars, where it is 3.71 meters per second squared. Example 3-1, which you can find in *ch03/ex1-atoms*, shows one way to build code that supports this.

Example 3-1. Pattern matching on atoms as well as function names

```
defmodule Drop do

  def fall_velocity(:earth, distance) do
    :math.sqrt(2 * 9.8 * distance)
  end

  def fall_velocity(:moon, distance) do
    :math.sqrt(2 * 1.6 * distance)
  end

  def fall_velocity(:mars, distance) do
    :math.sqrt(2 * 3.71 * distance)
  end

end
```

It looks like the fall_velocity function gets defined three times here, and it certainly provides three processing paths for the same function. However, because Elixir will choose which version of the function to call by pattern matching, they aren't duplicate definitions. As in English, these pieces are called *clauses*. All of the clauses for a given function name must be grouped together in the module.

Once you have this, you can calculate velocities for objects falling a given distance on Earth, the Earth's moon, and Mars. Rather than using recompile, which compiles all the *.ex* files in your project, you can also reload a single module with IEx's r() command:

```
iex(1)> r(Drop)
warning: redefining module Drop (current version loaded from
  _build/dev/lib/drop/ebin/Elixir.Drop.beam)
  lib/drop.ex:1

{:reloaded, Drop, [Drop]}
iex(2)> Drop.fall_velocity(:earth, 20)
19.79898987322333
iex(3)> Drop.fall_velocity(:moon, 20)
8.0
```

```
iex(4)> Drop.fall_velocity(:mars, 20)
12.181953866272849
```

If you try to find the velocity for a pattern that doesn't have a matching clause, you get an error:

```
iex(5)> Drop.fall_velocity(:jupiter, 20)
** (FunctionClauseError) no function clause matching in Drop.fall_velocity/2
    drop.ex:3: Drop.fall_velocity(:jupiter, 20)
```

You'll quickly find that atoms are a critical component for writing readable Elixir code.

 If you want to do a pattern match against a value stored in a variable, you'll need to put a ^ in front of the variable name.

Atomic Booleans

Elixir uses the values `true` and `false` to represent the Boolean logic values of the same names. Although underneath these are atoms, `:true` and `:false`, they are common enough that you don't need to use the colons. Elixir will return these values if you ask it to compare something:

```
iex(1)> 3 < 2
false
iex(2)> 3 > 2
true
iex(3)> 10 == 10
true
iex(4)> :true == true
true
iex(5)> :false == false
true
```

Elixir also has special operators that work on these atoms (and on comparisons that resolve to these atoms):

```
iex(6)> true and true
true
iex(7)> true and false
false
iex(8)> true or false
true
iex(9)> false or false
false
iex(10)> not true
false
```

The and and or operators both take two arguments. For and, the result is true if and only if the two arguments are true. For or, the result is true if at least one of the arguments is true. If you're comparing expressions more complicated than true and false, it's wise to put them in parentheses.

Elixir will automatically take shortcuts on its logic. If it finds, for example, that the first argument in an and is false, it won't evaluate the second argument and will return false. Likewise, if the first argument in an or is true, it won't evaluate the second argument and will return true.

The not operator is simpler, taking just one argument. It turns true into false and false into true. Unlike the other Boolean operators, which go between their arguments, not goes before its single argument.

If you try to use these operators with any other atoms, you'll get an argument error:

```
iex(11)> not :bonkers
** (ArgumentError) argument error
    :erlang.not(:bonkers)
```

 Like true and false, Elixir lets you write the atom :nil as nil. There are other atoms that often have an accepted meaning, like :ok and :error, but those are more conventions than a formal part of the language and don't get special treatment. Their colons are required.

Guards

The fall_velocity calculations work fairly well, but there's still one glitch. If the function gets a negative value for distance, the square root (sqrt) function in the calculation will be unhappy:

```
iex(1)> Drop.fall_velocity(:earth, -20)
** (ArithmeticError) bad argument in arithmetic expression
    (stdlib) :math.sqrt(-392.0)
          drop.ex:4: Drop.fall_velocity/2
```

Since you can't dig a hole 20 meters down, release an object, and marvel as it accelerates to the surface, this isn't a terrible result. However, it might be more elegant to at least produce a different kind of error.

In Elixir, you can specify which data a given function will accept with *guards*. Guards, indicated by the when keyword, let you fine-tune the pattern matching based on the content of arguments, not just their shape. Guards have to stay simple, can use only a very few built-in functions, and are limited by a requirement that they evaluate only data without any side effects—but they can still transform your code.

You can find a list of functions that can safely be used in guards in Appendix A.

Guards evaluate their expressions to `true` or `false`, as previously described, and the first one with a `true` result wins. That means that you can write `when true` for a guard that always gets called if it is reached, or block out some code you don't want to call (for now) with `when false`.

In this simple case, you can keep negative numbers away from the square root function by adding guards to the `fall_velocity` clauses, as shown in Example 3-2, which you can find in *ch03/ex2-guards*.

Example 3-2. Adding guards to the function clauses

```
defmodule Drop do

  def fall_velocity(:earth, distance) when distance >= 0 do
    :math.sqrt(2 * 9.8 * distance)
  end

  def fall_velocity(:moon, distance) when distance >= 0 do
    :math.sqrt(2 * 1.6 * distance)
  end

  def fall_velocity(:mars, distance) when distance >= 0 do
    :math.sqrt(2 * 3.71 * distance)
  end

end
```

The `when` expression describes a condition or set of conditions in the function head. In this case, the condition is simple: the `distance` must be greater than or equal to zero. In Elixir, greater than or equal to is written >=, and less than or equal to is written <=, just as they're described in English. If you compile that code and ask for the result of a positive distance, the result is the same. Ask for a negative distance, and the result is different:

```
iex(1)> recompile
Compiling 1 file (.ex)
:ok
iex(2)> Drop.fall_velocity(:earth, 20)
19.79898987322333
iex(3)> Drop.fall_velocity(:earth, -20)
** (FunctionClauseError) no function clause matching in Drop.fall_velocity/2
    drop.ex:3: Drop.fall_velocity(:earth, -20)
```

Because of the guard, Elixir doesn't find a function clause that works with a negative argument. The error message may not seem like a major improvement, but as you add layers of code, "not handled" may be a more appealing response than "broke my formula."

A clearer, though still simple, use of guards might be code that returns an absolute value. Yes, Elixir has a built-in function, abs(), for this, but Example 3-3 makes clear how this works.

Example 3-3. Calculating absolute value with guards

```
defmodule MathDemo do

  def absolute_value(number) when number < 0 do
    -number
  end

  def absolute_value(number) when number == 0 do
    0
  end

  def absolute_value(number) when number > 0 do
    number
  end

end
```

When `Mathdemo.absolute_value()` is called with a negative (less than zero) argument, Elixir calls the first clause, which returns the negation of that negative argument, making it positive. When the argument equals (==) zero, Elixir calls the second clause, returning 0. Finally, when the argument is positive (greater than zero), Elixir calls the third clause, just returning the number. (The first two clauses have processed everything that isn't positive, so the guard on the last clause is unnecessary and will go away in Example 3-4.)

> All the examples from this point forward are built using Mix and started with `iex -S mix`. This will automatically compile the code if necessary. To save space and avoid needless repetition, we will generally omit the IEx startup and initial compilation messages.

Here are a few examples:

```
iex(1)> MathDemo.absolute_value(-20)
20
iex(2)> MathDemo.absolute_value(0)
0
```

```
iex(3)> MathDemo.absolute_value(20)
20
```

This may seem like an unwieldy way to calculate. Don't worry—Elixir has simpler logic switches you can use inside of functions. However, guards are critically important to choosing among function clauses, which will be especially useful as you start to work with recursion in Chapter 4.

Elixir runs through the function clauses in the order you list them and stops at the first one that matches. If you find your information is heading to the wrong clause, you may want to reorder your clauses or fine-tune your guard conditions.

Also, when your guard clause is testing for just one value, you can easily switch to using pattern matching instead of a guard. The `absolute_value()` function in Example 3-4 does the same thing as the one in Example 3-3.

Example 3-4. Calculating absolute value with guards and pattern matching

```
defmodule MathDemo do

  def absolute_value(number) when number < 0 do
    -number
  end

  def absolute_value(number) do
    number
  end

end
```

In this case, it's up to you whether you prefer the simpler form or preserving a parallel approach.

 You can also have multiple comparisons in a single guard. If you separate them with the or operator, it succeeds if any of the comparisons succeeds. If you separate them with the and operator, they all have to succeed for the guard to succeed.

Underscoring That You Don't Care

Guards let you specify more precise handling of incoming arguments. Sometimes you may actually want handling that is less precise, though. Not every argument is essential to every operation, especially when you start passing around complex data structures. You could create variables for arguments and then never use them, but you'll get warnings from the compiler (which suspects you must have made a mistake), and you may confuse other people using your code who are surprised to find your code cares about only half of the arguments they sent.

You might, for example, decide that you're not concerned with what planemo (for *planetary mass object*, including planets, dwarf planets, and moons) a user of your velocity function specifies, and you're just going to use Earth's value for gravity. Then you might write something like Example 3-5, found in *ch03/ex3-underscore*.

Example 3-5. Declaring a variable and then ignoring it

```
defmodule Drop do

  def fall_velocity(planemo, distance) when distance >= 0 do
  :math.sqrt(2 * 9.8 * distance)
  end

end
```

This will compile, but you'll get a warning, and if you try to use it for, say, Mars, you'll get the wrong answer:

```
iex(1)> r(Drop)
r(Drop)
warning: redefining module Drop (current version loaded from
  _build/dev/lib/drop/ebin/Elixir.Drop.beam)
  lib/drop.ex:1

warning: variable planemo is unused
  lib/drop.ex:3

{:reloaded, Drop, [Drop]}
iex(2)> Drop.fall_velocity(:mars,20)
19.79898987322333
```

On Mars, that should be more like 12 than 19, so the compiler was right to scold you.

Other times, though, you really only care about some of the arguments. In these cases, you can use a simple underscore (_). The underscore accomplishes two things: it tells the compiler not to bother you, and it tells anyone reading your code that you're not going to be using that argument. In fact, Elixir won't let you. You can try to assign values to the underscore, but Elixir won't give them back to you. It considers the underscore permanently unbound:

```
iex(3)> _ = 20
20
iex(4)> _
** (CompileError) iex:4 unbound variable _
```

If you really wanted your code to be Earth-centric and ignore any suggestions of other planemos, you could instead write something like Example 3-6.

Example 3-6. Deliberately ignoring an argument with an underscore

```
defmodule Drop2 do

  def fall_velocity(_, distance) when distance >= 0 do
   :math.sqrt(2 * 9.8 * distance)
  end

end
```

This time there will be no compiler warning, and anyone who looks at the code will know that first argument is useless:

```
iex(4)> r(Drop2)
warning: redefining module Drop2 (current version loaded from
  _build/dev/lib/drop/ebin/Elixir.Drop2.beam)
  lib/drop2.ex:1

{:reloaded, Drop2, [Drop2]}
iex(5)> Drop2.fall_velocity(:you_dont_care, 20)
19.79898987322333
```

You can use the underscore multiple times to ignore multiple arguments. It matches anything for the pattern match and never binds, so there's never a conflict.

 You can also start variable names with underscores—like _planemo —and the compiler won't warn if you never use those variables. Those variables do get bound, though, and you can reference them later in your code if you change your mind. Consequently, if you use the same variable name more than once in a set of arguments, even if one of the names starts with an underscore, you'll get an error from the compiler for trying to bind twice to the same name.

Adding Structure: Tuples

Elixir's tuples let you combine multiple items into a single composite datatype. This makes it easier to pass messages between components, letting you create your own complex datatypes as needed. Tuples can contain any kind of Elixir data, including numbers, atoms, other tuples, and the lists and strings you'll encounter in later chapters.

Tuples themselves are simple—a group of items surrounded by curly braces:

```
iex(1)> {:earth, 20}
{:earth, 20}
```

Tuples might contain one item, or they might contain a hundred. Two to five seems typical (and useful, and readable). Often (but not always) an atom at the beginning of the tuple indicates what it's really for, providing an informal identifier of the complex information structure stored in the tuple.

Elixir includes built-in functions that give you access to the contents of a tuple on an item-by-item basis. You can retrieve the values of items with the elem function, set values in a new tuple with the put_elem function, and find out how many items are in a tuple with the tuple_size function. Elixir (unlike Erlang) counts from zero, so the first item in a tuple is referenced as 0, the second as 1, and so on:

```
iex(2)> tuple={:earth,20}
{:earth,20}
iex(3)> elem(tuple,1)
20
iex(4)> new_tuple=put_elem(tuple,1,40)
{:earth,40}
iex(5)> tuple_size(new_tuple)
2
```

If you can stick with pattern matching tuples, however, you'll likely create more readable code.

Pattern Matching with Tuples

Tuples make it easy to package multiple arguments into a single container and let the receiving function decide what to do with them. Pattern matching on tuples looks much like pattern matching on atoms, except that there is, of course, a pair of curly braces around each set of arguments, as Example 3-7 (which you'll find in *ch03/ex4-tuples*) demonstrates.

Example 3-7. Encapsulating arguments in a tuple

```
defmodule Drop do

  def fall_velocity({:earth, distance}) when distance >= 0 do
    :math.sqrt(2 * 9.8 * distance)
  end

  def fall_velocity({:moon, distance}) when distance >= 0 do
    :math.sqrt(2 * 1.6 * distance)
  end

  def fall_velocity({:mars, distance}) when distance >= 0 do
    :math.sqrt(2 * 3.71 * distance)
  end

end
```

The arity changes: this version is fall_velocity/1 instead of fall_velocity/2 because the tuple counts as only one argument. The tuple version works much like the atom version but requires the extra curly braces when you call the function as well:

```
iex(1)> Drop.fall_velocity({:earth, 20})
19.79898987322333
iex(2)> Drop.fall_velocity({:moon, 20})
8.0
iex(3)> Drop.fall_velocity({:mars, 20})
12.181953866272849
```

Why would you use this form when it requires a bit of extra typing? Using tuples opens more possibilities. Other code could package different things into tuples—more arguments, different atoms, even functions created with fn(). The ability to pass a single tuple rather than a pile of arguments is what gives Elixir much of its flexibility, especially when you get to passing messages between different processes.

Processing Tuples

There are many ways to process tuples, not just the simple pattern matching shown in Example 3-7. If you receive the tuple as a single variable, you can do many different things with it. A simple place to start is using the tuple as a pass-through to a private version of the function. That part of Example 3-8, which you can find in *ch03/ex5-tuplesMore*, may look familiar, as it's the same as the fall_velocity/2 function in Example 3-1.

Example 3-8. Encapsulating arguments in a tuple and passing them to a private function

```
defmodule Drop do

  def fall_velocity({planemo, distance}) when distance >= 0 do
    fall_velocity(planemo, distance)
  end


  defp fall_velocity(:earth, distance) do
    :math.sqrt(2 * 9.8 * distance)
  end

  defp fall_velocity(:moon, distance) do
    :math.sqrt(2 * 1.6 * distance)
  end

  defp fall_velocity(:mars, distance) do
    :math.sqrt(2 * 3.71 * distance)
  end

end
```

The use of defp for the private versions means that *only* fall_velocity/1, the tuple version, is public. The fall_velocity/2 function is available within the module, however. It's not especially necessary here, but this "make one version public, keep another version with different arity private" approach is common in situations where you want to make a function accessible but don't necessarily want its inner workings directly available.

If you call this function—the tuple version, so curly braces are necessary— fall_velocity/1 calls the private fall_velocity/2, which returns the proper value to fall_velocity/1, which will return it to you. The results should look familiar:

```
iex(1)> Drop.fall_velocity({:earth, 20})
19.79898987322333
iex(2)> Drop.fall_velocity({:moon, 20})
8.0
iex(3)> Drop.fall_velocity({:mars, 20})
12.181953866272849
```

There are a few different ways to extract the data from the tuple. You could reference the components of the tuple by number using the built-in Kernel macro elem/2, which takes a tuple and a numeric position as its arguments. The first component of a tuple can be reached at position 0, the second at position 1, and so on:

```
def fall_velocity(where) do
  fall_velocity(elem(where,0), elem(where,1))
end
```

You could also break things up a bit and do pattern matching after getting the variable:

```
def fall_velocity(where) do
  {planemo, distance} = where
  fall_velocity(planemo,distance)
end
```

The result of that last line will be the value the fall_velocity/1 function returns.

The pattern matching is a little different from that in Example 3-8. The function accepted a tuple as its argument and assigned it to the variable where. (If where is not a tuple, the {planemo, distance} = where will fail with an error.) Extracting the contents of that tuple, since we know its structure, can be done with a pattern match inside the function. The planemo and distance variables will be bound to the values contained in the where tuple and can then be used in the call to fall_velocity/2.

## CHAPTER 4

Logic and Recursion

So far, Elixir seems logical but fairly simple. Pattern matching controls the flow through a program, and requests that match a form return certain responses. While this is enough to get many things done, sometimes you'll want more powerful options, especially as you start working with larger and more complicated data structures.

Logic Inside of Functions

Pattern matching and guards are powerful tools, but there are times when it's much easier to do some comparisons inside of a function clause instead of creating new functions. Elixir's designers agreed and created two constructs for evaluating conditions inside of functions: the case expression and the less frequently used cond and if expressions.

The case construct lets you use pattern matching and guards inside of a function clause. It reads most clearly when a single value (or set of values) needs to be compared with multiple possibilities. The cond construct evaluates only a series of expressions, without pattern matching. The cond construct tends to produce more readable code in situations where the multiple possibilities are specified by combinations of different values. The if construct evaluates only a single expression.

All these constructs return a value your code can capture.

Evaluating Cases

The case construct lets you perform pattern matching inside of your function clause. If you found the multiple function clauses of Example 3-2 hard to read, you might prefer to create a version that looks like Example 4-1, which you can find in *ch04/ex1-case*.

Example 4-1. Moving pattern matching inside the function with case

```
defmodule Drop do

  def fall_velocity(planemo, distance) when distance >= 0 do
    case planemo do
      :earth -> :math.sqrt(2 * 9.8 * distance)
      :moon  -> :math.sqrt(2 * 1.6 * distance)
      :mars  -> :math.sqrt(2 * 3.71 * distance)
    end
  end

end
```

The `case` construct will compare the atom in `planemo` to the values listed, going down the list in order. It won't process beyond the first match it finds. Each matching value is followed by a `->`, which you can read as "yields." The `case` construct will return the result of different calculations based on which atom is used, and because the `case` construct returns the last value in the function clause, the function will return that value as well.

 You can use the underscore (_) for your pattern match if you want a choice that matches "everything else." However, you should always put that last—nothing that comes after it will ever be evaluated.

The results should look familiar:

```
iex(1)> Drop.fall_velocity(:earth, 20)
19.79898987322333
iex(2)> Drop.fall_velocity(:moon, 20)
8.0
iex(3)> Drop.fall_velocity(:mars, -20)
** (FunctionClauseError) no function clause matching in Drop.fall_velocity/2
    (drop) lib/drop.ex:3: Drop.fall_velocity(:mars, -20)
```

The `case` construct switches among planemos, while the guard clause on the function definition keeps out negative distances, producing (rightly) the error on line 3. This way the guard needs to appear only once.

You can also use the return value from the `case` construct to reduce duplicate code and make the logic of your program clearer. In this case, the only difference between the calculations for `earth`, `moon`, and `mars` is a gravitational constant. Example 4-2, which you can find in *ch04/ex2-case*, shows how to make the `case` construct return the gravitational constant for use in a single calculation at the end.

Example 4-2. Using the return value of the case construct to clean up the function

```
defmodule Drop do

  def fall_velocity(planemo, distance) when distance >= 0 do
    gravity = case planemo do
      :earth -> 9.8
      :moon  -> 1.6
      :mars  -> 3.71
    end
    :math.sqrt(2 * gravity * distance)
  end

end
```

This time, the `gravity` variable is set to the return value of the `case` construct. The now more readable formula `math:sqrt(2 * gravity * distance)` is the last line of the function, and the value it produces will be the return value.

You can also use guards with a `case` statement, as shown, perhaps less than elegantly, in Example 4-3, which is in *ch04/ex3-case*. This might make more sense if there were different planemos with different rules about distances.

Example 4-3. Moving guards into the case statement

```
defmodule Drop do

  def fall_velocity(planemo, distance)  do
    gravity = case planemo do
      :earth when distance >= 0 -> 9.8
      :moon when distance >= 0  -> 1.6
      :mars when distance >= 0  -> 3.71
    end
    :math.sqrt(2 * gravity * distance)
  end

end
```

This produces similar results, except that the error message at the end changes from a `FunctionClauseError` to a `CaseClauseError`:

```
iex(3)> r(Drop)
warning: redefining module Drop (current version defined in memory)
  lib/drop.ex:1

{:reloaded, Drop, [Drop]}
iex(4)> Drop.fall_velocity(:earth, 20)
```

```
19.79898987322333
iex(5)> Drop.fall_velocity(:moon, 20)
8.0
iex(6)> Drop.fall_velocity(:mars, -20)
** (CaseClauseError) no case clause matching: :mars
    (drop) lib/drop.ex:4: Drop.fall_velocity/2
```

The error is correct, in that the case construct is trying to match :mars, but misleading because the problem isn't with :mars but rather with the guard that's checking the distance variable. If Elixir tells you that your case doesn't match, but a match is obviously right there in front of you, check your guard statements.

Adjusting to Conditions

The cond construct is broadly similar to the case statement, but without the pattern matching. If you would like, this allows you to write a catch-all clause—an expression matching true at the end. This often makes it easier to express logic based on broader comparisons than simple matching.

Suppose, for example, that the precision of the fall_velocity function is too great. Instead of an actual speed, you'd like to describe the relative speed produced by dropping from a tower of a given height. You can add a cond construct that does that to the earlier code from Example 4-2, as shown in Example 4-4 (in *ch04/ex4-cond*).

Example 4-4. Adding a cond construct to convert numbers into atoms

```
defmodule Drop do

  def fall_velocity(planemo, distance) when distance >= 0 do
    gravity = case planemo do
      :earth -> 9.8
      :moon  -> 1.6
      :mars  -> 3.71
    end

    velocity = :math.sqrt(2 * gravity * distance)

    cond do
      velocity == 0 -> :stable
      velocity < 5 -> :slow
      velocity >= 5 and velocity < 10 -> :moving
      velocity >= 10 and velocity < 20 -> :fast
      velocity >= 20 -> :speedy
    end
  end

end
```

This time, the cond construct returns a value (an atom describing the velocity) based on the many guards it includes. Because that value is the last thing returned within the function, that becomes the return value of the function.

The results are a little different from our past trials:

```
iex(6)> r(Drop)
warning: redefining module Drop (current version defined in memory)
  lib/drop.ex:1

{:reloaded, Drop, [Drop]}
iex(7)> Drop.fall_velocity(:earth, 20)
:fast
iex(8)> Drop.fall_velocity(:moon, 20)
:moving
iex(9)> Drop.fall_velocity(:mars, 20)
:fast
iex(10)> Drop.fall_velocity(:earth, 30)
:speedy
```

If you want to capture the value produced by the cond construct in a variable, you can. Just replace the cond do in the first line with something like description = cond do.

 Elixir evaluates the cond and if statements on the basis of *truthiness*. All values are considered to be true except nil and false.

if, or else

For simpler cases, Elixir also offers an if function that tests only a single clause, and allows an else to follow if a failed test also requires action.

Example 4-5, in *ch04/ex5-if*, sends a warning to standard output (in this case IEx) if you drop an object too fast. It uses the simpler cousin of cond, if, to decide whether to put out the extra message.

Example 4-5. Sending an extra warning if the velocity is too high

```
defmodule Drop do

  def fall_velocity(planemo, distance) when distance >= 0 do
    gravity = case planemo do
      :earth -> 9.8
      :moon  -> 1.6
      :mars  -> 3.71
    end
```

```
velocity = :math.sqrt(2 * gravity * distance)

if velocity > 20 do
  IO.puts("Look out below!")
else
  IO.puts("Reasonable...")
end

velocity

end

end
```

The new if clause checks the velocity variable to see if it's above 20. If it is, it calls IO.puts, which creates a side effect: a message on the screen. If not, the else clause puts a milder message on the screen (the velocity at the end makes sure that the calculated result is the return value):

```
iex(1)> Drop.fall_velocity(:earth, 50)
Look out below!
31.304951684997057
iex(2)> Drop.fall_velocity(:moon, 100)
Reasonable...
17.88854381999832
```

You can write if statements in a few different ways. If the if statement is compact enough, it can be tempting to put it on a single line:

```
iex(3)> x=20
20
iex(4)> if x>10 do :large end
:large
```

That works well, and you can even add an else:

```
iex(5)> if x>10 do :large else :small end
:large
```

As an alternative, Elixir lets you put a colon after the do and then use a shorter form:

```
iex(6)> if x>10, do: :large, else: :small
:large
```

You may also find Elixir's unless statement more readable than an if when you want to test against an opposite:

```
iex(7)> unless x>10, do: :small, else: :large
:large
```

Variable Assignment in case and if Constructs

Every possible path created in a case, cond, or if statement has the opportunity to bind values to variables. This is usually a wonderful thing, but it can let you create unstable programs by assigning different variables in different clauses. This might look something like Example 4-6, which you can find in *ch04/ex6-broken*.

Example 4-6. A badly broken cond construct

```
defmodule Broken do

  def bad_cond(test_val) do

    cond do
      test_val < 0 -> x=1
      test_val >= 0 -> y=2
    end

    x+y

  end
end
```

The Elixir compiler warns you about this sort of questionable behavior and suggests how you can rewrite it. The output has been reformatted to fit the page:

```
$ iex -S mix
Erlang/OTP 19 [erts-8.0] [source] [64-bit] [smp:4:4] [async-threads:10] [hipe]
  [kernel-poll:false]

Compiling 1 file (.ex)

warning: the variable "x" is unsafe as it has been set inside a
case/cond/receive/if/&&/||. Please explicitly return the variable value instead.
For example:

    case int do
      1 -> atom = :one
      2 -> atom = :two
    end

should be written as

    atom =
      case int do
        1 -> :one
        2 -> :two
      end

Unsafe variable found at:
  lib/broken.ex:10
```

```
;; similar warning for variable "y"
Generated broken app
Interactive Elixir (1.3.1) - press Ctrl+C to exit (type h() ENTER for help)
iex(1)>
```

If you decide to ignore the warnings and insist upon using the broken function, you will get an error at runtime:

```
iex(1)> Broken.bad_cond(20)
** (ArithmeticError) bad argument in arithmetic expression
    (broken) lib/broken.ex:10: Broken.bad_cond/1
```

 Elixir also lifts Erlang's tight rules on what can happen in the clause being evaluated by if and cond. Erlang only lets you use the features available in guards, ensuring that there will be no side effects. Elixir doesn't have those limits.

The Gentlest Side Effect: IO.puts

Up until Example 4-5, all of our Elixir examples focused on a single path through a group of functions. You put an argument or arguments in, and got a return value back. That approach is the cleanest way to do things: you can count on things that worked before to work again because there's no opportunity to muck up the system with leftovers of past processing.

Example 4-5 stepped outside of that model, creating a side effect that will linger after the function is complete. The side effect is just a message that appears in the shell (or in standard output when you start running Elixir outside of the shell). Applications that share information with multiple users or keep information around for longer than a brief processing cycle will need stronger side effects, like storing information in databases.

Elixir best practice suggests using side effects *only* when you really need to. An application that presents an interface to a database, for example, really will need to read from and write to that database. An application that interacts with users will need to put information on the screen (or other interface) so that users can figure out what they're expected to do.

Side effects are also extremely useful for tracing logic when you are first starting out. The simplest way to see what a program is doing, before you've learned how to use the built-in tracing and debugging tools for processes, is to have the program report its status at points you consider interesting. This is not a feature you want to leave in shipping code, but when you're getting started, it can give you an easily understandable window into your code's behavior.

The `IO.puts` function lets you send information to the console, or, when you're eventually running code outside of the console, to other places. For now, you'll just use it to send messages from the program to the console. Example 4-5 showed the simplest way to use `IO.puts`, just printing a message it takes in double quotes:

```
IO.puts("Look out below!")
```

`IO.puts` adds a *newline* to the end, telling the console to start any new messages it sends at the beginning of the next line. This makes your results look a bit neater. If you don't want a newline, you can use `IO.write` instead. If you want to print a variable that isn't a string, you can use `IO.inspect`.

Elixir flatly prohibits operations that could cause side effects in guard expressions. If side effects were allowed in guards, then any time a guard expression was evaluated—whether it returned `true` or `false`—the side effect would happen. `IO.puts` wouldn't likely do anything terrible, but these rules mean that it too is blocked from use in guard expressions.

Simple Recursion

The main tool you'll use to repeat actions is *recursion*: having a function call itself until it's (hopefully) reached a conclusion. This can sound complicated, but it doesn't have to be.

There are two basic kinds of useful recursion. In some situations, you can count on the recursion to reach a natural end. The process runs out of items to work on or reaches a natural limit. In other situations, there is no natural end, and you need to keep track of the result so the process will end. If you can master these two basic forms, you'll be able to create many more complex variations.

There is a third form, in which the recursive calls never reach an end. This is called an *infinite loop* and is best known as an error you'll want to avoid. As you'll see in Chapter 9, though, even unending recursion can be useful when you want to continually receive messages from a process.

Counting Down

The simplest model of recursion with a natural limit is a countdown, like the one used for rockets. You start with a large number and count down to zero. When you reach zero, you're done (and the rocket takes off, if there is one).

To implement this in Elixir, you'll pass a starting number to an Elixir function. If the number is greater than zero, it will then announce the number and call itself with the number minus one as the argument. If the number is zero (or less), it will announce blastoff! and end. Example 4-7, found in *ch04/ex7-countdown*, shows one way to do this.

Example 4-7. Counting down

```
defmodule Count do

  def countdown(from) when from > 0 do
    IO.inspect(from)
    countdown(from-1)
  end

  def countdown(from) do
    IO.puts("blastoff!")
  end

end
```

The last clause could have a guard—when from <= 0—but it would be useful only to make it clear to human readers when the blastoff happens . Unnecessary guard clauses may lead to later confusion, so brevity is probably the best option here. However, you'll get a warning that from is unused in the final clause. Here's a test run:

```
$ iex -S mix
Erlang/OTP 19 [erts-8.0] [source] [64-bit] [smp:4:4] [async-threads:10] [hipe]
 [kernel-poll:false]

Compiling 1 file (.ex)
warning: variable from is unused
  lib/count.ex:8

Generated count app
Interactive Elixir (1.3.1) - press Ctrl+C to exit (type h() ENTER for help)
iex(1)> Count.countdown(2)
2
1
blastoff!
:ok
```

The first time through, Elixir chose the first clause of countdown(from), passing it a value of 2. That clause printed 2, plus a newline, and then it called the countdown function again, passing it a value of 1. That triggered the first clause again. It printed 1, plus a newline, and then it called the countdown function again—this time passing it a value of 0.

The value of 0 triggered the second clause, which printed blastoff! and ended. After running three values through the same set of code, the function comes to a neat conclusion.

You could also implement this conclusion with an `if` statement inside a single `countdown(from)` function clause, although this is unusual in Elixir. We find guards more readable in these cases, but you may see things differently.

Counting Up

Counting up is trickier because there's no natural endpoint, so you can't model your code on Example 4-7. Instead, you can use an *accumulator*. An accumulator is an extra argument that keeps track of the current result of past work, passing it back into a recursive function. (You can have more than one accumulator argument if you need, though one is often sufficient.) Example 4-8, which you can find in *ch04/ex8-countup*, shows how to add a `countup()` function to the `count` module. This function lets Elixir count up to a number.

Example 4-8. Counting up

```
defmodule Count do

  def countup(limit) do
    countup(1,limit)
  end

  defp countup(count, limit) when count <= limit do
    IO.inspect(count)
    countup(count+1, limit)
  end

  # use underscore to avoid "unused variable" warnings

  defp countup(_count, _limit) do
    IO.puts("finished!")
  end

end
```

It produces results like the following:

```
iex(1)> Count.countup(2)
1
2
finished!
:ok
```

The `countup/2` function, which does most of the work, remains private and is not exported. This isn't mandatory—you might make it public if you wanted to support counting between arbitrary values—but it's a common practice. Keeping the recursive internal functions private makes it less likely that someone will misuse them for purposes they're not well suited to. In this case, it doesn't matter at all, but it can make a big difference in other more complex situations, especially when data is modified.

When you call countup/1, it calls countup/2 with an argument of 1 (for the current count) and the limit value you provided for the upper limit.

If the current count is less than or equal to the upper limit, the first clause of the countup/2 function reports the current count value with IO.puts. Then it calls itself again, increasing the count by one but leaving the limit alone.

If the current count is greater than the upper limit, it fails the guard on the first clause, so the second clause kicks in: it reports "Finished." and is done.

 The guards here are sufficient to avoid infinite loops. You can enter zero, negative numbers, or decimals as arguments to countup/1 and it will terminate neatly. You can get into serious trouble, however, if your termination test relies on == or === for comparison to a single value rather than >= or <= for comparison to a range.

Recursing with Return Values

The counting examples we've seen so far are simple—they demonstrate how recursion works, but just discard the return values. There are return values—the IO.puts calls return the atom :ok—but they aren't of much use. More typically, a recursive function call will make use of the return value.

A classic recursive call calculates factorials. A factorial is the product of all positive integers equal to or less than the argument. The factorial of 1 is 1; 1 by itself yields 1. The factorial of 2 is 2; 2 × 1 yields 2. It starts to get interesting at 3, where 3 × 2 × 1 is 6. At 4, 4 × 3 × 2 × 1 is 24, and the results get rapidly larger with larger arguments.

There was a pattern to that, though. You can calculate the factorial of any integer by multiplying the integer by the factorial of one less than that integer. That makes it a perfect case for using recursion, using the results of smaller integers to calculate the larger ones. This approach is similar to the countdown logic, but instead of just counting, the program collects calculated results. That could look like Example 4-9, which you'll find in *ch04/ex9-factorial-down*.

Example 4-9. A factorial written with the counting-down approach

```
defmodule Fact do

  def factorial(n) when n > 1 do
    n * factorial(n - 1)
  end
```

```
  def factorial(n) when n <= 1 do
    1
  end
end
```

The first clause of factorial, used for numbers greater than 1, uses the pattern previously described. It returns a value that is the number, *n*, times the factorial of the next integer down. The second clause returns the value 1 when *n* reaches 1. Using <= in that comparison, rather than ==, gives the function more resilience against non-integer or negative arguments, though the answers it returns aren't quite right: factorials really only work for integers of 1 or higher. The results are as previously suggested:

```
iex(1)> Fact.factorial(1)
1
iex(2)> Fact.factorial(3)
6
iex(3)> Fact.factorial(4)
24
iex(4)> Fact.factorial(40)
815915283247897734345611269596115894272000000000
```

This works, but it may not be clear why it works. Yes, the function counts down and collects the values, but if you want to see the mechanism, you need to add some IO.puts calls into the code, as shown in Example 4-10. (You can find this in *ch04/ ex10-factorial-down-instrumented*.)

Example 4-10. Looking into the factorial recursion calls

```
defmodule Fact do

  def factorial(n) when n > 1 do
    IO.puts("Calling from #{n}.")
    result = n * factorial(n - 1)
    IO.puts("#{n} yields #{result}.")
    result
  end

  def factorial(n) when n <= 1 do
    IO.puts("Calling from 1.")
    IO.puts("1 yields 1.")
    1
  end
end
```

There's a bit more overhead here. To present the result of the recursive call and still return that value to the next recursive call requires storing it in a variable, here called result. The IO.puts call makes visible which value produced the result. Then, because the last value expression in a function clause is the return value, result appears again. The second clause, for 1, is similar, except that it can report simply that 1 yields 1. because it always will.

When you compile this and run it, you'll see something like the following:

```
iex(1)> Fact.factorial(4)
Calling from 4.
Calling from 3.
Calling from 2.
Calling from 1.
1 yields 1.
2 yields 2.
3 yields 6.
4 yields 24.
24
```

Although the calls count down the values, as the function logic would suggest, the messages about results don't appear until the countdown is complete, and then they all appear in order, counting up.

The reason this happens is that the function calls don't return values until the countdown is complete. Until then, Elixir builds a stack of frames corresponding to the function calls. You can think of the frames as paused versions of the function logic, waiting for an answer to come back. Once the call with an argument of 1 returns a simple value, not calling any further, Elixir can unwind those frames and calculate the result. That unwinding presents the results—"X yields Y."—in the order that the frames unwind.

That "unwinding" also means that the code in Examples 4-9 and 4-10 is not *tail recursive*. When Elixir encounters code that ends with a simple recursive call, it can optimize the handling to avoid keeping that stack of calls around. This probably doesn't matter for a one-time calculation, but it makes a huge difference when you write code that will stay running for a long time.

You can achieve tail recursion for factorials by applying the counting-up approach to factorials. You'll get the same results—at least for integer values—but the calculations will work a little differently, as shown in Example 4-11 (in *ch04/ex11-factorial-up*).

Example 4-11. A factorial written with the counting-up approach

```
defmodule Fact do

  def factorial(n) do
    factorial(1, n, 1)
  end

  defp factorial(current, n, result) when current <= n do
    new_result = result * current
    IO.puts("#{current} yields #{new_result}.")
```

```
    factorial(current + 1, n, new_result)
  end

  defp factorial(_current, _n, result) do
    IO.puts("finished!")
    result
  end

end
```

As in the counting-up example, the main function call (here, factorial/1) calls a private function, factorial/3. In this case, there are two accumulators. current stores the current position in the count, whereas result is the answer from the previous multiplication. When the value of current climbs past the limiting value n, the first guard fails, the second clause is invoked, and the function is finished and returns the result. (To avoid a compiler warning, we precede the accumulator variables current and n with an underscore, because the final clause doesn't use them.)

Because factorial/3's last call in the recursive section is to itself, without any complications to track, it is tail recursive. Elixir can minimize the amount of information it has to keep around while the calls all happen.

The calculation produces the same results, but does the math in a different order:

```
iex(1)> Fact.factorial(4)
1 yields 1.
2 yields 2.
3 yields 6.
4 yields 24.
finished!
24
```

Although the code is tracking more values, the runtime has less to do. When it finally hits the final result, there's no further calculation needed. That result is the result, and it passes back through to the original call. This also makes it easier to structure the IO.puts calls. If you remove them or comment them out, the rest of the code stays the same.

## CHAPTER 5

Communicating with Humans

Elixir rebuilds the Erlang tools for working with strings from scratch, bringing them up to speed for Unicode (UTF-8) and recognizing that strings deserve more focus than just a list of characters. Chapter 4 showed you a bit of string handling and presentation (`IO.puts`), but there are more pieces you'll want to learn to handle communications with people and sometimes with other applications. At the very least, this chapter will let you build more convenient interfaces for testing your code than calling functions from IEx.

 If you're feeling completely excited about the recursion you learned about in Chapter 4, you may want to jump ahead to Chapter 6, where that recursion will once again be front and center.

Strings

Atoms are great for sending messages within a program, even messages that the programmer can remember, but they're not really designed for communicating outside of the context of Erlang processes. If you need to be assembling sentences or even presenting information, you'll want something more flexible. Strings are the structure you need. You've already used strings a little bit, as the double-quoted arguments to `IO.puts` in Example 4-5:

```
IO.puts("Look out below!")
```

The double-quoted content (`Look out below!`) is a string. A string is a sequence of characters. If you want to include a double quote within the string, you can escape it with a backslash, like \". \n gives you a newline. To include a backslash, you have to use \\. Appendix A includes a complete list of escapes and other options.

If you create a string in the shell, Elixir will report back the string *with* the escapes. To see what it "really" contains, use IO.puts:

```
iex(1)> x= "Quote -  \" in a string. \n  Backslash, too: \\ . \n"
"Quote -  \" in a string. \n  Backslash, too: \\ . \n"
iex(2)> IO.puts(x)
Quote -  " in a string.
  Backslash, too: \ .

:ok
```

 If you start entering a string and don't close the quotes, when you press Enter IEx will just give you a newline with the same number. This lets you include newlines in strings, but it can be very confusing. If you think you're stuck, usually entering " will get you out of it.

Elixir also provides operations for creating new strings. The simplest is *concatenation*, where you combine two strings into one. Elixir uses the unusual-looking but functional <> operator:

```
iex(3)> "el" <> "ixir"
"elixir"
iex(4)> a="el"
"el"
iex(5)> a <> "ixir"
"elixir"
```

Elixir also has string interpolation, using {} as a wrapper around content to be added to the string. You used this in Example 4-10 to see the value of variables:

```
IO.puts("#{n} yields #{result}.")
```

When Elixir encounters #{} in a string, it evaluates the expression in the braces to get a value, converts it to a string if necessary, and combines the pieces into a single string. That interpolation happens only once. Even if the variable used in the string changes, the contents of the interpolated string will remain the same:

```
iex(6)> a = "this"
"this"
iex(7)> b = "The value of a is #{a}."
"The value of a is this."
iex(8)> a = "that"
"that"
iex(9)> b
"The value of a is this."
```

You can put anything that returns a value in the interpolation: a variable, a function call, or an operation on parts. We find it most readable to just have variables, but your usage may vary. As with any other calculation, if the value to be interpolated can't be calculated, you'll get an error.

Interpolation works only for values that are already strings or can naturally be converted to strings (such as numbers). If you want to interpolate any other sort of value, you must wrap it in a call to the inspect function:

```
iex(10)> x = 7 * 5
35
iex(11)> "x is now #{x}"
"x is now 35"
iex(12)> y = {4, 5, 6}
{4,5,6}
iex(13)> "y is now #{y}"
** (Protocol.UndefinedError) protocol String.Chars not
implemented for {4, 5, 6}
    (elixir) lib/string/chars.ex:3:
      String.Chars.impl_for!/1
    (elixir) lib/string/chars.ex:17:
      String.Chars.to_string/1
iex(14)> "y is now #{inspect y}"
"y is now {4,5,6}"
```

Elixir also offers two options for comparing string equality, the == operator and the === (exact or strict equality) operator. The == operator is generally the simplest for this, though the other produces the same results:

```
iex(15)> "el" == "el"
true
iex(16)> "el" == "ixir"
false
iex(17)> "el" === "el"
true
iex(18)> "el" === "ixir"
false
```

Elixir doesn't offer functions for changing strings in place, as that would work badly with a model where variable contents don't change. However, it does offer a set of functions for finding content in strings and dividing or padding those strings, which together let you extract information from a string (or multiple strings) and recombine it into a new string.

If you want to do more with your strings, you should definitely explore the documentation for the String and Regex (regular expressions) Elixir modules.

Multiline Strings

Multiline strings, sometimes called *heredocs*, let you create strings containing new-lines. Chapter 2 mentioned them briefly, as a convenience for creating documentation, but you can use them for other purposes as well.

Unlike regular strings, multiline strings open and close with three double quotes:

```
iex(1)> multi = """
...(1)> This is a multiline
...(1)> string, also called a heredoc.
...(1)> """
"This is a multiline\nstring, also called a heredoc.\n"
iex(2)> IO.puts(multi)
This is a multiline
string, also called a heredoc.

:ok
```

Apart from the different way you enter them, you process multiline strings the same way as any other strings.

Unicode

Elixir works well with Unicode (UTF-8) strings. The `String.length/1` function returns the number of Unicode graphemes in its argument. This is not necessarily the same as the number of bytes in the string, as more than one byte is needed to represent many Unicode characters. If you do need to know the number of bytes, you can use the `byte_size/1` function:

```
iex(1)> str="서울 - 대한민국" # Seoul, Republic of Korea
"서울 - 대한민국"
iex(2)> String.length(str)
9
iex(3)> byte_size(str)
21
```

Character Lists

Elixir's string handling is a major change from Erlang's approach. In Erlang, all the strings are lists of characters; the same kind of lists you'll learn about in Chapter 6. As many Elixir programs will need to work with Erlang libraries, Elixir provides support for character lists as well as strings.

Character lists are slower to work with and take up more memory than strings, so they shouldn't be your first choice.

To create a character list, you use single quotes instead of double quotes:

```
iex(1)> x = 'ixir'
'ixir'
```

You concatenate character lists with ++ instead of <>:

```
iex(2)> 'el' ++ 'ixir'
'elixir'
```

You can convert character lists to strings with `List.to_string/1` and strings to character lists with `String.to_char_list/1`:

```
iex(3)> List.to_string('elixir')
"elixir"
iex(4)> String.to_char_list("elixir")
'elixir'
```

For purposes other than working with Erlang libraries, you should probably stick with strings. (Chapter 6 will explain more about working with lists, and these may be helpful if you have data that you want to treat explicitly as a list of characters.)

String Sigils

Elixir offers another way to create strings, character lists, and regular expressions you can apply to the other two formats. *String sigils* tell the interpreter, "This is going to be this kind of content."

Sigils start with a ~ (tilde), then one of the letters s (for binary string), c (for character list), r (for regular expression), or w (to produce a list split into words by whitespace). If the letter is lowercase, then interpolation and escaping happen as usual. If the letter is uppercase (S, C, R, or W), then the string is created exactly as shown, with no escaping or interpolation. After the letter, in addition to quotes, you can use slashes, square brackets, pipe symbols (|), parentheses, braces, or angle brackets to start and end the string.

This sounds complicated, but it works pretty easily. For example, if you needed to create a string that contained escapes that some other tool was going to process, you might write:

```
iex(1)> pass_through = ~S"This is a {#msg}, she said.\n  This is only a {#msg}."
"This is a {#msg}, she said.\\n  This is only a {#msg}."
iex(2)> IO.puts(pass_through)
```

```
This is a {#msg}, she said.\n  This is only a {#msg}.
:ok
```

Elixir also offers w and W, for lists of words. This sigil takes a binary string and splits it into a list of strings separated by whitespace:

```
iex(3)> ~w/Elixir is great!/
["Elixir", "is", "great!"]
```

 You can also create your own sigils for your own formats. See the Elixir website (*http://bit.ly/1lbMOnw*) for more on these possibilities.

Asking Users for Information

Many Elixir applications run kind of like wholesalers—in the background, providing goods and services to retailers who interact directly with users. Sometimes, however, it's nice to have a direct interface to code that is a little more customized than the IEx command line. You probably won't write many Elixir applications whose primary interface is the command line, but you may find that interface very useful when you first try out your code. (Odds are good that if you're working with Elixir, you don't mind using a command-line interface, either.)

You *can* mix input and output with your program logic, but for this kind of simple facade, it probably makes better sense to put it in a separate module. In this case, the Ask module will work with the Drop module from Example 3-8.

Gathering Characters

The IO.getn function will let you get just a few characters from the user. This seems like it should be convenient if, for example, you have a list of options: present the options to the user, and wait for a response. In Example 5-1, which you can find in *ch05/ex1-ask*, the options are the list of planemos, which are numbered 1 through 3. That means you just need a single-character response.

Example 5-1. Presenting a menu and waiting for a single-character response

```
defmodule Ask do

  def chars() do
    IO.puts("""
    Which planemo are you on?
      1. Earth
      2. Moon
      3. Mars
```

```
    """)

    IO.getn("Which? > ")

  end
end
```

Most of that code is presenting the menu. The key piece is the IO.getn call at the end. The first argument is a prompt, and the second is the number of characters you want returned, with a default value of 1. The function still lets users enter whatever they want until they press Enter, but it will tell you only the first character (or however many characters you specified), and it will return it as a string:

```
iex(1)> c("ask.ex")
[Ask]
iex(2)> Ask.chars
Which planemo are you on?
1. Earth
2. Earth's Moon
3. Mars

Which? > 3
"3"
iex(3)>
nil
iex(4)>
```

The IO.getn function returns the string "3", the character the user entered before pressing Enter. However, as you can tell by the nil and the duplicated command prompt, the Enter still gets reported to IEx. This can get stranger if users enter more content than is needed:

```
iex(5)> Ask.chars
Which planemo are you on?
1. Earth
2. Earth's Moon
3. Mars

Which? > 23456
"2"
iex(6)> 3456
3456
iex(7)>
```

There may be times when IO.getn is exactly what you want, but odds are good, at least when working within IEx, that you'll get cleaner results by taking in a complete line of user input and picking what you want from it.

Reading Lines of Text

Elixir offers a few different functions that pause to request information from users. The IO.gets function waits for the user to enter a complete line of text terminated by a newline. You can then process the line to extract the information you want, and nothing will be left in the buffer. Example 5-2, in *ch05/ex2-ask*, shows how this could work, though extracting the information is somewhat more complicated than we might like.

Example 5-2. Collecting user responses a line at a time

```
defmodule Ask do

  def line() do
    planemo=get_planemo()
    distance=get_distance()
    Drop.fall_velocity({planemo, distance})
  end

  defp get_planemo() do
    IO.puts("""
    Which planemo are you on?
      1. Earth
      2. Earth's Moon
      3. Mars
    """)

    answer = IO.gets("Which? > ")
    value=String.first(answer)
    char_to_planemo(value)
  end

defp get_distance() do
   input = IO.gets("How far? (meters) > ")
   value = String.strip(input)
   String.to_integer(value)
end

defp char_to_planemo(char) do
   case char do
       "1" -> :earth
       "2" -> :moon
       "3" -> :mars
   end
  end

end
```

The line function just calls three other functions. It calls get_planemo to present a menu to the user and get a reply, and it similarly calls get_distance to ask the user the distance of the fall. Then it calls `Drop.fall_velocity` to return the velocity at which a frictionless object will hit the ground when dropped from that height at that location.

The `get_planemo` function uses `IO.puts` and a multiline string to present information and an `IO.gets` call to retrieve information from the user. Unlike `IO.getn`, `IO.gets` returns the entire value the user entered as a string, including the newline, and leaves nothing in the buffer:

```
defp get_planemo() do
  IO.puts("""
  Which planemo are you on?
    1. Earth
    2. Earth's Moon
    3. Mars
  """)

  answer = IO.gets("Which? > ")
  value=String.first(answer)
  char_to_planemo(value)
end
```

The last two lines process the result. The only piece of the response that matters to this application is the first character of the response. The easy way to grab that is with the built-in function `String.first`, which pulls the first character from a string.

The `Drop.fall_velocity()` function won't know what to do with a planemo listed as 1, 2, or 3; it expects an atom of `:earth`, `:moon`, or `:mars`. The `get_planemo` function concludes by returning the value of that conversion, performed by the function `char_to_planemo()`:

```
defp char_to_planemo(char) do
  case char do
    "1" -> :earth
    "2" -> :moon
    "3" -> :mars
  end
end
```

The `case` statement matches against the string. The atom returned by the `case` statement will be returned to the `get_planemo/0` function, which will in turn return it to the `line/0` function for use in the calculation.

Getting the distance is somewhat easier:

```
defp get_distance() do
  input = IO.gets("How far? (meters) > ")
  value = String.strip(input)
  String.to_integer(value)
end
```

The `input` variable collects the user's response to the question, "How far?" The processing for `value` uses `String.strip` to remove any surrounding whitespace from `input`, including the newline at the end. Finally, the `String.to_integer` function extracts an integer from `value`. Using `String.to_integer` isn't perfect, but for these purposes, it's probably acceptable.

A sample run demonstrates that it produces the right results given the right input:

```
iex(1)> c("ask.ex")
[Ask]
iex(2)> c("drop.ex")
[Drop]
iex(3)> Ask.line
Which planemo are you on?
1. Earth
2. Earth's Moon
3. Mars

Which? > 1
How far? (meters) > 20
19.79898987322333
iex(4)> Ask.line
Which planemo are you on?
1. Earth
2. Earth's Moon
3. Mars

Which? > 2
How far? (meters) > 20
8.0
```

Chapter 10 will return to this code, looking at better ways to handle the errors users can provoke by entering unexpected answers.

The get_planemo() function works, but it is possible to write it in a more idiomatc form. First, you can change the case to three separate functions, each written on a single line with do:

```
defp char_to_planemo("1"), do: :earth
defp char_to_planemo("2"), do: :moon
defp char_to_planemo("3"), do: :mars
```

Also, instead of using intermediate variables in get_planemo and get_distance/1, you can use the |> pipe operator:

```
defp get_planemo() do
  IO.puts("""elixir enum.unzip
  Which planemo are you on?
  1. Earth
  2. Earth's Moon
  3. Mars
  """)

  IO.gets("Which? > ")
  |> String.first()
  |> char_to_planemo()
end

defp get_distance() do
  IO.gets("How far? (meters) > ")
  |> String.strip()
  |> String.to_integer()
end
```

This updated version is in *ch05/ex3-ask*. If you do not feel comfortable writing the one-line functions or using |>, you don't have to, but you should recognize it when you see such code in other people's programs, as these techniques are very commonly used.

## CHAPTER 6

Lists

Elixir is great at handling lists, long series of similar (or not) values. List processing makes it easy to see the value of recursion and offers opportunities to get a lot of work done for very little effort.

List Basics

An Elixir list is an ordered set of elements. Generally you will process a list in order, from the first item (the *head*) to the last item, though there are times when you may want to grab a particular item from the list. Elixir also provides built-in functions for manipulating lists when you don't want to go through the entire sequence.

Elixir syntax encloses lists in square brackets and separates elements with commas. A list of numbers might look like the following:

```
[1,2,4,8,16,32]
```

The elements can be of any type, including numbers, atoms, tuples, strings, and other lists. When you're starting out, it's definitely easiest to work with lists that contain only a single type of element, rather than mixing all the possibilities, but Elixir itself has no such constraint. There is also no limit on the number of items a list can contain, though eventually you may find practical limits of memory.

You can pattern match with lists just as you can with other Elixir data structures:

```
iex(1)> [1, x, 4, y] = [1, 2, 4, 8]
[1, 2, 4, 8]
iex(2)> x
2
iex(3)> y
8
```

Your code will usually make more sense if you use tuples to handle data structures containing various kinds of data in a known sequence, and lists to handle structures containing less-varied data in unknown quantities. Tuples are expected to come in a certain order and can also contain lists, so if you have a data structure that's mostly known except for an expanding part or two, including a list inside of a tuple can be a workable solution.

Lists can contain lists, and sometimes this can produce surprising results. If, for example, you want to add a list to a list, you may end up with more levels of list than you planned:

```
iex(4)> insert = [2, 4, 8]
[2, 4, 8]
iex(5)> full = [1, insert, 16, 32]
[1, [2, 4, 8], 16, 32]
```

You can fix that (if you want to) with the List.flatten/1 function:

```
iex(6)> neat = List.flatten(full)
[1, 2, 4, 8, 16, 32]
```

This also means that if you want to append lists, you need to decide whether you're creating a list of lists or a single list containing the contents of the component lists. To create a list of lists, you just put lists into lists:

```
iex(7)> a = [1, 2, 4]
[1, 2, 4]
iex(8)> b = [8, 16, 32]
[8, 16, 32]
iex(9)> list_of_lists = [a, b]
[[1, 2, 4], [8, 16, 32]]
```

To create a single list from multiple lists, you can use the Enum.concat/2 function or the equivalent ++ operator:

```
iex(10)> combined = Enum.concat(a, b)
[1, 2, 4, 8, 16, 32]
iex(11)> combined2 = a ++ b
[1, 2, 4, 8, 16, 32]
```

Both produce the same result: a combined and flattened list.

The ++ operator is right associative, which can change the order of the resulting list when you append multiple lists.

If you have a set of lists you'd like combined, you can use the `Enum.concat/1` function, which takes a list of lists as its argument and returns a single list containing their contents:

```
iex(12)> c = [64, 128, 256]
[64, 128, 256]
iex(13)> combined3 = Enum.concat([a, b, c])
[1, 2, 4, 8, 16, 32, 64, 128, 256]
```

Splitting Lists into Heads and Tails

Lists are a convenient way to hold piles of similar data, but their great strength in Elixir is the way they make it easy to do recursion. Lists are a natural fit for the counting-down style of logic explored in "Counting Down" on page 47: you can run through a list until you run out of items. In many languages, running through a list means finding out how many items it contains and going through them sequentially. Elixir takes a different approach, letting you process the first item in a list, the *head*, while extracting the rest of the list, the *tail*, so that you can pass it to another call recursively.

To extract the head and the tail, you use pattern matching, with a special form of the list syntax on the left:

```
[head | tail] = [1,2,4]
```

The two variables separated by a vertical bar (|), or *cons*, for list constructor, will be bound to the head and tail of the list on the right. In the console, Elixir will just report the contents of the right side of the expression, not the fragments created by the pattern match, but if you work through a list you can see the results:

```
iex(1)> list = [1, 2, 4]
[1, 2, 4]
iex(2)> [h1 | t1] = list
[1, 2, 4]
iex(3)> h1
1
iex(4)> t1
[2, 4]
iex(5)> [h2 | t2] = t1
[2, 4]
iex(6)> h2
2
iex(7)> t2
[4]
iex(8)> [h3 | t3] = t2
[4]
iex(9)> h3
4
iex(10)> t3
[]
```

```
iex(11)> [h4 | t4] = t3
** (MatchError) no match of right hand side value: []
```

Line 2 copies the initial list into two smaller pieces. h1 will contain the first item of the list, whereas t1 will contain a list that has everything *except* the first element. Line 5 repeats the process on the smaller list, breaking t1 into an h2 and a t2. This time t2 is still a list, as shown on line 7, but it contains only one item. Line 8 breaks that single-item list again, putting the value into h3 and an *empty* list into t3.

What happens when you try to split an empty list, as shown on line 11? Elixir reports an error, "no match...". This fortunately does not mean that recursion on lists is doomed to produce errors. That lack of a match will naturally stop the recursive process, which is probably what you want.

 Since extracting the head and tail gives you the first and remaining elements in a list, you use them when you want to move forward through a list. If order matters and you really need to go through a list backward, you'll need to use the Enum.reverse function and then walk through the reversed list.

Processing List Content

The head-and-tail notation was built for recursive processing. Actually making that work typically follows a pattern in which a list arrives as an argument and is then passed to another (usually private) function with an accumulator argument. A simple case might perform a calculation on the contents of the list. Example 6-1, in *ch06/ex1-product*, shows this pattern in use, multiplying the values of a list together.

Example 6-1. Calculating the product of values in a list

```
defmodule Overall do
  def product([]) do
    0
  end

  def product(list) do
    product(list, 1)
  end

  def product([], accumulated_product) do
    accumulated_product
  end

  def product([head | tail], accumulated_product) do
    product(tail, head * accumulated_product)
  end
end
```

In this module, the product/1 function is the gateway, passing the list (if the list has content) plus an accumulator to product/2, which does the real work. If you wanted to test the arriving list to make sure it meets your expectations, it would probably make the most sense to do that work in product/1, and let product/2 focus on recursive processing.

 Is the product of an empty list really zero? It might make more sense for an empty list to fail and produce a crash. Elixir's "let it crash" philosophy is, as you'll see later, pretty calm about such things. In the long run, you'll have to decide which cases are better left to crash and which shouldn't.

The product/2 function has two clauses. The first matches the empty list and will get called at the end of the recursive process when there are no more entries to process, or if the list arrives empty. It returns its second argument, the accumulator.

The second clause does more work if the arriving list is not empty. First, the pattern match ([head|tail]) splits off the first value in the list from the rest of the list. Next, it calls product/2 again, with the remaining (if any) portion of the list and a new accumulator that is multiplied by the value of the first entry in the list. The result will be the product of the values included in the list:

```
iex(1)> Overall.product([1, 2, 3, 5])
30
```

That went smoothly, but what happened? After product/1 called product/2, it made five iterations over the list, concluding with an empty list, as shown in Table 6-1.

Table 6-1. Recursive processing of a simple list in product/2

Arriving list	Arriving product	Head	Tail
[1, 2, 3, 5]	1	1	[2, 3, 5]
[2, 3, 5]	1 (1*1)	2	[3, 5]
[3, 5]	2 (1*2)	3	[5]
[5]	6 (2*3)	5	[]
[]	30 (6*5)	None	None

The last arriving accumulated_product, 30, will be handled by the clause for the empty list and reported as the return value for product/2. When product/1 receives that value, it will also report 30 as its return value and exit.

Because strings in single quotes are lists, you can do strange things like enter `Overall.product('funny')`. `product/1` will interpret the character values as numbers and return `17472569400`.

Creating Lists with Heads and Tails

While there are times you want to calculate a single value from a list, much list processing involves modifying lists or converting a list into another list. Because you can't actually change a list, modifying or converting a list means creating a new list. To do that, you use the same vertical bar head/tail syntax, but on the right side of the pattern match instead of the left. You can try this out in the console, though it's more useful in a module:

```
iex(1)> x = [1 | [2, 3]]
[1, 2, 3]
```

Elixir interprets `[1|[2,3]]` as creating a list. If the value to the right of the vertical bar is a list, the head gets prepended to that list (put on the front of it). In this case, the result is a neat list of numbers. There are a few other forms you should be aware of:

```
iex(2)> y = [1, 2 | [3]]
[1, 2, 3]
iex(3)> z = [1, 2 | 3]
[1, 2 | 3]
```

In line 2, there isn't a list wrapped around the now two items in the head, but the constructor still blends the head and the tail together seamlessly. (If you do wrap them in square brackets, the list constructor assumes that you want a list as the first item in the list, so `[[1,2] | [3]]` will produce `[[1,2],3]`.)

However, line 3 demonstrates what happens if you don't wrap the tail in square brackets—you get a list, called an *improper list*, that still contains a constructor, with a strange tail. Until you've learned your way quite thoroughly around Elixir, you definitely should avoid this, as it will create runtime errors if you try to process it as a normal list. Eventually you may find rare reasons to do this or encounter code that uses it.

More typically, you'll use list constructors to build lists inside recursive functions. Example 6-2, which you can find in *ch06/ex2-drop*, starts from a set of tuples representing planemos and distances. With the help of the `Drop` module from Example 3-8, it creates a list of velocities for the corresponding falls.

Example 6-2. Calculating a series of drop velocities, with an error

```
defmodule ListDrop do
  def falls(list) do
```

```
    falls(list, [])
  end

  def falls([], results) do
    results
  end

  def falls([head|tail], results) do
    falls(tail, [Drop.fall_velocity(head) | results])
  end
end
```

Much of this is familiar, except that the results variable gets a list instead of a number, and the last line of falls/2 creates a list instead of a single value. If you run it, however, you'll see one minor problem:

```
$ iex -S mix
Erlang/OTP 19 [erts-8.0] [source] [64-bit] [smp:4:4] [async-threads:10] [hipe]
 [kernel-poll:false]

Compiling 2 files (.ex)
Generated list_drop app
Interactive Elixir (1.3.1) - press Ctrl+C to exit (type h() ENTER for help)
iex(1)>> ListDrop.falls([{:earth, 20}, {:moon, 20}, {:mars, 20}])
[12.181953866272849, 8.0, 19.79898987322333]
```

The resulting velocities are reversed: the Earth has more gravity than Mars, and objects should fall faster on Earth. What happened? That last key line in falls/2 is reading a list from the beginning to the end and creating a list from the end to the beginning. That puts the values in the wrong order. Fortunately, as Example 6-3 (in *ch06/ex3-drop*) demonstrates, this is easy to fix. You need to call Enum.reverse/1 in the clause of the falls/2 function that handles the empty list.

Example 6-3. Calculating a series of drop velocities, with the error fixed

```
defmodule ListDrop do
  def falls(list) do
    falls(list, [])
  end

  def falls([], results) do
    Enum.reverse(results)
  end

  def falls([head|tail], results) do
    falls(tail, [Drop.fall_velocity(head) | results])
  end
end
```

Now it works:

```
iex(2)> r(ListDrop)
warning: redefining module ListDrop (current version loaded from
  _build/dev/lib/list_drop/ebin/Elixir.ListDrop.beam)
  lib/list_drop.ex:1
iex(3)> ListDrop.falls([{:earth, 20}, {:moon, 20}, {:mars, 20}])
[19.79898987322333, 8.0, 12.181953866272849]
```

You could instead have put the Enum.reverse/1 call in the falls/1 gateway function. Either way is fine, though we prefer to have falls/2 return a finished result.

Mixing Lists and Tuples

As you get deeper into Elixir and pass around more complex data structures, you may find that you're processing lists full of tuples, or that it would be more convenient to rearrange two lists into a single list of tuples or vice versa. The Enum module includes easy solutions to these kinds of transformations and searches.

The simplest tools are the Enum.zip/2 and Enum.unzip/1 functions. They can turn two lists of the same size into a list of tuples or a list of tuples into a tuple of two lists:

```
iex(1)> list1 = ["Hydrogen", "Helium", "Lithium"]
["Hydrogen", "Helium", "Lithium"]
iex(2)> list2 = ["H", "He", "Li"]
["H", "He", "Li"]
iex(3)> element_list = Enum.zip(list1, list2)
[{"Hydrogen", "H"}, {"Helium", "He"}, {"Lithium", "Li"}]
iex(4)> separate_lists = Enum.unzip(element_list)
{["Hydrogen", "Helium", "Lithium"], ["H", "He", "Li"]}
```

The two lists, list1 and list2, have different contents but the same number of items. The List.zip/1 function returns a list containing a tuple for each of the items in the original lists. The List.unzip/1 function takes that list of two-component tuples and splits it out into a tuple containing two lists.

Building a List of Lists

While simple recursion isn't too complicated, list processing has a way of turning into lists of lists in various stages. Pascal's triangle, a classic mathematical tool, is relatively simple to create but demonstrates more intricate work with lists. It starts with a 1 at the top, and then each new row is composed of the sum of the two numbers above it:

```
        1
      1   1
    1   2   1
  1   3   3   1
1   4   6   4   1
  . . .
```

If those numbers seem familiar, it's probably because they're the binomial coefficents that appear when you put (*x*+*y*) to a power. That's just the beginning of this mathematical marvel!

Pascal's triangle is easily calculated with Elixir in a number of ways. You can apply the list techniques already discussed in this chapter by treating each row as a list, and the triangle as a list of lists. The code will be seeded with the first row—the top 1—represented as [0,1,0]. The extra zeros make the addition much simpler.

 This is not intended to be an efficient, elegant, or maximally compact implementation. At this point, a naive implementation likely explains more about lists.

For a first step, Example 6-4, found in *ch06/ex4-pascal*, calculates rows individually. This is a simple recursive process, walking over the old list and adding its contents to create a new list.

Example 6-4. Calculating a row

```
defmodule Pascal do
  def add_row(initial) do
    add_row(initial, 0, [])
  end

  def add_row([], 0, final) do
    [0 | final]
  end

  def add_row([h | t], last, new) do
    add_row(t, h, [last + h | new])
  end
end
```

The add_row/1 function sets things up, sending the current row a 0 to get the math started and an empty list you can think of as "where the results go," though it is really an accumulator. The add_row/3 function has two clauses. The first checks to see if the list being added is empty. If it is, then the function reports back the final row, adding a 0 at the front.

Most of the work gets done in the second clause of add_row/3. When it receives its arguments, the [h | t] pattern match splits the head of the list into the h value (a number) and the tail into t (a list, which may be empty if that was the last number). It also gets values for the last number processed and the current new list being built.

It then makes a recursive call to add_row/3. In that new call, the tail of the old list, t, is the new list to process; the h value becomes the last number processed; and the third argument, the list, opens with the actual addition being performed, which is then combined with the rest of the new list being built.

 Because the lists in the triangle are symmetrical, there is no need to use Enum.reverse/1 to flip them. You can, of course, if you want to.

You can test this easily from the console, but remember that your test lists need to be wrapped in zeros:

```
iex(1)> Pascal.add_row([0, 1, 0])
[0, 1, 1, 0]
iex(2)> Pascal.add_row([0, 1, 1, 0])
[0, 1, 2, 1, 0]
iex(3)> Pascal.add_row([0, 1, 2, 1, 0])
[0, 1, 3, 3, 1, 0]
```

Now that you can create a new row from an old one, you need to be able to create a set of rows from the top of the triangle, as shown in Example 6-5, which you can find in *ch06/ex4-pascal*. The add_row/3 function effectively counted down to the end of the list, but triangle/3 will need to count up to a given number of rows. The trian gle/1 function sets things up, defining the initial row, setting the counter to 1 (because that initial row *is* the first row), and passing on the number of rows to be created.

The triangle/3 function has two clauses. The first, the stop clause, halts the recursion when enough rows have been created and reverses the list. (The individual rows may be symmetrical, but the triangle itself is not.) The second clause does the actual work of generating new rows. It gets the previous row generated from the list, and then it passes that to the add_row/1 function, which will return a new row. Then it calls itself with the new list, an incremented count, and the rows value the stop clause needs.

Example 6-5. Calculating the whole triangle with both functions

```
defmodule Pascal do
  def triangle(rows) do
    triangle([[0,1,0]], 1, rows)
  end

  def triangle(list, count, rows) when count >= rows do
    Enum.reverse(list)
  end

  def triangle(list, count, rows) do
    [previous | _] = list
    triangle([add_row(previous) | list], count + 1, rows)
  end

  def add_row(initial) do
    add_row(initial, 0, [])
  end

  def add_row([], 0, final) do
    [0 | final]
  end

  def add_row([h | t], last, new) do
    add_row(t, h, [last + h | new])
  end
end
```

Happily, this works:

```
iex(4)> r(Pascal)
warning: redefining module Pascal (current version loaded from
  _build/dev/lib/pascal/ebin/Elixir.Pascal.beam)
  lib/pascal.ex:1

{:reloaded, Pascal, [Pascal]}
iex(5)> Pascal.triangle(4)
[[0, 1, 0], [0, 1, 1, 0], [0, 1, 2, 1, 0], [0, 1, 3, 3, 1, 0]]
iex(6)> Pascal.triangle(6)
[[0, 1, 0], [0, 1, 1, 0], [0, 1, 2, 1, 0], [0, 1, 3, 3, 1, 0],
 [0, 1, 4, 6, 4, 1, 0], [0, 1, 5, 10, 10, 5, 1, 0]]
```

Pascal's triangle may be a slightly neater set of lists than most you will process, but this kind of layered list processing is a very common tactic for processing and generating lists of data.

## CHAPTER 7

Name-Value Pairs

Tuples and lists are powerful tools for creating complex data structures, but there are two key pieces missing from the story so far. Tuples are relatively anonymous structures. Relying on a specific order and number of components in tuples can create major maintenance headaches. Lists have similar problems: the usual approaches to list processing in Elixir assume that lists are just sequences of (often) similar parts.

Sometimes you want to call things out by name instead of number, or pattern match to a specific location. Elixir has many different options for doing just that.

Maps and structs appeared late in Elixir's development. They layer directly on features Erlang introduced in R17. In the long run, maps and structs will probably become the key pieces to know, but you may need the rest for compatibility with older Erlang code.

Keyword Lists

Sometimes you need to process lists of tuples containing two elements that can be considered as a "key and value" pair, where the key is an atom. Elixir displays them in *keyword list* format, and you may enter them in that format as well:

```
iex(1)> planemo_list = [{:earth, 9.8}, {:moon, 1.6}, {:mars, 3.71}]
[earth: 9.8, moon: 1.6, mars: 3.71]
iex(2)> atomic_weights = [hydrogen: 1.008, carbon: 12.011, sodium: 22.99]
[hydrogen: 1.008, carbon: 12.011, sodium: 22.99]
iex(3)> ages = [david: 59, simon: 40, cathy: 28, simon: 30]
[david: 59, simon: 40, cathy: 28, simon: 30]
```

A keyword list is always sequential and can have duplicate keys. Elixir's Keyword module lets you access, delete, and insert values via their keys.

Use Keyword.get/3 to retrieve the first value in the list with a given key. The optional third argument to Keyword.get provides a default value to return in case the key is not in the list. Keyword.fetch!/2 will raise an error if the key is not found. Keyword.get_values/2 will return all the values for a given key:

```
iex(4)> Keyword.get(atomic_weights, :hydrogen)
1.008
iex(5)> Keyword.get(atomic_weights, :neon)
nil
iex(6)> Keyword.get(atomic_weights, :carbon, 0)
12.011
iex(7)> Keyword.get(atomic_weights, :neon, 0)
0
iex(8)> Keyword.fetch!(atomic_weights, :neon)
** (KeyError) key :neon not found in:
    [hydrogen: 1.008, carbon: 12.011, sodium: 22.99]
    (elixir) lib/keyword.ex:312: Keyword.fetch!/2
iex(8)> Keyword.get_values(ages, :simon)
[40,30]
```

You can use Keyword.has_key?/2 to see if a key exists in the list:

```
iex(9)> Keyword.has_key?(atomic_weights, :carbon)
true
iex(10)> Keyword.has_key?(atomic_weights, :neon)
false
```

To add a new value, use Keyword.put_new/3. If the key already exists, its value remains unchanged:

```
iex(11)> weights2 = Keyword.put_new(atomic_weights, :helium, 4.0026)
[helium: 4.0026, hydrogen: 1.008, carbon: 12.011, sodium: 15.999]
iex(12)> weights3 = Keyword.put_new(weights2, :helium, -1)
[helium: 4.0026, hydrogen: 1.008, carbon: 12.011, sodium: 22.99]
```

To replace a value, use Keyword.put/3. If the key doesn't exist, it will be created. If it does exist, *all* entries for that key will be removed and the new entry added:

```
iex(13)> ages2 = Keyword.put(ages, :chung, 19)
[chung: 19, david: 59, simon: 40, cathy: 28, simon: 30]
iex(14)> ages3 = Keyword.put(ages2, :simon, 22)
[simon: 22, chung: 19, david: 59, cathy: 28]
```

 All of these functions are copying lists or creating new modified versions of a list. As you'd expect in Elixir, the original list remains untouched.

If you want to delete all entries for a key, use Keyword.delete/2. To delete only the first entry for a key, use Keyword.delete_first/2:

```
iex(15)> ages2
[chung: 19, david: 59, simon: 40, cathy: 28, simon: 30]
iex(16)> ages4 = Keyword.delete(ages2, :simon)
[chung: 19, david: 59, cathy: 28]
```

Lists of Tuples with Multiple Keys

If you create the list of atomic weights with tuples that include both the element name and its chemical symbol, you can use either the first or the second element in the tuple as a key:

```
iex(1)> atomic_info = [{:hydrogen, :H, 1.008}, {:carbon, :C, 12.011},
...(1)> {:sodium, :Na, 22.99}]
[{:hydrogen, :H, 1.008}, {:carbon, :C, 12.011}, {:sodium, :Na, 22.99}]
```

If you have data structured this way, you can use the List.keyfind/4, List.keymember?/3, List.keyreplace/4, List.keystore/4, and List.keydelete/3 functions to manipulate the list. Each of these functions takes the list as its first argument. The second argument is the key you want to find, and the third argument is the position within the tuple that should be used as the key, with 0 as the first element:

```
iex(2)> List.keyfind(atomic_info, :H, 1)
{:hydrogen, :H, 1.008}
iex(3)> List.keyfind(atomic_info, :carbon, 0)
{:carbon, :C, 12.011}
iex(4)> List.keyfind(atomic_info, :F, 1)
nil
iex(5)> List.keyfind(atomic_info, :fluorine, 0, {})
{}
iex(6)> List.keymember?(atomic_info, :Na, 1)
true
iex(7)> List.keymember?(atomic_info, :boron, 0)
false
iex(8)> atomic_info2 = List.keystore(atomic_info, :boron, 0,
...(8)> {:boron, :B, 10.081})
[{:hydrogen, :H, 1008}, {:carbon, :C, 12.011}, {:sodium, :Na, 22.99},
 {:boron, :B, 10.081}]
iex(9)> atomic_info3 = List.keyreplace(atomic_info2, :B, 1,
...(9)> {:boron, :B, 10.81})
[{:hydrogen, :H, 1008}, {:carbon, :C, 12.011}, {:sodium, :Na, 22.99},
 {:boron, :B, 10.81}]
iex(10)> atomic_info4 = List.keydelete(atomic_info3, :fluorine, 0)
[{:hydrogen, :H, 1008}, {:carbon, :C, 12.011}, {:sodium, :Na, 22.99},
 {:boron, :B, 10.81}]
iex(11)> atomic_info5 = List.keydelete(atomic_info3, :carbon, 0)
[{:hydrogen, :H, 1008}, {:sodium, :Na, 22.99}, {:boron, :B, 10.81}]
```

Lines 2 and 3 show that you can search the list by chemical name (position 0) or symbol (position 1). By default, trying to find a key that doesn't exist returns nil (line 4), but you may return any value you choose (line 5). Lines 6 and 7 show the use of List.keymember?.

To add new values, you must give a complete tuple as the last argument, as shown in line 8. The value for the atomic weight of boron was deliberately entered incorrectly. Line 9 uses List.keyreplace to correct the error.

 You can also use List.keyreplace to replace the entire tuple. If you wanted to replace boron with zinc, you would have typed:

```
iex(9)> atomic_info3 = List.keyreplace(atomic_info2, :B,
...(9)> 1, {:zinc, :Zn, 65.38})
```

Lines 10 and 11 show what happens when you use List.keydelete on an entry that is not in the list and on one that is in the list.

Hash Dictionaries

If you know that your keys will be unique, you can create a *hash dictionary* (Hash Dict), which is an associative array. Hash dictionaries aren't really lists, but we're including them in this chapter because all of the functions that you have used with a keyword list will work equally well with a HashDict. The advantage of a HashDict over a keyword list is that it works well for large amounts of data. In order to use a hash dictionary, you must explicitly create it with the HashDict.new function:

```
iex(1)> planemo_hash = Enum.into([earth: 9.8, moon: 1.6, mars: 3.71],
...(1)> HashDict.new())
#HashDict<[earth: 9.8, mars: 3.71, moon: 1.6]>
iex(2)> HashDict.has_key?(planemo_hash, :moon)
true
iex(3)> HashDict.has_key?(planemo_hash, :jupiter)
false
iex(4)> HashDict.get(planemo_hash, :jupiter)
nil
iex(5)> HashDict.get(planemo_hash, :jupiter, 0)
0
iex(6)> planemo_hash2 = HashDict.put_new(planemo_hash, :jupiter, 99.9)
#HashDict<[moon: 1.6, mars: 3.71, jupiter: 99.9, earth: 9.8]>
iex(7)> planemo_hash3 = HashDict.put_new(planemo_hash2, :jupiter, 23.1)
#HashDict<[moon: 1.6, mars: 3.71, jupiter: 99.9, earth: 9.8]>
iex(8)> planemo_hash4 = HashDict.put(planemo_hash3, :jupiter, 23.1)
#HashDict<[moon: 1.6, mars: 3.71, jupiter: 23.1, earth: 9.8]>
iex(9)> planemo_hash5 = HashDict.delete(planemo_hash4,:saturn)
#HashDict<[moon: 1.6, mars: 3.71, jupiter: 23.1, earth: 9.8]>
iex(10)> planemo_hash6 = HashDict.delete(planemo_hash4, :jupiter)
#HashDict<[moon: 1.6, mars: 3.71, earth: 9.8]>
```

Line 6 deliberately sets Jupiter's gravity to an incorrect value. Line 7 shows that Hash Dict.put_new/2 will not update an existing value; line 8 shows that HashDict.put will update existing values. Line 9 shows that attempting to delete a nonexistent key from a hash dictionary leaves it unchanged.

 Use of HashDicts is deprecated, and they will be removed from Elixir in version 2.0. Instead, use maps, which are much faster.

From Lists to Maps

Keyword lists are a convenient way to address content stored in lists by key, but underneath, Elixir is still walking through the list. That might be OK if you have other plans for that list requiring walking through all of it, but it can be unnecessary overhead if you're planning to use keys as your only approach to the data.

The Erlang community, after dealing with these issues for years, added a new set of tools to R17: maps. (The initial implementation is partial but will get you started.) Elixir simultaneously added support for the new feature, with, of course, a distinctive Elixir syntax.

Creating Maps

The simplest way to create a map is to use %{} to create an empty map:

```
iex(1)> new_map = %{}
%{}
```

Frequently, you'll want to create maps with at least some initial values. Elixir offers two ways to do this. You use the same %{} syntax, but put some extra declarations inside:

```
iex(2)> planemo_map = %{:earth => 9.8, :moon => 1.6, :mars => 3.71}
%{earth: 9.8, mars: 3.71, moon: 1.6}
```

The map now has keys that are the atoms :earth, :moon, and :mars, pointing to the values 9.8, 1.6, and 3.71, respectively. The nice thing about this syntax is that you can use any kind of value as the key. It's perfectly fine, for example, to use numbers for keys:

```
iex(3)> number_map=%{2 => "two", 3 => "three"}
%{2 => "two", 3 => "three"}
```

However, atoms are probably the most common keys, and Elixir offers a more concise syntax for creating maps that use atoms as keys:

```
iex(4)> planemo_map_alt = %{earth: 9.8, moon: 1.6, mars: 3.71}
%{earth: 9.8, mars: 3.71, moon: 1.6}
```

The responses created by IEx in lines 2 and 4 are identical, and Elixir itself will use the more concise syntax if appropriate.

Updating Maps

If the strength of a planemo's gravitational field changes, you can easily fix that with:

```
iex(5)> altered_planemo_map = %{planemo_map | earth: 12}
%{earth: 12, mars: 3.71, moon: 1.6}
```

or:

```
iex(6)> altered_planemo_map = %{planemo_map | :earth => 12}
%{earth: 12, mars: 3.71, moon: 1.6}
```

You can update multiple key-value pairs if you want, with syntax like %{planemo_map | earth: 12, mars:3} or %{planemo_map | :earth => 12, :mars => 3}. The | notation will work only if a key already exists in the map. If it does not exist, you will get a KeyError.

You may also want to add another key-value pair to a map. You can't, of course, change the map itself, but the Map.put_new library function can easily create a new map that includes the original map plus an extra value:

```
iex(7)> extended_planemo_map = Map.put_new(planemo_map, :jupiter, 23.1)
%{earth: 9.8, jupiter: 23.1, mars: 3.71, moon: 1.6}
```

Reading Maps

Elixir lets you extract information from maps through pattern matching. The same syntax works whether you're matching in a variable line or in a function clause. Need the gravity for Earth?

```
iex(8)> %{earth: earth_gravity} = planemo_map
%{earth: 9.8, mars: 3.71, moon: 1.6}
iex(9)> earth_gravity
9.8
```

If you ask for a value for a key that doesn't exist, you'll get an error. If you need to pattern match "any map," just use the empty map, %{}.

From Maps to Structs

One shortcoming of tuples, keyword lists, and maps is that they are fairly unstructured. When you use tuples, you are responsible for remembering the order in which the data items occur in the tuple. With keyword lists and maps, you can add a new key at any time or misspell a key name, and Elixir will not complain. Elixir *structs*

---

overcome these problems. They are based on maps, so the order of key-value pairs doesn't matter, but a struct also keeps track of the key names and makes sure you don't use invalid keys.

Setting Up Structs

Using structs requires telling Elixir about them with a special declaration. You use a defstruct declaration (actually a macro, as you'll see later) inside of a defmodule declaration:

```
defmodule Planemo do
    defstruct name: :nil, gravity: 0, diameter: 0, distance_from_sun: 0
end
```

That defines a struct named Planemo, containing fields named name, gravity, diameter, and distance_from_sun with their default values. This declaration creates structs for different towers for dropping objects:

```
defmodule Tower do
    defstruct location: "", height: 20, planemo: :earth, name: ""
end
```

Creating and Reading Structs

Find these in *ch07/ex1-struct*, compile them in IEx, and you can start using the structs to store data. As you can see on line 1, creating a new struct with empty {} applies the default values, while specifying values as shown on line 4 overrides all the defaults:

```
$ iex -S mix
Erlang/OTP 19 [erts-8.0] [source] [64-bit] [smp:4:4] [async-threads:10] [hipe]
  [kernel-poll:false]

Compiling 2 files (.ex)
Generated tower app
Interactive Elixir (1.3.1) - press Ctrl+C to exit (type h() ENTER for help)
iex(1)> tower1 = %Tower{}
%Tower{height: 20, location: "", name: "", planemo: :earth}
iex(2)> tower2 = %Tower{location: "Grand Canyon"}
%Tower{height: 20, location: "Grand Canyon", name: "", planemo: :earth}
iex(3)> tower3 = %Tower{location: "NYC", height: 241, name: "Woolworth Building"}
%Tower{height: 241, location: "NYC", name: "Woolworth Building",
  planemo: :earth}
iex(4)> tower4 = %Tower{location: "Rupes Altat 241", height: 500,
...(4)> planemo: :moon, name: "Piccolini View"}
%Tower{height: 500, location: "Rupes Altat 241", name: "Piccolini View",
  planemo: :moon}
iex(5)> tower5 = %Tower{planemo: :mars, height: 500,
...(5)> name: "Daga Vallis", location: "Valles Marineris"}
%Tower{height: 500, location: "Valles Marineris", name: "Daga Vallis",
  planemo: :mars}
```

```
iex(6)> tower5.name
"Daga Vallis"
```

These towers (or at least drop sites) demonstrate a variety of ways to use the record syntax to create variables as well as interactions with the default values:

- Line 1 just creates `tower1` with the default values. You can add real values later.
- Line 2 creates a `tower2` with a `location`, but otherwise relies on default values.
- Line 3 overrides the default values for `location`, `height`, and `name`, but leaves the `planemo` alone.
- Line 4 overrides all of the default values.
- Line 5 replaces all of the default values, and also demonstrates that *it doesn't matter in what order you list the name-value pairs.* Elixir will sort it out.

Once you have values in your structs, you can extract the values using the dot notation shown on line 6, which may be familiar from other programming languages.

Pattern Matching Against Structs

Since structures are maps, pattern matches against structures work in exactly the same way as they do for maps:

```
iex(7)> %Tower{planemo: p, location: where} = tower5
%Tower{height: 500, location: "Valles Marineris", name: "Daga Vallis",
 planemo: :mars}
iex(8)> p
:mars
iex(9)> where
"Valles Marineris"
```

Using Structs in Functions

You can pattern match against structures submitted as arguments. The simplest way to do this is to just match against the struct, as shown in Example 7-1, which is in *ch07/ex2-struct-match.*

Example 7-1. A method that pattern matches a complete record

```
defmodule StructDrop do

  def fall_velocity(t = %Tower{}) do
    fall_velocity(t.planemo, t.height)
  end

  def fall_velocity(:earth, distance) when distance >= 0 do
    :math.sqrt(2 * 9.8 * distance)
  end
```

```
def fall_velocity(:moon, distance) when distance >= 0 do
  :math.sqrt(2 * 1.6 * distance)
end

def fall_velocity(:mars, distance) when distance >= 0 do
  :math.sqrt(2 * 3.71 * distance)
end
```

```
end
```

This uses a pattern match that will match only Tower structs, and puts the matched struct into a variable t. Then, like its predecessor in Example 3-8, it passes the individual arguments to fall_velocity/2 for calculations, this time using the struct syntax:

```
iex(10)> r(StructDrop)
warning: redefining module StructDrop (current version loaded from
  _build/dev/lib/struct_drop/ebin/Elixir.StructDrop.beam)
  lib/struct_drop.ex:1

{:reloaded, StructDrop, [StructDrop]}
[StructDrop]
iex(11)> StructDrop.fall_velocity(tower5)
60.909769331364245
iex(12)> StructDrop.fall_velocity(tower1)
19.79898987322333
```

The StructDrop.fall_velocity/1 function shown in Example 7-2 pulls out the planemo field and binds it to the variable planemo.[1] It pulls out the height field and binds it to distance. Then it returns the velocity of an object dropped from that distance, just like earlier examples throughout this book.

You can also extract the specific fields from the structure in the pattern match, as shown in Example 7-2, which is in *ch07/ex3-struct-components*.

Example 7-2. A method that pattern matches components of a structure

```
defmodule StructDrop do
  def fall_velocity(%Tower{planemo: planemo, height: distance}) do
    fall_velocity(planemo, distance)
  end

  def fall_velocity(:earth, distance) when distance >= 0 do
    :math.sqrt(2 * 9.8 * distance)
  end
```

---

1 It is possible to have a variable whose name is the same as a field name, as in this example.

```
  def fall_velocity(:moon, distance) when distance >= 0 do
    :math.sqrt(2 * 1.6 * distance)
  end

  def fall_velocity(:mars, distance) when distance >= 0 do
    :math.sqrt(2 * 3.71 * distance)
  end
end
```

You can take each of the Tower structures you have created and feed them into this function, and it will tell you the velocity resulting from a drop from the top of that tower to the bottom.

Finally, you can pattern match against both the fields and the structure as a whole. Example 7-3, in *ch07/ex4-struct-multi*, demonstrates using this mixed approach to create a more detailed response than just the fall velocity.

Example 7-3. A method that pattern matches the whole structure as well as components of a structure

```
defmodule StructDrop do
  def fall_velocity(t = %Tower{planemo: planemo, height: distance}) do
    IO.puts("From #{t.name}'s elevation of #{distance} meters on #{planemo},")
    IO.puts("the object will reach #{fall_velocity(planemo, distance)} m/s")
    IO.puts("before crashing in #{t.location}")
  end

  def fall_velocity(:earth, distance) when distance >= 0 do
    :math.sqrt(2 * 9.8 * distance)
  end

  def fall_velocity(:moon, distance) when distance >= 0 do
    :math.sqrt(2 * 1.6 * distance)
  end

  def fall_velocity(:mars, distance) when distance >= 0 do
    :math.sqrt(2 * 3.71 * distance)
  end
end
```

If you pass a Tower structure to StructDrop.fall_velocity/1, it will match against individual fields it needs to do the calculation and match the whole structure into t so that it can produce a more interesting, if not necessarily grammatically correct, report:

```
iex(1)> StructDrop.fall_velocity(tower5)
From Daga Vallis's elevation of 500 meters on mars,
the object will reach 60.909769333136424520399 m/s
before crashing in Valles Marineris
:ok
```

```
iex(2)> StructDrop.fall_velocity(tower3)
From Woolworth Building's elevation of 241 meters on earth,
the object will reach 68.72845116834803036454 m/s
before crashing in NYC
:ok
```

Adding Behavior to Structs

Elixir lets you attach behavior to structures (and, in fact, any type of data) with *protocols*. For example, you may want to test to see if a structure is valid or not. Clearly, the test for what is a valid structure varies from one type of structure to another. For example, you may consider a Planemo valid if its gravity, diameter, and distance from the sun are nonnegative. A Tower is valid if its height is nonnegative and it has a nonnil value for planemo.

Example 7-4 shows the definition of a protocol for testing validity. The files for this example are in *ch07/ex5-protocol*.

Example 7-4. Defining a protocol for valid structures

```
defprotocol Valid do
  @doc "Returns true if data is considered nominally valid"
  def valid?(data)
end
```

The interesting line here is def valid?(data); it is, in essence, an incomplete function definition. Every datatype whose validity you want to test will have to provide a complete function with the name valid?, so let's add some code to the definition of the Planemo structure:

```
defmodule Planemo do
  defstruct name: nil, gravity: 0, diameter: 0, distance_from_sun: 0
end

defimpl Valid, for: Planemo do
  def valid?(p) do
    p.gravity >= 0 and p.diameter >= 0 and
    p.distance_from_sun >= 0
  end
end
```

Let's test that out right now.

```
iex(1)> p = %Planemo{}
%Planemo{diameter: 0, distance_from_sun: 0, gravity: 0, name: nil}
iex(2)> Valid.valid?(p)
true
iex(3)> p2 = %Planemo{name: :weirdworld, gravity: -2.3}
%Planemo{diameter: 0, distance_from_sun: 0, gravity: -2.3, name: :weirdworld}
iex(4)> Valid.valid?(p2)
```

```
false
iex(5)> t = %Tower{}
%Tower{height: 20, location: "", name: "", planemo: :earth}
iex(6)> Valid.valid?(t)
** (Protocol.UndefinedError) protocol Valid not implemented for
    %Tower{height: 20, location: "", name: "", planemo: :earth}
    valid_protocol.ex:1: Valid.impl_for!/1
    valid_protocol.ex:3: Valid.valid?/1
```

Lines 1 and 2 show the creation and testing of a valid Planemo; lines 3 and 4 show the results for an invalid one. Line 6 shows that you cannot test a Tower structure for validity yet, as the valid? function has not yet been implemented. Here is the updated code for the Tower struct, which you can find in *ch07/ex6-protocol*:

```
defmodule Tower do
  defstruct location: "", height: 20, planemo: :earth, name: ""
end

defimpl Valid, for: Tower do
  def valid?(%Tower{height: h, planemo: p}) do
    h >= 0 and p != nil
  end
end
```

Here is the test:

```
iex(6)> r(Tower)
warning: redefining module Tower (current version loaded from
  _build/dev/lib/valid/ebin/Elixir.Tower.beam)
  lib/tower.ex:1

{:reloaded, Tower, [Tower]}
iex(7)> Valid.valid?(t)
true
iex(8)> t2 = %Tower{height: -2, location: "underground"}
%Tower{height: -2, location: "underground", name: "", planemo: :earth}
iex(9)> Valid.valid?(t2)
false
```

Adding to Existing Protocols

When you inspect a Tower, you get rather generic output:

```
iex(10)> t3 = %Tower{location: "NYC", height: 241, name: "Woolworth Building"}
%Tower{height: 241, location: "NYC", name: "Woolworth Building",
 planemo: :earth}
iex(11)> inspect t3
"%Tower{height: 241, location: \"NYC\", name: \"Woolworth Building\",
planemo: :earth}"
```

Wouldn't it be nice to have better-looking output? You can enable this by implementing the Inspect protocol for Tower structures. Example 7-5 shows the code to add to *tower.ex*; you will find the source in *ch07/ex7-inspect*.

Example 7-5. Implementing the Inspect protocol for the Tower structure

```
defimpl Inspect, for: Tower do
  import Inspect.Algebra
  def inspect(item, _options) do
    metres = concat(to_string(item.height), "m:")
    msg = concat([metres, break, item.name, ",", break,
      item.location, ",", break,
      to_string(item.planemo)])
  end
end
```

The Inspect.Algebra module implements "pretty printing" using an algebraic approach (hence the name). In the simplest form, it puts together *documents* that may be separated by optional line breaks (break) and connected with concat. Every place that you put a break in a document is replaced by a space, or, if there is not enough space for the next item on the line, a line break.

The inspect/2 function takes the item you want to inspect as its first argument. The second argument is a structure that lets you specify options that give you greater control over how inspect/2 produces its output.

The first concat puts the height and abbreviation for metres together without any intervening space. The second concat connects all the items in the list, so the function returns a string containing the pretty-printed document. Since Valid is a protocol rather than a module, we have to compile the file:

```
iex(12)> c("lib/valid.ex")
warning: redefining module Valid (current version loaded from
  _build/dev/consolidated/Elixir.Valid.beam)
  lib/valid.ex:1

[Valid]
iex(13)> inspect t3
"241m: Woolworth Building, NYC, earth"
```

## CHAPTER 8

Higher-Order Functions and List Comprehensions

Higher-order functions, or functions that accept other functions as arguments, are a key place where Elixir's power really starts to shine. It's not that you can't do higher-order functions in other languages—you can in many—but rather that Elixir treats higher-order functions as a native and natural part of the language rather than an oddity.

Simple Higher-Order Functions

Way back in Chapter 2, you saw how to use fn to create a function:

```
iex(1)> fall_velocity = fn(distance) -> :math.sqrt(2 * 9.8 * distance) end
#Function<6.106461118/1 in :erl_eval.expr/5>
iex(2)> fall_velocity.(20)
19.79898987322333
iex(3)> fall_velocity.(200)
62.609903369994115
```

Elixir not only lets you put functions into variables, it lets you pass functions as arguments. This means that you can create functions whose behavior you modify at the time you call them, in much more intricate ways than is normally possible with parameters. A very simple function that takes another function as an argument might look like Example 8-1, which you can find in *ch08/ex1-hof*.

Example 8-1. An extremely simple higher-order function

```
defmodule Hof do
  def tripler(value, function) do
    3 * function.(value)
```

```
      end
end
```

The argument names are generic, but fit. `tripler/2` will take a value and a function as arguments. It runs the value through the function and multiplies the result by three. In the shell, this might look like the following:

```
iex(1)> my_function = fn(value) -> 20 * value end
#Function<6.106461118/1 in :erl_eval.expr/5>
iex(2)> Hof.tripler(6, my_function)
360
```

Line 1 defines another simple function taking one argument (and returning that number multiplied by 20) and stores it in the variable `my_function`. Then line 2 calls the `Hof.tripler/2` function with a value of 6 and the `my_function` function. In the `Hof.tripler/2` function, it feeds the `value` to the `function`, getting back 120. Then it triples that, returning 360.

You can skip assigning the function to a variable if you want, and just include the `fn` declaration inside the `Hof.tripler/2` function call:

```
iex(3)> Hof.tripler(6, fn(value) -> 20 * value end)
360
```

That may or may not be easier to read, depending on the functions and your expectations. This case is trivially simple, but demonstrates that it works.

Elixir gives you another way to specify the function: you can use & as the capture operator, &1 to stand for the first argument, and so on. Using this notation, you can make the previous examples even simpler:

```
iex(4)> ampersand_function = &(20 * &1)
#Function<6.106461118/1 in :erl_eval.expr/5>
iex(5)> Hof.tripler(6, ampersand_function)
360
iex(6)> Hof.tripler(6, &(20 * &1))
360
```

 While this is a powerful technique, you can outsmart yourself with it easily (speaking from experience!). Just as with normal code, you need to make sure the number and sometimes the type of your arguments line up. The extra flexibility and power can create new problems if you aren't careful.

`fn` has a few other tricks up its sleeve that you should know. You can use a `fn` to preserve context, even context that has since changed or vanished:

```
iex(7)> x = 20
20
iex(8)> my_function2 = fn(value) -> x * value end
#Function<6.106461118/1 in :erl_eval.expr/5>
iex(9)> x = 0
0
iex(10)> my_function2.(6)
120
```

Line 7 assigns a variable named x a value, and line 8 uses that variable in a fn. Line 9 changes the x variable, but line 10 shows that my_function2 still remembers that x was 20. Even though the value of x has been changed, the fn preserves the value and can act upon it. (This is called a *closure*.)

Again, you can use the ampersand notation:

```
iex(11)> x = 20
20
iex(12)> my_function3 = &(x * &1)
#Function<6.106461118/1 in :erl_eval.expr/5>
iex(13)> x = 0
0
iex(14)> Hof.tripler(6, my_function3)
360
```

You may also want to pass a function from a module, even a built-in module, to your (or any) higher-order function. That's simple, too:

```
iex(15)> Hof.tripler(:math.pi, &:math.cos(&1))
-3.0
```

In this case, the Hof.tripler function receives the value pi and a function, which is the :math.cos/1 function from the built-in math module. Since the function has arity 1, you must indicate this with &1. Because the cosine of pi is –1, the tripler returns -3.0.

Creating New Lists with Higher-Order Functions

Lists are one of the best and easiest places to apply higher-order functions. Applying a function to all the components of a list to create a new list, sort a list, or break a list into smaller pieces is popular work. You don't need to do much difficult work to make this happen, though: Elixir's built-in List and Enum modules offer a variety of higher-order functions, listed in Appendix A, that take a function and list and do something with them. You can also use *list comprehensions* to do much of the same work. The List and Enum modules may seem easier at first, but as you'll see, list comprehensions are powerful and concise.

The functions in the Enum module will work on any *collection* of data (for example, the individual lines in a file); the functions in List make sense only for lists.

Reporting on a List

The simplest of these functions is Enum.each/2, which always returns the atom :ok. That may sound strange, but Enum.each/2 is a function you'll call if and only if you want to do something to the list with side effects—like presenting the contents of a list to the console. To do that, define a list and a simple function that applies IO.puts/1, here stored in the variable print, and then pass them both to Enum.each/2:

```
iex(1)> print = fn(value) -> IO.puts(" #{value}") end
#Function<6.106461118/1 in :erl_eval.expr/5>
iex(2)> list = [1, 2, 4, 8, 16, 32]
iex(3)> Enum.each(list, print)
 1
 2
 4
 8
 16
 32
:ok
```

The Enum.each/2 function walked through the list, in order, and called the function in print with each item of the list as a value. The IO.puts function inside of print presented the list item, slightly indented. When it reached the end of the list, Enum.each/2 returned the value :ok, which the console also displayed.

Most of the demonstrations in this chapter will be operating on that same list variable containing [1, 2, 4, 8, 16, 32].

Running List Values Through a Function

You might also want to create a new list based on what a function does with all of the values in the original list. You can square all of the values in a list by creating a function that returns the square of its argument and passing that to Enum.map/2. Instead of returning :ok, it returns a new list reflecting the work of the function it was given:

```
iex(4)> square = &(&1 * &1)
#Function<6.106461118/1 in :erl_eval.expr/5>
```

```
iex(5)> Enum.map(list, square)
[1, 4, 16, 64, 256, 1024]
```

 If you want to generate a list of sequential integers (or characters), you can use the notation *start..end*. You normally use this notation with integers, but you can also use it with characters, with rather unusual results:

```
iex(6)> Enum.map(1..3, square)
[1, 4, 9]
iex(7)> Enum.map(-2..2, square)
[4, 1, 0, 1, 4]
iex(8)> Enum.map(?a..?d, square)
[9409, 9604, 9801, 10000]
```

There's another way to accomplish the same thing that Enum.map/2 does, with what Elixir calls a *list comprehension*:

```
iex(9)> for value <- list, do: value * value
[1, 4, 16, 64, 256, 1024]
```

That produces the same resulting list, with different (and more flexible) syntax.

You can read this list comprehension as "For each value in list list, create an entry value * value in a new list." You can also use ranges in a list comprehension: for value <- 1..3, do: value * value.

Filtering List Values

The Enum module offers a few different functions for filtering the content of a list based on a function you provide as a parameter. The most obvious, Enum.filter/2, returns a list composed of the members of the original list for which the function returned true. For example, if you wanted to filter a list of integers down to values that could be represented as four binary digits—so, numbers 0 or greater but less than 16—you could define a function and store it in four_bits:

```
iex(10)> four_bits = fn(value) -> (value >= 0) and (value < 16) end
#Function<6.106461118/1 in :erl_eval.expr/5>
```

Then, if you apply it to the previously defined list of [1, 2, 4, 8, 16, 32], you'll get just the first four values:

```
iex(11)> Enum.filter(list, four_bits)
[1, 2, 4, 8]
```

Once again, you can create the same effect with a list comprehension. This time, you don't actually need to create a function, but instead use a guard-like construct (written *without* the when) on the right side of the comprehension:

```
iex(12)> for value <- list, value >= 0, value < 16, do: value
[1, 2, 4, 8]
```

 If you also want a list of the values that didn't match, instead use Enum.partition/2, which returns a tuple containing both the matched and unmatched values as separate lists. See "Splitting Lists" on page 99 for an example.

Beyond List Comprehensions

for comprehensions are concise and powerful, but they lack a few key features available in other recursive processing. They return a list, but there will be many times when you want to process a list and return something else, like a Boolean, a tuple, or a number. List comprehensions also lack support for accumulators and don't let you suspend processing completely when certain conditions are met.

You could write your own recursive functions to process lists, but much of the time, you'll find that the Enum and List modules already offer a function that takes a function you define and a list and returns what you need.

Testing Lists

Sometimes you just want to know if all the values—or any of the values—in a list meet specific criteria. Are they all of a specific type, or do they meet certain conditions?

The Enum.all?/2 and Enum.any?/2 functions let you test a list against rules you specify in a function. If your function returns true for all of the list values, both of these functions will return true. Enum.any?/2 will also return true if one or more values in the list results in your function return true. Both will return false if your function consistently returns false:

```
iex(1)> int? = fn(value) -> is_integer(value) end
#Function<erl_eval.6.17052888>
iex(2)> Enum.all?(list, int?)
true
iex(3)> Enum.any?(list, int?)
true
iex(4)> greater_than_ten? = &(&1 > 10)
#Function<6.106461118/1 in :erl_eval.expr/5>
iex(5)> Enum.all?(list, greater_than_ten?)
false
iex(6)> Enum.any?(list, greater_than_ten?)
true
```

You can think of Enum.all?/2 as an and function applied to lists because it stops processing as soon as it encounters a false result. Similarly, Enum.any?/2 is like or, in this case stopping as soon as it finds a true result. As long as you only need to test individual values within lists, these two higher-order functions can save you writing a lot of recursive code.

 By convention, functions that return a Boolean value (also called *predicates*) have names that end with a question mark. We have followed that convention in the preceding example. Functions whose names begin with is_ (such as is_integer) are usually used for guards.

Splitting Lists

Filtering lists is useful, but sometimes you want to know what didn't go through the filter, and sometimes you just want to separate items.

The Enum.partition/2 function returns a tuple containing two lists. The first list contains the items from the original list that met the conditions specified in the function you provided, while the second list contains the items that didn't. If the compare variable is defined as shown in line 4 of the previous demonstration, returning true when a list value is greater than 10, then you can easily split a list into a list of items greater than 10 and a list of items less than or equal to 10:

```
iex(7)> Enum.partition(list, compare)
{[16, 32], [1, 2, 4, 8]}
```

Sometimes you'll want to split a list by starting from the beginning—the head—and stopping when a list value no longer meets a condition. The Enum.take_while/2 and Enum.drop_while/2 functions create a new list that contains the parts of an old list before or after encountering a boundary condition. These functions aren't filters, and to make that clear, the examples use a different list than the rest in this chapter:

```
iex(8)> test = &(&1 < 4)
#Function<6.106461118/1 in :erl_eval.expr/5>
iex(9)> Enum.drop_while([1, 2, 4, 8, 4, 2, 1], test)
[4, 8, 4, 2, 1]
iex(10)> Enum.take_while([1, 2, 4, 8, 4, 2, 1], test)
[1, 2]
```

Both functions run through a list from head to tail and stop when they reach a value for which the function you provide as the first argument returns false. The Enum.drop_while/2 function returns what's left of the list, including the value that flunked the test. It does not, however, filter out later list entries that it might have dropped if they had appeared earlier in the list. The Enum.take_while/2 function returns what was already processed, *not* including the value that flunked the test.

Folding Lists

Adding an accumulator to list processing lets you turn lists into much more than other lists and opens the door to much more sophisticated processing. Elixir's `List.foldl/3` and `List.foldr/3` functions let you specify a function, an initial value for an accumulator, and a list. Instead of the one-argument functions you've seen so far, you need to create a two-argument function. The first argument is the current value in the list traversal, and the second argument is an accumulator. The result of that function will become the new value of the accumulator.

Defining a function that works within the folding functions looks a little different, because of the two arguments:

```
iex(11)> sumsq = fn(value, accumulator) -> accumulator + value * value end
#Function<12.54118792/2 in :erl_eval.expr/5>
```

This function squares each `value` coming from a list and adds it to the `accumulator` passed to it by the function doing the folding. You can use `List.foldl/3` with this function to get the sum of squares of a list of numbers, with zero as the starting value of the accumulator:

```
iex(12)> List.foldl([2, 4, 6], 0, sumsq)
56
```

Folding has one other key twist. You can choose whether you want the function to traverse the list from head to tail, with `List.foldl/3`, or from tail to head, with `List.foldr/3`. If order doesn't change the result, you should go with `List.foldl/3`, as its implementation is tail recursive and more efficient in most situations. In the preceding example, efficiency aside, it doesn't matter if you use `List.foldl/3` or `List.foldr/3`, since addition is commutative.

Consider, however, this function to be used in a fold:

```
iex(13)> divide = fn(value, accumulator) -> value / accumulator end
#Function<12.106461118/2 in :erl_eval.expr/5>
```

This function divides its first argument, the `value` coming from the list, by the second, the `accumulator` passed to it by the function doing the folding.

The `divide` function is one of those cases that will produce very different results depending on the direction in which you process the list (and the initial accumulator value). In this case, folding also produces different results than you might expect in a simple division. Given the usual `list` of [1, 2, 4, 8, 16, 32], it seems like going from left to right will produce 1/2/4/8/16/32 and going from right to left will produce 32/16/8/4/2/1, at least if you use an initial accumulator of 1. Those aren't the results produced, however:

```
iex(14)> divide = fn(value, accumulator) -> value / accumulator end
#Function<12.106461118/2 in :erl_eval.expr/5>
```

```
iex(15)> 1/2/4/8/16/32
3.0517578125e-5
iex(16)> List.foldl(list, 1, divide)
8.0
iex(17)> 32/16/8/4/2/1
0.03125
iex(18)> List.foldr(list, 1, divide)
0.125
```

This code seems too simple to have a bug, so what's going on? Table 8-1 walks through the calculations for List.foldl(list, 1, divide), and Table 8-2 walks through List.foldr(list, 1, divide) step by step.

Table 8-1. Recursive division of a list forward with List.foldl/3

Value from list	Accumulator	Result of division
1	1	1
2	1 (1/1)	2
4	2 (2/1)	2
8	2 (4/2)	4
16	4 (8/2)	4
32	4 (16/4)	8

Table 8-2. Recursive division of a list backward with List.foldr/3

Value from list	Accumulator	Result of division
32	1	32
16	32 (32/1)	0.5
8	0.5 (16/32)	16
4	16 (8/0.5)	0.25
2	0.25 (4/16)	8
1	8 (2/0.25)	0.125

Moving through a list step by step produces very different values. In this case, the simple divide function's behavior changes drastically above and below the value 1, and combining that with walking through a list item by item yields results that might not be precisely what you expected.

The result of the List.foldl is the same as 32/(16/(8/(4/(2/(1/1))))), while the result of the List.foldr is the same as 1/(2/(4/(8/(16/(32/1))))). The parentheses in those perform the same restructuring as the fold, and the concluding 1 in each is where the initial accumulator value fits in.

Folding is an incredibly powerful operation. This simple if slightly weird example just used a single value, a number, as an accumulator. If you use a tuple as the accumulator, you can store all kinds of information about a list as it passes by and even perform multiple operations. You probably won't want to try to define the functions you use for that as one-liners, but the possibilities are endless.

## CHAPTER 9

Playing with Processes

Elixir is a functional language, but Elixir programs are rarely structured around simple functions. Instead, Elixir's key organizational concept is the *process*, an independent component (built from functions) that sends and receives messages. Programs are deployed as sets of processes that communicate with each other. This approach makes it much easier to distribute work across multiple processors or computers, and also makes it possible to do things like upgrade programs in place without shutting down the whole system.

Taking advantage of those features, though, means learning how to create (and end) processes, how to send messages among them, and how to apply the power of pattern matching to incoming messages.

The Shell Is a Process

You've been working within a single process throughout this book so far, the Elixir shell. None of the previous examples sent or received messages, of course, but the shell is an easy place to send and (for test purposes, at least) receive messages.

The first thing to explore is the *process identifier*, often called a *pid*. The easiest pid to get is your own, so in the shell you can just try the self() function:

```
iex(1)> self()
#PID<0.26.0>
```

#PID<0.26.0> is the shell's representation of a process identifier; the three integers constitute a triple that provides a unique identifier for this process. You may get a different set of numbers when you try it. This group of numbers is guaranteed to be unique within this run of Elixir, not permanently the same in future use. Elixir uses pids internally, but while you can read them in the shell, you can't type pids directly into the shell or into functions. Elixir much prefers that you treat pids as abstractions.

Pids can even identify processes running on different computers within a cluster. You'll need to do more work to set up a cluster, but you won't have to throw away code you wrote with pids and processes built on them when you get there.

Every process gets its own pid, and those pids function like addresses for mailboxes. Your programs will send messages from one process to another by sending them to a pid. When that process gets time to check its mailbox, it will be able to retrieve and process the messages there.

Elixir, however, will *never* report that a message send failed, even if the pid doesn't point to a real process. It also won't report that a message was ignored by a process. You need to make sure your processes are assembled correctly.

The syntax for sending a message is pretty simple. You use the send/2 function with two arguments, an expression containing the pid and the message:

```
iex(2)> send(self(), :test1)
:test1
iex(3)> pid = self()
#PID<0.26.0>
iex(4)> send(pid, :test2)
:test2
```

Line 2 sent a message to the shell containing the atom :test1. Line 3 assigned the pid for the shell, retrieved with the self() function, to a variable named pid, and then line 4 used that pid variable to send a message containing the atom :test2. (The send/2 function always returns the message, which is why it appears right after the sends in lines 2 and 4.)

Where did those messages go? What happened to them? Right now, they're just waiting in the shell's mailbox, doing nothing.

There's a shell function—flush()—that you can use to see what's in the mailbox, but it also removes those messages from the mailbox. The first time you use it you'll get a report of what's in the mailbox, but the second time the messages are gone, already read:

```
iex(5)> flush()
:test1
:test2
:ok
iex(6)> flush()
:ok
```

The proper way to read the mailbox, which gives you a chance to do something with the messages, is the receive...end construct. You can test this out in the shell. The first of the following tests just reports what the message was, whereas the second expects a number and doubles it:

```
iex(7)> send(self(), :test1)
:test1
iex(8)> receive do
...(8)>    x -> x
...(8)> end
:test1
iex(9)> send(self(), 23)
23
iex(10)> receive do
...(10)>    y -> 2 * y
...(10)> end
46
```

So far, so good. However, if you screw up—if there isn't a message waiting, or if you provide a pattern match that doesn't work—the shell will just sit there, hung. Actually, it's waiting for something to arrive in the mailbox (in technical terms, receive *blocks* until it receives a message), but you'll be stuck. The easiest way out of that is to hit Ctrl+G, and then type q. You'll have to restart IEx. (x and y become bound variables, and even though they are not immutable, it is considered in the spirit of functional programming to not reuse them.)

Spawning Processes from Modules

While sending messages to the shell is an easy way to see what's happening, it's not especially useful. Processes at their heart are just functions, and you know how to build functions in modules. The receive...end statement is structured like a case...end statement, so it's easy to get started.

Example 9-1, which is in *ch09/ex1-simple*, shows a simple—excessively simple—module containing a function that reports messages it receives.

Example 9-1. An overly simple process definition

```
defmodule Bounce do
  def report do
    receive do
      msg -> IO.puts("Received #{msg}")
    end
  end
end
```

When the report/0 function receives a message, it will report that it received it. Setting this up means compiling the module and then using the spawn/3 function, which turns the function into a freestanding process. The arguments are the module name, the function name (as an atom), and a list of arguments for the function. Even if you don't have any arguments, you need to include an empty list in square brackets. The spawn/3 function will return the pid, which you should capture in a variable (here, pid):

```
iex(1)> pid = spawn(Bounce, :report, [])
#PID<0.43.0>
```

Once you have the process spawned, you can send a message to that pid, and the process will report that it received the message:

```
iex(2)> send(pid, 23)
Received 23
23
```

However, there's one small problem. The report process exited—it went through the receive clause only once, and when it was done, it was done. If you try to send the process another message, you'll get back the message, and nothing will report an error, but you also won't get any notification that the message was received because nothing is listening any longer:

```
iex(3)> send(pid, 23)
23
```

To create a process that keeps processing messages, you need to add a recursive call, as shown in the receive statement in Example 9-2 (in *ch09/ex2-recursion*).

Example 9-2. A function that creates a stable process

```
defmodule Bounce do
  def report do
    receive do
      msg -> IO.puts("Received #{msg}")
      report()
    end
  end
end
```

That extra call to report() means that after the function shows the message that arrived, it will run again, ready for the next message. If you recompile the bounce module and spawn it to a new pid2 variable, you can send multiple messages to the process, as shown here:

```
iex(4)> r(Bounce)
warning: redefining module Bounce (current version loaded from
  _build/dev/lib/bounce/ebin/Elixir.Bounce.beam)
  /Users/elixir/code/ch09/ex2-recursion/lib/bounce.ex:1

{:reloaded, Bounce, [Bounce]}
iex(5)> pid2 = spawn(Bounce, :report, [])
#PID<0.43.0>
```

```
iex(6)> send(pid2, 23)
Received 23
23
iex(7)> send(pid2, :message)
Received message
:message
```

Because processes are asynchronous, the output from send/2 may appear before the output from report/0.

You can also pass an accumulator from call to call if you want, for a simple example, to keep track of how many messages have been received by this process. Example 9-3 shows the addition of an argument, in this case just an integer that gets incremented with each call. You can find it in *ch09/ex3-counter*.

Example 9-3. A function that adds a counter to its message reporting

```
defmodule Bounce do
  def report(count) do
    receive do
      msg -> IO.puts("Received #{count}: #{msg}")
      report(count + 1)
    end
  end
end
```

The results are pretty predictable, but remember that you need to include an initial value in the arguments list in the spawn/3 call:

```
$ iex -S mix
Erlang/OTP 19 [erts-8.0] [source] [64-bit] [smp:4:4] [async-threads:10] [hipe]
  [kernel-poll:false]

Compiling 1 file (.ex)
Interactive Elixir (1.3.1) - press Ctrl+C to exit (type h() ENTER for help)
iex(1)> pid2 = spawn(Bounce, :report, [1])
#PID<0.43.0>
iex(2)> send(pid2, :test)
:test
Received 1: test
iex(3)> send(pid2, :test2)
:test2
Received 2: test2
iex(4)> send(pid2, :another)
:another
Received 3: another
```

Whatever you do in your recursive call, keeping it simple (and preferably tail recursive) is best, as these functions can get called many, many times in the life of a process.

 If you want to create impatient processes that stop after waiting a given amount of time for a message, you should investigate the after construct of the receive clause.

You can write this function in a slightly different way that may make what's happening clearer and easier to generalize. Example 9-4, in *ch09/ex4-state*, shows how to use the return value of the receive clause, here the count plus one, to pass state from one iteration to the next.

Example 9-4. Using the return value of the receive clause as state for the next iteration

```
defmodule Bounce do
  def report(count) do
    new_count = receive do
      msg -> IO.puts("Received #{count}: #{msg}")
      count + 1
    end
    report(new_count)
  end
end
```

In this model, all (though there's just one here) of the receive clauses return a value that gets passed to the next iteration of the function. If you use this approach, you can think of the return value of the receive clause as the state to be preserved between function calls. That state can be much more intricate than a counter—it might be a tuple, for instance, that includes references to important resources or work in progress.

Lightweight Processes

If you've worked in other programming languages, you may be getting worried. Threads and process spawning are notoriously complex and often slow in other contexts, but Elixir expects an application to be a group of easily spawned processes? That run recursively?

Yes, absolutely. Elixir was written specifically to support that model, and its processes are more lightweight than those of pretty much any of its competitors. The Erlang scheduler that Elixir uses gets processes started and distributes processing time among them, as well as splitting them out across multiple processors.

It is certainly possible to write processes that perform badly and to structure applications so that they wait a long time before doing anything. You don't, though, have to worry about those problems happening just because you're using multiple processes.

Registering a Process

Much of the time, pids are all you need to find and contact a process. However, you will likely create some processes that need to be more findable. Elixir provides a process registration system that is extremely simple: you specify an atom and a pid, and then any process that wants to reach that registered process can just use the atom to find it. This makes it easier, for example, to add a new process to a system and have it connect with previously existing processes.

To register a process, just use the `Process.register/2` built-in function. The first argument is the pid of the process, and the second argument is an atom, effectively the name you're assigning the process. Once you have it registered, you can send it messages using the atom instead of a pid:

```
iex(1)> pid1 = spawn(Bounce, :report, [1])
#PID<0.39.0>
iex(2)> Process.register(pid1, :bounce)
true
iex(3)> send(:bounce, :hello)
:hello
Received 1: hello
iex(4)> send(:bounce, "Really?")
Received 2: Really?
"Really?"
```

If you attempt to call a process that doesn't exist (or one that has crashed), you'll get a bad arguments error:

```
iex(5)> send(:zingo, :test)
** (ArgumentError) argument error
    :erlang.send(:zingo, :test)
```

If you attempt to register a process to a name that is already in use, you'll also get an error, but if a process has exited (or crashed), the name is effectively no longer in use and you can reregister it.

You can also use `Process.whereis/1` to retrieve the pid for a registered process (or `nil`, if there is no process registered with that atom), and `unregister/1` to take a process out of the registration list without killing it. Remember that you must use an atom for the process name:

```
iex(5)> get_bounce = Process.whereis(:bounce)
#PID<0.39.0>
iex(6)> Process.unregister(:bounce)
true
```

```
iex(7)> test_bounce = Process.whereis(:bounce)
nil
iex(8)> send(get_bounce, "Still there?")
Received 3: Still there?
"Still there?"
```

If you want to see which processes are registered, you can use the
Process.registered/0 function.

If you've worked in other programming languages and learned the gospel of "no
global variables," you may be wondering why Elixir permits a systemwide list of processes like this. Most of the rest of this book, after all, has been about isolating change
and minimizing shared context.

If you think of registered processes as more like services than functions, however, it
may make more sense. A registered process is effectively a service published to the
entire system, something usable from multiple contexts. Used sparingly, registered
processes create reliable entry points for your programs—something that can be very
valuable as your code grows in size and complexity.

When Processes Break

Processes are fragile. If there's an error, the function stops and the process goes away.
Example 9-5, in *ch09/ex5-division*, shows a report/0 function that can break if it gets
input that isn't a number.

Example 9-5. A fragile function

```
defmodule Bounce do
  def report do
    receive do
      x -> IO.puts("Divided to #{x / 2}")
      report()
    end
  end
end
```

If you compile and run this (deliberately) error-inviting code, you'll find that it works
well so long as you only send it numbers. Send anything else, and you'll see an error
report in the shell, and no more responses from that pid. It died:

```
iex(1)> pid3 = spawn(Bounce, :report, [])
#PID<0.50.0>
iex(2)> send(pid3, 38)
38
```

```
Divided to 19.0
iex(3)> send(pid3, 27.56)
Divided to 13.78
27.56
iex(4)> send(pid3, :seven)
:seven
iex(5)>
14:18:59.471 [error] Process #PID<0.65.0> raised an exception
** (ArithmeticError) bad argument in arithmetic expression
    bounce.ex:4: Bounce.report/0
iex(5)> send(pid3, 14)
14
```

As you get deeper into Elixir's process model, you'll find that "let it crash" is not an unusual design decision in Elixir, though being able to tolerate such things and continue requires some extra work. Chapter 10 will also show you how to find and deal with errors of various kinds.

Processes Talking Amongst Themselves

Sending messages to Elixir processes is easy, but it's hard for them to report back responses if you don't leave information about where they can find you again. Sending a message without including the sender's pid is kind of like leaving a phone message without including your own number: it might trigger action, but the recipient might not get back to you.

To establish process-to-process communications without registering lots of processes, you need to include pids in the messages. Passing the pid requires adding an argument to the message. It's easy to get started with a test that calls back the shell. Example 9-6, in *ch09/ex6-talking*, builds on the Drop module from Example 3-2, adding a drop/0 function that receives messages and making the fall_velocity/2 function private.

Example 9-6. A process that sends a message back to the process that called it

```
defmodule Drop do
  def drop do
    receive do
      {from, planemo, distance} ->
        send(from, {planemo, distance, fall_velocity(planemo, distance)})
        drop()
    end
  end

  defp fall_velocity(:earth, distance) when distance >= 0 do
    :math.sqrt(2 * 9.8 * distance)
  end
```

```
  defp fall_velocity(:moon, distance) when distance >= 0 do
    :math.sqrt(2 * 1.6 * distance)
  end

  defp fall_velocity(:mars, distance) when distance >= 0 do
    :math.sqrt(2 * 3.71 * distance)
  end
end
```

To get started, it's easy to test this from the shell:

```
iex(1)> pid1 = spawn(Drop, :drop, [])
#PID<0.43.0>
iex(2)> send(pid1, {self(), :moon, 20})
{#PID<0.26.0>,:moon,20}
iex(3)> flush()
{:moon,20,8.0}
:ok
```

Example 9-7, which you'll find in *ch09/ex7-talkingProcs*, shows a process that calls
that process, just to demonstrate that this can work with more than just the shell. We
use IO.write/1 so that the code listing doesn't stretch off the page, but the output
will all appear on one line.

Example 9-7. Calling a process from a process, and reporting the results

```
defmodule MphDrop do
  def mph_drop do
    drop_pid = spawn(Drop, :drop, [])
    convert(drop_pid)
  end

  def convert(drop_pid) do
    receive do
      {planemo, distance} ->
        send(drop_pid, {self(), planemo, distance})
        convert(drop_pid)
      {planemo, distance, velocity} ->
        mph_velocity = 2.23693629 * velocity
        IO.write("On #{planemo}, a fall of #{distance} meters ")
        IO.puts("yields a velocity of #{mph_velocity} mph.")
        convert(drop_pid)
    end
  end
end
```

The mph_drop/1 function spawns a Drop.drop/0 process when it is first set up, using
the same module you saw in Example 9-6, and stores the pid in drop_pid. Then it
calls convert/1, which will listen for messages recursively.

If you don't separate the initialization from the recursive listener, your code will work, but it will spawn new `Drop.drop/0` processes every time it processes a message instead of using the same one repeatedly.

The `receive` clause relies on the call from the shell (or another process) including only two arguments, while the `Drop.drop/0` process sends back a result with three. (As your code grows more complex, you will likely want to use more explicit flags about the kind of information contained in a message.) When the `receive` clause gets a message with two arguments, it sends a message to `drop_pid`, identifying itself as the sender and passing on the arguments. When the `drop_pid` process returns a message with the result, the `receive` clause reports on the result, converting the velocity to miles per hour. (Yes, it leaves the distance metric, but it makes the velocity more intelligible to Americans.)

Using this from the shell looks like the following after invoking `iex -S mix`:

```
iex(1)> pid1 = spawn(MphDrop, :mph_drop, [])
#PID<0.47.0>
iex(2)> send(pid1, {:earth, 20})
On earth, a fall of 20 meters
yields a velocity of 44.289078952755766 mph.
{:earth,20}
iex(3)> send(pid1, {:mars, 20})
On mars, a fall of 20 meters
yields a velocity of 27.250254686571544 mph.
{:mars,20}
```

This simple example might look like it behaves as a more complex version of a function call, but there is a critical difference. In the shell, with nothing else running, the result will come back quickly—so quickly that it reports before the shell puts up the message—but this was a series of asynchronous calls. Nothing held and waited specifically for a returned message.

The shell sent a message to `pid1`, the process identifier for `MphDrop.convert/1`. That process sent a message to `drop_pid`, the process identifier for `Drop.drop/0`, which `MphDrop.mph_drop/0` set up when it was spawned. That process returned another message to `MphDrop.convert/1`, which reported to standard output (in this case, the shell). Those messages passed and were processed rapidly, but in a system with thousands or millions of messages in motion, those passages might have been separated by many messages and come in later.

Watching Your Processes

Erlang provides a simple but powerful tool for keeping track of your processes and seeing what's happening. *Observer*, a tool that lets you observe and manage processes, offers a GUI that lets you look into the current state of your processes and see what's happening. Depending on how you installed Erlang when you installed Elixir, you may be able to start it from a toolbar, but you can always start it from the shell:

```
iex(4)> :observer.start
#PID<0.49.0>
```

In order to use Observer, you need wxwidgets installed and Erlang compiled to support it.

When you click the Processes tab you'll see something like Figure 9-1 appear. It's a long list of processes, more than you probably wanted to know about. If you click the Current Function column header twice to sort the list in reverse order, you will see the Elixir processes at the top, similar to Figure 9-2.

Pid	Name or Initial Func	Reds	Memory	MsgQ	Current Function
<0.45.0>	wxe_server:init/1	208979	8404	0	gen_server:loop/6
<0.65.0>	gen:init_it/6	134687	98892	20	wxe_util:rec/1
<0.54.0>	erlang:apply/2	62755	17256	0	observer_pro_wx:table_holder/1
<0.3.0>	erl_prim_loader	35036	27564	0	erl_prim_loader:loop/3
<0.53.0>	gen:init_it/6	29306	6052	0	wxe_util:rec/1
<0.64.0>	gen:init_it/6	29196	8456	0	wxe_util:rec/1
<0.48.0>	gen:init_it/6	3894	27664	0	wx_object:loop/6
<0.20.0>	code_server	3170	142368	0	code_server:loop/1
<0.47.0>	erlang:apply/2	1936	1392	0	timer:sleep/1
<0.44.0>	observer	1582	8556	0	wx_object:loop/6
<0.52.0>	gen:init_it/6	1137	2996	0	wx_object:loop/6
<0.42.0>	erlang:apply/2	328	21228	0	Elixir.IEx.Evaluator:loop/1
<0.0.0>	init	267	14792	0	init:loop/1
<0.66.0>	erlang:apply/2	148	1412	0	io:wait_io_mon_reply/2

Figure 9-1. Observer's process list when first loaded

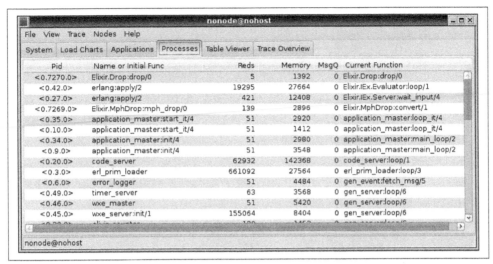

Figure 9-2. Observer's process list after sorting by Current Function

Observer will update the process list every 10 seconds. If you would prefer to control the refresh yourself, choose Refresh Interval from the View menu, and uncheck Periodical Refresh.

Watching Messages Among Processes

The list of processes is useful, but Observer also lets you look inside of process activity. This is a slightly more complex process, so take a deep breath!

1. Find the `Elixir.MphDrop:mph_drop/0` process and right-click it.

2. Choose "Trace selected processes by name (all nodes)" and select all items in the left of the dialog, as shown in Figure 9-3. Then click OK.

3. Click the Trace Overview tab.

4. Click Start Trace, and you will get a warning message as shown in Figure 9-4. You may safely ignore that message.

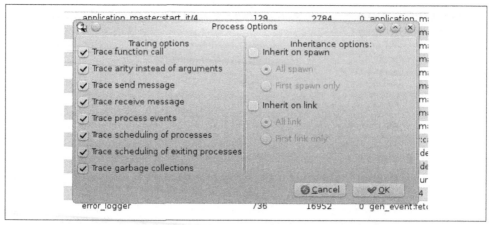

Figure 9-3. Options in trace processes

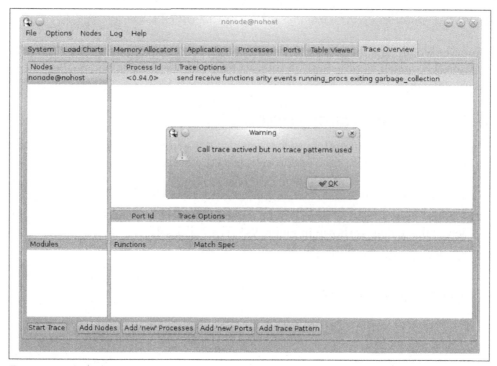

Figure 9-4. Starting a trace

This will open up a new window, which may display a message like "Dropped 10 messages." Now make the process do something:

```
iex(5)> send(pid1, {:mars, 20})
On mars, a fall of 20 meters
yields a velocity of 27.25025468657154448238 mph.
{:mars,20}
```

The Observer window for that process will update to show messages and calls, as shown in Figure 9-5. << means a message was received, whereas ! indicates a message sent.

```
╳ ○                            Trace Log                        ⌄ ⌃ ⊗
File
 {bin_old_vheap_size,0},
 {bin_old_vheap_block_size,46422}]
15:09:55:369318 (<0.94.0>)  <0.50.0> ! {io_request,<0.94.0>,#Ref<0.0.1.9641>,
                                        {put_chars,unicode,<<"On mars, a fall of 20 mete
15:09:55:369337 (<0.94.0>)  out {io,execute_request,2}
15:09:55:369523 (<0.94.0>)  << {io_reply,#Ref<0.0.1.9641>,ok}
15:09:55:369562 (<0.94.0>)  in {io,execute_request,2}
15:09:55:369582 (<0.94.0>)  code_server ! {code_call,<0.94.0>,
                                        {ensure_loaded,'Elixir.String.Chars.Float'}}
15:09:55:369597 (<0.94.0>)  out {code_server,call,1}
15:09:55:375286 (<0.94.0>)  << {code_server,{module,'Elixir.String.Chars.Float'}}
15:09:55:375586 (<0.94.0>)  in {code_server,call,1}
15:09:55:375643 (<0.94.0>)  <0.50.0> ! {io_request,<0.94.0>,#Ref<0.0.1.9644>,
                                        {put_chars,unicode,
                                        <<"yields a velocity of 27.250254686571544 m
15:09:55:375657 (<0.94.0>)  out {io,execute_request,2}
15:09:55:375923 (<0.94.0>)  << {io_reply,#Ref<0.0.1.9644>,ok}
15:09:55:376106 (<0.94.0>)  in {io,execute_request,2}
15:09:55:376122 (<0.94.0>)  out {'Elixir.MphDrop',convert,1}
```

Figure 9-5. Tracing calls when you send mph_drop a message

Observer is generally the easiest place to turn when you're having difficulty figuring out what is happening among your processes.

Breaking Things and Linking Processes

When you send a message, you'll always get back the message as the return value. This doesn't mean that everything went well and the message was received and processed correctly, however. If you send a message that doesn't match a pattern at the receiving process, nothing will happen (for now at least), with the message landing in the mailbox but not triggering activity. Sending a message that gets through the pattern matching but creates an error will halt the process where the error occurred, possibly even a few messages and processes down the line.

 Messages that don't match a pattern in the receive clause don't vanish; they just linger in the mailbox without being processed. It is possible to update a process with a new version of the code that retrieves those messages.

Because processes are fragile, you often want your code to know when another process has failed. In this case, if bad inputs halt Drop.drop/0, it doesn't make much sense to leave the MphDrop.convert/1 process hanging around. You can see how this works through the shell and Observer. First, start up Observer, go to the process window, and then, from the command line, spawn MphDrop.mph_drop/0:

```
iex(1)> :observer.start()
:ok
iex(2)> pid1 = spawn(MphDrop, :mph_drop, [])
#PID<0.82.0>
```

You'll see something like Figure 9-6 in Observer. Then, feed your process some bad data, an atom (:zoids) instead of a number for the distance, and Observer will look more like Figure 9-7:

```
iex(3)> send(pid1, {:moon, :zoids})

19:28:27.825 [error] Process #PID<0.83.0> raised an exception
** (ArithmeticError) bad argument in arithmetic expression
    (mph_drop) lib/drop.ex:15: Drop.fall_velocity/2
    (mph_drop) lib/drop.ex:5: Drop.drop/0
```

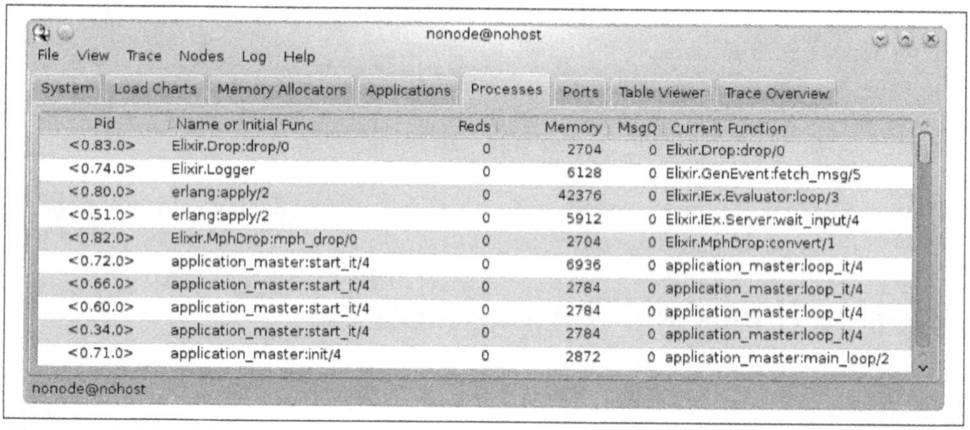

Figure 9-6. A healthy set of processes

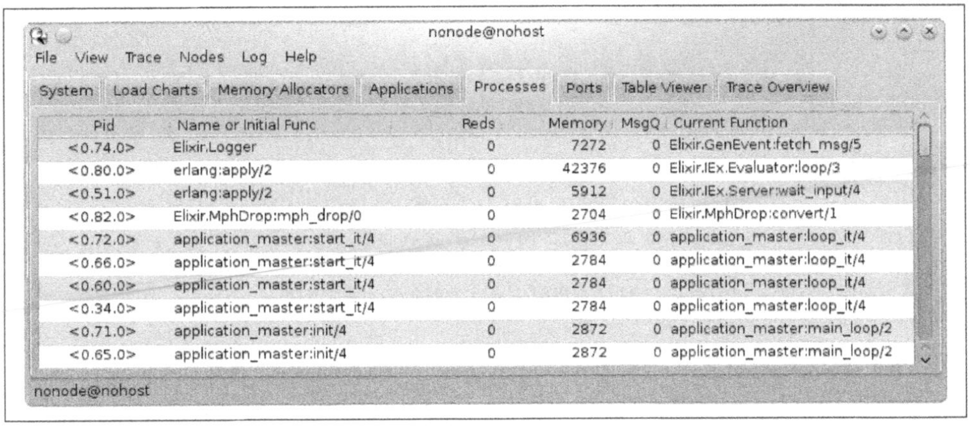

Figure 9-7. Only the drop:drop/0 process is gone

Since the remaining `MphDrop.convert/1` process is now useless, it would be better for it to halt when `Drop.drop/0` fails. Elixir lets you specify that dependency with a link. The easy way to do that while avoiding potential race conditions is to use `spawn_link/3` instead of just `spawn/3`. Everything else in the module remains the same. This is shown in Example 9-8, which you can find in *ch09/ex8-linking*.

Example 9-8. Calling a linked process from a process so failures propagate

```
defmodule MphDrop do
  def mph_drop do
    drop_pid = spawn_link(Drop, :drop, [])
    convert(drop_pid)
  end

  def convert(drop_pid) do
    receive do
      {planemo, distance} ->
        send(drop_pid, {self(), planemo, distance})
        convert(drop_pid)
      {planemo, distance, velocity} ->
        mph_velocity = 2.23693629 * velocity
        IO.write("On #{planemo}, a fall of #{distance} meters ")
        IO.puts("yields a velocity of #{mph_velocity} mph.")
        convert(drop_pid)
    end
  end
end
```

Now, if you recompile and test this out with Observer, you'll see that both processes vanish when drop:drop/0 fails, as shown in Figure 9-8:

```
iex(1)> :observer.start()
:ok
iex(2)> pid1 = spawn(MphDrop, :mph_drop, [])
#PID<0.162.0>
iex(3)> send(pid1, {:moon, :zoids})
{:moon,:zoids}
iex(4)>

19:30:26.822 [error] Process #PID<0.163.0> raised an exception
** (ArithmeticError) bad argument in arithmetic expression
    (mph_drop) lib/drop.ex:15: Drop.fall_velocity/2
    (mph_drop) lib/drop.ex:5: Drop.drop/0
```

Pid	Name or Initial Func	Reds	Memory	MsgQ	Current Function
<0.137.0>	Elixir.Logger	0	7272	0	Elixir.GenEvent:fetch_msg/5
<0.143.0>	erlang:apply/2	0	34472	0	Elixir.IEx.Evaluator:loop/3
<0.51.0>	erlang:apply/2	0	5912	0	Elixir.IEx.Server:wait_input/4
<0.135.0>	application_master:start_it/4	0	5792	0	application_master:loop_it/4
<0.84.0>	application_master:start_it/4	0	2784	0	application_master:loop_it/4
<0.66.0>	application_master:start_it/4	0	2784	0	application_master:loop_it/4
<0.60.0>	application_master:start_it/4	0	2784	0	application_master:loop_it/4
<0.34.0>	application_master:start_it/4	0	2784	0	application_master:loop_it/4

Figure 9-8. Both processes now depart when there is an error

Links are bidirectional. If you kill the the MphDrop.mph_drop/0 process—with, for example, Process.exit(pid1,:kill).—the Drop.drop/0 process will also vanish. (:kill is the harshest reason for an exit, and isn't trappable because sometimes you really need to halt a process.)

That kind of failure may not be what you have in mind when you think of linking processes. It's the default behavior for linked Elixir processes, and makes sense in many contexts, but you can also have a process trap exits. When an Elixir process fails, it sends an explanation, in the form of a tuple, to other processes that are linked to it. The tuple contains the atom :EXIT, the pid of the failed process, and the error as a complex tuple. If your process is set to trap exits, through a call to Process .flag(:trap_exit, true), these error reports arrive as messages, rather than just killing your process.

Example 9-9, in *ch09/ex9-trapping*, shows how the initial mph_drop/0 method changes to include this call to set the process flag, and adds another entry to the receive clause which will listen for exits and report them more neatly.

Example 9-9. Trapping a failure, reporting an error, and exiting

```
defmodule MphDrop do
  def mph_drop do
    Process.flag(:trap_exit, true)
    drop_pid = spawn_link(Drop, :drop, [])
    convert(drop_pid)
  end

  def convert(drop_pid) do
    receive do
      {planemo, distance} ->
        send(drop_pid, {self(), planemo, distance})
        convert(drop_pid)
      {:EXIT, pid, reason} ->
        IO.puts("Failure: #{inspect(pid)} #{inspect(reason)}")
      {planemo, distance, velocity} ->
        mph_velocity = 2.23693629 * velocity
        IO.write("On #{planemo}, a fall of #{distance} meters ")
        IO.puts("yields a velocity of #{mph_velocity} mph.")
        convert(drop_pid)
    end
  end
end
```

If you run this and feed it bad data, the convert/1 method will report an error message (mostly duplicating the shell) before exiting neatly:

```
iex(1)> pid1 = spawn(MphDrop, :mph_drop, [])
#PID<0.144.0>
iex(2)> send(pid1, {:moon, 20})
On moon, a fall of 20 meters
yields a velocity of 17.89549032 mph.
{:moon,20}
iex(3)> send(pid1, {:moon, :zoids})
Failure: #PID<0.145.0> {:badarith, [{Drop, :fall_velocity, 2,
  [file: 'lib/drop.ex', line: 15]},
  {Drop, :drop, 0, [file: 'lib/drop.ex', line: 5]}]}
  {:moon, :zoids}
iex(4)>
12:04:31.360 [error] Process #PID<0.145.0> raised an exception
** (ArithmeticError) bad argument in arithmetic expression
    (mph_drop) lib/drop.ex:15: Drop.fall_velocity/2
    (mph_drop) lib/drop.ex:5: Drop.drop/0

    nil
iex(5)>
```

A more robust alternative would set up a new drop_pid variable, spawning a new process. That version, shown in Example 9-10, which you can find in *ch09/ex10-resilient*, is much hardier. Its receive clause sweeps away failure, soldiering on with a new copy (new_drop_pid) of the drop calculator if needed.

Example 9-10. Trapping a failure, reporting an error, and setting up a new process

```
defmodule MphDrop do
  def mph_drop do
    Process.flag(:trap_exit, true)
    drop_pid = spawn_link(Drop, :drop, [])
    convert(drop_pid)
  end

  def convert(drop_pid) do
    receive do
      {planemo, distance} ->
        send(drop_pid, {self(), planemo, distance})
        convert(drop_pid)
      {:EXIT, _pid, _reason} ->
        new_drop_pid = spawn_link(Drop, :drop, [])
        convert(new_drop_pid)
      {planemo, distance, velocity} ->
        mph_velocity = 2.23693629 * velocity
        IO.write("On #{planemo}, a fall of #{distance} meters ")
        IO.puts("yields a velocity of #{mph_velocity} mph.")
        convert(drop_pid)
    end
  end
end
```

If you compile and run Example 9-10, you'll see Figure 9-9 when you first start Observer. If you feed it bad data, as shown on line 6 in the following code sample, you'll still get the error message from the shell, but the process will work just fine. As you'll see in Observer, as shown in Figure 9-10, it started up a new process to handle the Drop.drop/0 calculations, and as line 7 shows, it works like its predecessor:

```
iex(1)> pid1 = spawn(MphDrop, :mph_drop, [])
#PID<0.145.0>
iex(2)> :observer.start()
:ok
iex(3)> send(pid1, {:moon, 20})
On moon, a fall of 20 meters
yields a velocity of 17.89549032 mph.
{:moon,20}
iex(4)> send(pid1, {:mars, 20})
On mars, a fall of 20 meters
yields a velocity of 27.250254686571544 mph.
{:mars, 20}
iex(5)> send(pid1, {:mars, :zoids})
{:mars, :zoids}
Failure: #PID<0.109.0> {:badarith, [{Drop, :fall_velocity, 2,
  [file: 'lib/drop.ex', line: 19]},
  {Drop, :drop, 0, [file: 'lib/drop.ex', line: 5]}]}
iex(6)>
15:59:49.713 [error] Process #PID<0.146.0> raised an exception
** (ArithmeticError) bad argument in arithmetic expression
```

```
    (mph_drop) lib/drop.ex:19: Drop.fall_velocity/2
    (mph_drop) lib/drop.ex:5: Drop.drop/0

nil
iex(7)> send(pid1, {:moon, 20})
On moon, a fall of 20 meters
yields a velocity of 17.89549032 mph.
{:moon,20}
```

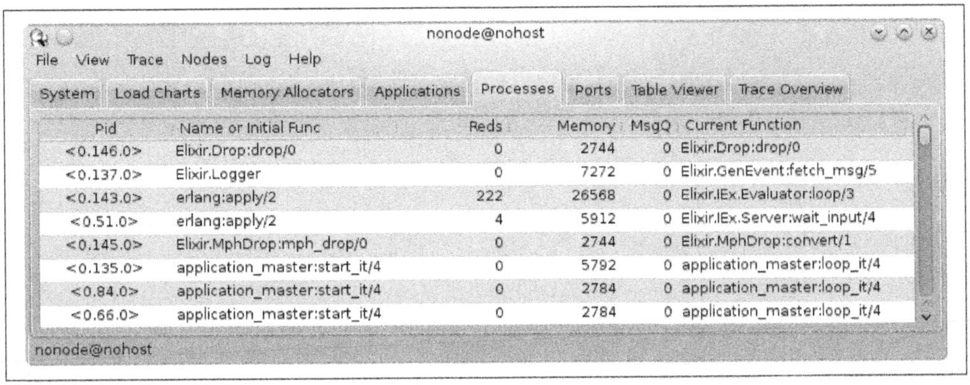

Figure 9-9. Processes before an error—note the Pid on the top line

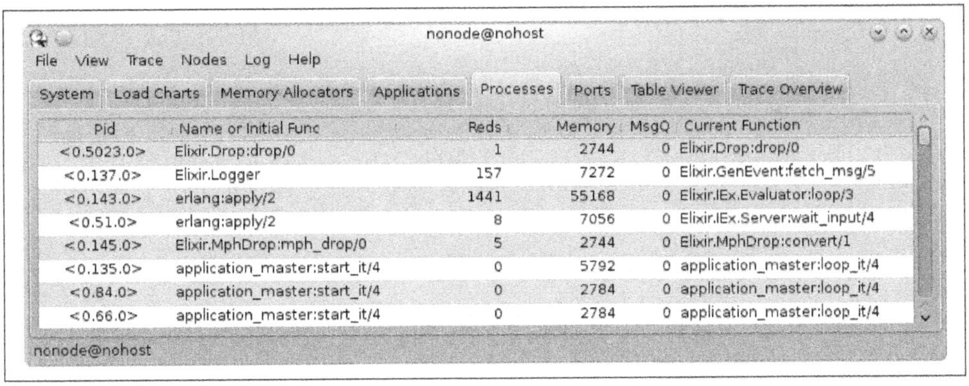

Figure 9-10. Processes after an error—note the top line Pid change

Elixir offers many more process management options. You can remove a link with Process.unlink/1, or establish a connection for just watching a process with Process.monitor/1. If you want to terminate a process, use Process.exit/2 to specify a process and reason. You may specify another process's pid or self().

Building applications that can tolerate failure and restore their functionality is at the core of robust Elixir programming. Developing in that style is probably a larger leap for most programmers than Elixir's shift to functional programming, but it's where the true power of Elixir becomes obvious.

## CHAPTER 10

Exceptions, Errors, and Debugging

"Let it crash" is a brilliant insight, but one whose application you probably want to control. While it's possible to write code that constantly breaks and recovers, it can be easier to write and maintain code that explicitly handles failure where it happens. However you choose to deal with errors, you'll definitely want to be able to track them down in your application.

Flavors of Errors

As you've already seen, some kinds of errors will keep Elixir from compiling your code, and the compiler will also give you warnings about potential issues, like variables that are declared but never used. Two other kinds of errors are common: runtime errors, which turn up when code is operating and can actually halt a function or process, and logic errors, which may not kill your program but can cause deeper headaches.

Logic errors are often the trickiest to diagnose, requiring careful thought and perhaps some time with the debugger, log files, or a test suite. Simple mathematical errors can take a lot of work to untangle. Sometimes issues are related to timing, when the sequence of operations isn't what you expect. In severe cases, race conditions can create deadlocks and halting, but more mild cases can produce bad results and confusion.

Runtime errors can also be annoying, but they are much more manageable. In some ways you can see handling runtime errors as part of the logic of your program, though you don't want to get carried away. In Elixir, unlike many other programs, handling errors as errors may offer only minor advantages over letting an error kill a process and then dealing with the problem at the process level, as Example 9-10 showed.

Rescuing Code from Runtime Errors as They Happen

If you want to catch runtime errors close to where they took place, the try...rescue construct lets you wrap suspect code and handle problems (if any) that code creates. It makes it clear to both the compiler and the programmer that something unusual is happening, and lets you deal with any unfortunate consequences of that work.

For a simple example, look back to Example 3-1, which calculated fall velocity without considering the possibility that it would be handed a negative distance. The :math.sqrt/1 function will produce a badarith error if it has a negative argument. Example 4-2 kept that problem from occurring by applying guards, but if you want to do more than block, you can take a more direct approach with try and rescue, as shown in Example 10-1. (You can find this and the following two variations in *ch10/ex1-tryCatch*.)

Example 10-1. Using try and catch to handle a possible error

```
defmodule Drop do
  def fall_velocity(planemo, distance) do
    gravity = case planemo do
      :earth -> 9.8
      :moon -> 1.6
      :mars -> 3.71
    end
    try do
      :math.sqrt(2 * gravity * distance)
    rescue
      error -> error
    end
  end
end
```

The calculation itself is now wrapped in a try. If the calculation succeeds, the statement following the do will be used, and the return value will become the result of the calculation.

If the calculation fails, in this case because of a negative argument, the pattern match in the rescue clause comes into play. In this case, the variable error will contain the exception type and message, and will return that as its value.

You can try the following on the command line:

```
iex(1)> Drop.fall_velocity(:earth, 20)
19.79898987322333
iex(2)> Drop.fall_velocity(:earth, -20)
%ArithmeticError{message: "bad argument in arithmetic expression"}
```

When the calculation is successful, you'll just get the result. When it fails, you see the exception. It's not a complete solution, but it's a foundation on which you can build.

You can have multiple statements in the try (much as you can in a case). At least when you're getting started, it's easiest to keep the code you are trying simple so you can see where failures happened. However, if you wanted to watch for requests that provided an atom that didn't match the planemos in the case, you could put it all into the try:

```
defmodule Drop do
  def fall_velocity(planemo, distance) do
    try do
      gravity = case planemo do
        :earth -> 9.8
        :moon -> 1.6
        :mars -> 3.71
      end
      :math.sqrt(2 * gravity * distance)
    rescue
      error -> error
    end
  end
end
```

If you try an unsupported planemo, you'll now see the code catch the problem (at least, once you recompile the code to use the new version):

```
iex(3)> Drop.fall_velocity(:jupiter, 20)
** (CaseClauseError) no case clause matching: :jupiter
    drop.ex:3: Drop.fall_velocity/2
iex(3)> r(Drop)
warning: redefining module Drop (current version defined in memory)
  lib/drop.ex:1

{:reloaded, Drop, [Drop]}
iex(4)> Drop.fall_velocity(:jupiter, 20)
%CaseClauseError{term: :jupiter}
```

The CaseClauseError indicates that a case failed to match and tells you the actual item that didn't match.

You can also have multiple pattern matches in the rescue. If the error doesn't match any of the patterns in the rescue clause, it gets reported as a runtime error, as if the try hadn't wrapped it. The following example will provide different messages for each type of error. The code doesn't store the exception in a variable since it doesn't use information stored in the exception:

```
defmodule Drop do
  def fall_velocity(planemo, distance) do
    try do
      gravity = case planemo do
```

```
        :earth -> 9.8
        :moon -> 1.6
        :mars -> 3.71
      end
    :math.sqrt(2 * gravity * distance)
  rescue
    ArithmeticError -> {:error, "Distance must be non-negative"}
    CaseClauseError -> {:error, "Unknown planemo #{planemo}"}
  end
  end
end
```

And here is what it looks like in action:

```
iex(5)> r(Drop)
warning: redefining module Drop (current version defined in memory)
  lib/drop.ex:1

{:reloaded, Drop, [Drop]}
iex(6)> Drop.fall_velocity(:earth, -20)
{:error,"Distance must be non-negative"}
iex(7)> Drop.fall_velocity(:jupiter, 20)
{:error,"Unknown planemo jupiter"}
```

 If you want to do the same actions for multiple exceptions, you can write code like this:

```
[ArithmeticError, CaseClauseError] -> "Generic Error"
err in [ErlangError, RuntimeError] -> {:error, err}
```

If the code that might fail can create a mess, you may want to include an `after` clause after the `rescue` clause and before the closing end. The code in an `after` clause is guaranteed to run whether the attempted code succeeds or fails and can be a good place to address any side effects of the code. It doesn't affect the return value of the clause.

Logging Progress and Failure

The `IO.puts` function is useful for simple communications with the shell, but as your programs grow (and especially as they become distributed processes), hurling text toward standard output is less likely to get you the information you need. Elixir offers a set of functions for more formal logging. They *can* hook into more sophisticated logging systems, but it's easy to get started with them as a way to structure messages from your application.

These functions in Elixir's `Logger` module give you four levels of reporting:

`:info`

> For information of any kind.

`:debug`

> For debug-related messages.

`:warn`

> For news that's worse. Someone should do something eventually.

`:error`

> For when something is just plain broken and needs to be looked at.

As you can see, these calls produce reports that are visually distinctive. If you run IEx and enter these statements, you will see that the messages also appear in different colors:

```
iex(1)> require Logger
Logger
iex(2)> counter=255
255
iex(3)> Logger.info("About to begin test")

18:57:36.846 [info]  About to begin test
:ok
iex(4)> Logger.debug("Current value of counter is #{counter}")

18:58:06.526 [debug] Current value of counter is 255
:ok
iex(5)> Logger.warn("Connection lost; will retry.")

18:58:21.759 [warn]  Connection lost; will retry.
:ok
iex(6)> Logger.error("Unable to read database.")

18:58:37.008 [error] Unable to read database.
:ok
```

These functions produce only a mild improvement over IO.puts, so why would you use them? Because there is much, much more lurking under the surface. By default, when Elixir starts up, it sets up the Logger module to report to the shell. However, you can design a custom backend to log information to any destination you please.

While logging information is useful, it's not unusual to write code with subtle errors where you're not positive what to log where. You could litter the code with reporting, or you could use the Erlang debugging tools that are also available in Elixir.

Tracing Messages

Elixir offers a wide variety of tools for tracing code, both with other code (using Erlang's trace and trace_pattern built-in functions) and with a text-based debugger/reporter. The dbg module is the easiest place to start into this toolset, letting you specify what you want traced and showing you the results in the shell.

The :dbg module is an Erlang module, but if you are getting tired of typing the leading : every time you use an Erlang function, you can make things feel more Elixir-like by typing this command:

```
iex(1)> alias :dbg, as: Dbg
:dbg
```

For now, we will continue to use :dbg.

An easy place to get started is tracing messages sent between processes. You can use :dbg.p to trace the messages sent between the mph_drop process defined in Example 9-8 and the drop process from Example 9-6. After compiling the modules, you call :dbg.tracer() to start reporting trace information to the shell. Then you spawn the mph_drop process as usual and pass that pid to the :dbg.p/2 process. The second argument here will be :m, meaning that the trace should report the messages. The code from Example 9-8 is duplicated in *ch10/ex2-debug* and is started here via iex -S mix:

```
iex(1)> :dbg.tracer()
{:ok,#PID<0.71.0>}
iex(2)> pid1 = spawn(MphDrop, :mph_drop, [])
#PID<0.148.0>
iex(3)> :dbg.p(pid1, :m)
{:ok, [{:matched, :nonode@nohost, 1}]}
```

Now when you send a message to the mph_drop process, you'll get a set of reports on the resulting flow of messages (<0.148.0> is the mph_drop process, and <0.149.0> is the drop process):

```
iex(4)> send(pid1, {:moon, 20})
On moon, a fall of 20 meters {:moon, 20}
(<0.148.0>) << {moon,20}
yields a velocity of 17.89549032 mph.
(<0.148.0>) <0.149.0> ! {<0.148.0>,moon,20}
(<0.148.0>) << {moon,20,8.0}
(<0.148.0>) <0.50.0> ! {io_request,<0.148.0>,#Ref<0.0.2.159>,
                        {put_chars,unicode,
                             <<"On moon, a fall of 20 meters ">>}}
(<0.148.0>) << {io_reply,#Ref<0.0.2.159>,ok}
(<0.148.0>) <0.50.0> ! {io_request,<0.148.0>,#Ref<0.0.3.350>,
                        {put_chars,unicode,
                             <<"yields a velocity of 17.89549032 mph.\n">>}}
(<0.148.0>)<< {io_reply,#Ref<0.0.3.350>,ok}
```

The << pointing to a pid indicates that that process received a message. Sends are indicated with the pid followed by ! followed by the message. This is much like what you saw when using Observer to view process messages in "Watching Your Processes" on page 114. Because :dbg is an Erlang module, the values in messages (both sent and received) are printed using the Erlang syntax rather than the Elixir syntax. Here is some explanation of the preceding debug output:

- On this run, the report from mph_drop that On moon, a fall of 20 meters yields a velocity of 17.89549032 mph. and the result of {:moon, 20} come through in the middle of the tracing information. The rest of the trace indicates how that report got there.
- mph_drop (<0.148.0>) receives the message tuple {moon,20}.
- It sends a further message, the tuple {<0.148.0>,moon,20}, to the drop process at pid <0.149.0>.
- mph_drop receives a tuple {moon,20,8.0} (from drop).
- Then it calls io:request/2, which triggers another set of process messages to make the report.

The trace reports come through interleaved with the actual execution of the code, but they make the flow of messages clear. You'll want to learn to use :dbg in its many variations to trace your code and may eventually want to use match patterns and the trace functions themselves to create more elegant systems for watching specific code.

Watching Function Calls

If you just want to keep track of arguments moving between function calls, you can use the tracer to report on the sequence of calls. Chapter 4 demonstrated recursion and reported results along the way through IO.puts. There's another way to see that work, again using the :dbg module.

Example 4-11, the upward factorial calculator, started with a call to Fact.factorial/1, which then called Fact.factorial/3 recursively. :dbg will let you see the actual function calls and their arguments, mixed with the IO.puts reporting. (You can find it in *ch10/ex3-debug*.)

Tracing functions is a little trickier than tracing messages because you can't just pass :dbg.p/2 a pid. As shown on line 2 in the following code sample, you need to tell it you want it to report on all processes (:all) and their calls (:c). Once you've done that, you have to specify which calls you want it to report, using :dbg.tpl as shown on line 3. It takes a module name (Fact), a function name as an atom (:facto rial), and optionally a match specification that lets you specify arguments more precisely. Variations on this function also let you specify arity.

So turn on the tracer, tell it you want to follow function calls, and specify a function (or functions, through multiple calls to :dbg.tpl) to watch. Then call the function, and you'll see a list of the calls:

```
iex(1)> :dbg.tracer()
{:ok,#PID<0.43.0>}
iex(2)> :dbg.p(:all, :c)
{:ok, [{:matched, :nonode@nohost, 51}]}
iex(3)> :dbg.tpl(Fact, :factorial, [])
{:ok, [{:matched, :nonode@nohost, 2}]}

iex(4)> Fact.factorial(4)
1 yields 1.
(<0.26.0>) call 'Elixir-Fact':factorial(4)
(<0.26.0>) call 'Elixir-Fact':factorial(1,4,1)
2 yields 2.
(<0.26.0>) call 'Elixir-Fact':factorial(2,4,1)
3 yields 6.
(<0.26.0>) call 'Elixir-Fact':factorial(3,4,2)
4 yields 24.
(<0.26.0>) call 'Elixir-Fact':factorial(4,4,6)
finished!
(<0.26.0>) call 'Elixir-Fact':factorial(5,4,24)
24
```

You can see that the sequence is a bit messy here, with the trace reporting coming a little bit after the IO.puts results from the function being traced. Because the trace is running in a separate process (at pid <0.43.0>) from the function (at pid <0.26.0>), its reporting may not line up smoothly (or at all, though it usually does).

When you're done tracing, call :dbg.stop/0 (if you might want to restart tracing with the same setup) or :dbg.stop_clear/0 (if you know that when you start again you'll want to set things up again).

The :dbg module and the trace functions on which it builds are incredibly powerful tools.

## CHAPTER 11

Static Analysis, Typespecs, and Testing

In programming, there are three major classes of errors: *syntax errors*, *runtime errors*, and *semantic errors*. The Elixir compiler takes care of finding syntax errors for you, and in Chapter 10 you learned how to handle runtime errors. That leaves *logic errors*, when you tell Elixir to do something that you didn't mean to say. While logging and tracing can help you find logic errors, the best way to solve them is to make sure that they never make their way into your program in the first place—and that is the role of *static analysis*, *typespecs*, and *unit testing*.

Static Analysis

Static analysis refers to debugging by analyzing the source code of a program without running it. The Dialyzer (*http://erlang.org/doc/man/dialyzer.html*) (DIscrepancy AnalYZer for ERlang programs) is a tool that does static analysis of Erlang source and *.beam* files to check for such problems as unused functions, code that can never be reached, improper lists, patterns that are unused or cannot match, etc. To make it easier to use Dialyzer with Elixir, use the Dialyxir (*https://github.com/jeremyjh/dialyxir*) tool. We followed the global install path with these commands:

```
$ git clone https://github.com/jeremyjh/dialyxir
$ cd dialyxir
$ mix archive.build
$ mix archive.install
$ mix dialyzer.plt
```

The last command builds a *Persistent Lookup Table* (PLT) that stores results of Dialyzer analyses; the PLT will analyze most of the commonly used Erlang and Elixir libraries so that they don't have to be scanned every time you use Dialyzer. This step will take several minutes to complete, so be patient and go out and enjoy a short break. As per the instructions on GitHub, you must rerun that command whenever you install newer versions of Elixir or Erlang.

Now that Dialyxir has set up Dialyzer, let's see it in action. Consider the code in Example 11-1, which you will find in *ch11/ex1-guards*, which adds a very wrong function to the example in *ch03/ex2-guards*.

Example 11-1. Erroneous calls to clauses

```elixir
defmodule Drop do

  def fall_velocity(:earth, distance) when distance >= 0 do
    :math.sqrt(2 * 9.8 * distance)
  end

  def fall_velocity(:moon, distance) when distance >= 0 do
    :math.sqrt(2 * 1.6 * distance)
  end

  def fall_velocity(:mars, distance) when distance >= 0 do
    :math.sqrt(2 * 3.71 * distance)
  end

  def wrongness() do
    total_distance = fall_velocity(:earth, 20) +
      fall_velocity(:moon, 20) +
      fall_velocity(:jupiter, 20) +
      fall_velocity(:earth, "20")
    total_distance
  end
end
```

If you go into IEx, the compiler will not detect any errors. It is only when you run the wrongness/0 function that things go bad:

```
$ iex -S mix
Erlang/OTP 19 [erts-8.0] [source] [64-bit] [smp:4:4] [async-threads:10] [hipe]
[kernel-poll:false]

Compiling 1 file (.ex)
Generated drop app
Interactive Elixir (1.3.1) - press Ctrl+C to exit (type h() ENTER for help)
iex(1)> Drop.wrongness()
** (FunctionClauseError) no function clause matching in Drop.fall_velocity/2
    (drop) lib/drop.ex:3: Drop.fall_velocity(:jupiter, 20)
    (drop) lib/drop.ex:18: Drop.wrongness/0
iex(1)>
```

Dialyzer, however, would have warned you about this problem in advance. The first mix clean command clears out any compiled files so that Dialyzer is starting "from scratch":

```
$ mix clean
$ mix dialyzer
Compiling 1 file (.ex)
Generated drop app
Starting Dialyzer
dialyzer --no_check_plt --plt /home/david/.dialyxir_core_19_1.3.1.plt
  -Wunmatched_returns -Werror_handling -Wrace_conditions -Wunderspecs
  /Users/elixir/code/ch11/ex1-guards/_build/dev/lib/drop/ebin
  Proceeding with analysis...
drop.ex:15: Function wrongness/0 has no local return
drop.ex:18: The call 'Elixir.Drop':fall_velocity('jupiter',20) will never return
  since it differs in the 1st argument from the success typing
  arguments: ('earth' | 'mars' | 'moon',number())
drop.ex:19: The call 'Elixir.Drop':fall_velocity('earth',<<_:16>>) will
  never return since it differs in the 2nd argument from the success
  typing arguments: ('earth' | 'mars' | 'moon',number())
 done in 0m3.27s
done (warnings were emitted)
```

Dialyzer compiles your file and then checks it. All the -W items on the dialyzer command line tell what things Dialyzer will give warning messages for in addition to the default things that it warns about.

The first error, Function wrongness/0 has no local return, means that the function never returns a value, because it has other errors in it. (If wrongness/0 had no errors but called functions that did have errors, Dialyzer would give you the same error.)

The second error tells you that the call fall_velocity(:jupiter, 20) (which Dialyzer punctuates differently, as it belongs to the Erlang universe) won't work because there is no pattern defined with :jupiter as the first argument.

The last error shows the power of Dialyzer. Even though the code hasn't given a @spec for drop/1, Dialyzer mystically divined that the second argument must be a number, which makes fall_velocity(:earth, "20") incorrect. (OK, it's not mystical. It's a really good algorithm.)

Typespecs

Dialyzer is an excellent tool and can do a lot on its own, but you can assist it in doing its job (and readers of your code in doing theirs) by explicitly specifying the types of parameters and return values of your functions. Consider the module in Example 11-2 (in *ch11/ex2-specs*), which implements several gravity-related equations.

Example 11-2. Explicitly specifying types

```elixir
defmodule Specs do

  @spec fall_velocity({atom(), number()}, number()) :: float()
  def fall_velocity({_planemo, gravity}, distance) when distance > 0 do
    :math.sqrt(2 * gravity * distance)
  end

  @spec average_velocity_by_distance({atom(), number()}, number()) :: float()
  def average_velocity_by_distance({planemo, gravity}, distance) when distance > 0 do
    fall_velocity({planemo, gravity}, distance) / 2.0
  end

  @spec fall_distance({atom(), number()}, number()) :: float()
  def fall_distance({_planemo, gravity}, time) when time > 0 do
    gravity * time * time / 2.0
  end

  def calculate() do
    earth_v = average_velocity_by_distance({:earth, 9.8}, 10)
    moon_v = average_velocity_by_distance({:moon, 1.6}, 10)
    mars_v = average_velocity_by_distance({3.71, :mars}, 10)
    IO.puts("After 10 seconds, average velocity is:")
    IO.puts("Earth: #{earth_v} m.")
    IO.puts("Moon: #{moon_v} m.")
    IO.puts("Mars: #{mars_v} m.")
  end
end
```

Each of these functions takes a tuple giving a planemo name and its gravitational acceleration as its first parameter, and a distance or time (as appropriate) for its second parameter. You may have noticed that the calculate/0 function has an error in the calculation for mars_v; the items in the initial tuple are in the wrong order. The compiler won't catch the error, so you get this result from IEx:

```
iex(1)> Specs.calculate()
** (ArithmeticError) bad argument in arithmetic expression
    (specs) lib/specs.ex:5: Specs.fall_velocity/2
    (specs) lib/specs.ex:10: Specs.average_velocity_by_distance/2
    (specs) lib/specs.ex:21: Specs.calculate/0
iex(1)>
```

Dialyzer, however, with the assistance of @spec, will tell you there is a problem:

```
$ mix dialyzer
Starting Dialyzer
dialyzer --no_check_plt --plt /home/david/.dialyxir_core_19_1.3.1.plt
  -Wunmatched_returns -Werror_handling -Wrace_conditions -Wunderspecs
  /Users/elixir/code/ch11/ex2-specs/_build/dev/lib/specs/ebin
    Proceeding with analysis...
specs.ex:23: Function calculate/0 has no local return
```

```
specs.ex:26:
  The call 'Elixir.Specs':average_velocity_by_distance(
    {3.70999999999999996447, 'mars'},10)
  will never return since the success typing is
  ({atom(),number()},number()) -> float()
  and the contract is ({atom(),number()},number()) -> float()
  done in 0m3.04s
done (warnings were emitted)
```

This is one of those instances when using a @spec gives a *less* clear message from Dialyzer—without the @spec, you get this error instead:

```
specs.ex:26: The call 'Elixir.Specs':average_velocity_by_
  distance({3.70999999999999996447, 'mars'},10)
  will never return since it differs in the 1st argument
  from the success typing arguments:
  ({atom(),number()},number())
```

In either case, however, Dialyzer alerts you to a problem.

There is a lot of duplication in the @specs. You can eliminate that duplication by creating a typespec (type specification) of your own. In Example 11-3, in *ch11/ex3-type*, we define a planetuple type and use it in the @spec for each function.

Example 11-3. Creating a type specification

```elixir
defmodule NewType do
  @type planetuple :: {atom(), number()}

  @spec fall_velocity(planetuple, number()) :: float()
  def fall_velocity({_planemo, gravity}, distance) when distance > 0 do
    :math.sqrt(2 * gravity * distance)
  end

  @spec average_velocity_by_distance(planetuple, number()) :: float()
  def average_velocity_by_distance({planemo, gravity}, distance) when distance > 0 do
    fall_velocity({planemo, gravity}, distance) / 2.0
  end

  @spec fall_distance(planetuple, number()) :: float()
  def fall_distance({_planemo, gravity}, time) when time > 0 do
    gravity * time * time / 2.0
  end

  def calculate() do
    earth_v = average_velocity_by_distance({:earth, 9.8}, 10)
    moon_v = average_velocity_by_distance({:moon, 1.6}, 10)
    mars_v = average_velocity_by_distance({3.71, :mars}, 10)
    IO.puts("After 10 seconds, average velocity is:")
    IO.puts("Earth: #{earth_v} m.")
```

```
    IO.puts("Moon: #{moon_v} m.")
    IO.puts("Mars: #{mars_v} m.")
  end
end
```

If you want a custom type to be private, use @typep instead of @type; if you want it to be public without showing its internal structure, use @opaque. For a complete list of all the built-in type specifications as well as those defined by Elixir, see the documentation (*http://elixir-lang.org/docs/stable/elixir/typespecs.html*).

Writing Unit Tests

In addition to static analysis and defining @specs for your functions, you can avoid some debugging by adequately testing your code beforehand, and Elixir has a unit-testing module named ExUnit to make this easy for you.

To demonstrate ExUnit, we used Mix to create a new project named drop. In the *lib/ drop.ex* file, we wrote a Drop module with an error in it. The gravity constant for Mars has been accidentally mistyped as 3.41 instead of 3.71 (someone's finger slipped on the numeric keypad):

```
defmodule Drop do
  def fall_velocity(planemo, distance) do
    gravity = case planemo do
      :earth -> 9.8
      :moon -> 1.6
      :mars -> 3.41
    end
    :math.sqrt(2 * gravity * distance)
  end
end
```

In addition to the *lib* directory, Mix has already created a *test* directory. If you look in that directory, you will find two files with an extension of *.exs*: *test_helper.exs* and *drop_test.exs*. The *.exs* extension indicates that these are script files, which don't write their compiled output to disk. The *test_helper.exs* file sets up ExUnit to run automatically. You then define tests in the *drop_test.exs* file using the test macro. Here are two tests. The first tests that a distance of zero returns a velocity of zero, and the second tests that a fall of 10 meters on Mars produces the correct answer. Save this in a file named *drop_test.exs*:

```
defmodule DropTest do
  use ExUnit.Case, async: true

  test "Zero distance gives zero velocity" do
    assert Drop.fall_velocity(:earth,0) == 0
  end
```

```
    test "Mars calculation correct" do
      assert Drop.fall_velocity(:mars, 10) == :math.sqrt(2 * 3.71 * 10)
    end
  end
```

The `async: true` in the use line allows Elixir to run test cases in parallel. In this instance there is only one module, so there is only one test case.

A test begins with the macro `test` and a string that describes the test. The content of the `test` consists of executing some code and then asserting some condition. The test passes if all the assertions pass; it fails if any of the assertions fail. In particular, `assert` passes when the code it executes returns a truthy value, and fails when the code returns a falsey value.

To run the tests, type `mix test` at the command line:

```
$ mix test
Compiling 1 file (.ex)
Generated drop app

.

  1) test Mars calculation correct (DropTest)
     test/drop_test.exs:8
     Assertion with == failed
     code: Drop.fall_velocity(:mars, 10) == :math.sqrt(2 * 3.71 * 10)
     lhs:  8.258329128825032
     rhs:  8.613942186943213
     stacktrace:
       test/drop_test.exs:9: (test)



Finished in 0.06 seconds
2 tests, 1 failure

Randomized with seed 585665
```

The line starting . indicates the status of each test; one . means that one test succeeded.

Fix the error by going into the `Drop` module and changing Mars's gravity constant to the correct value of 3.71. Then run the tests again, and you will see what a successful test run looks like:

```
$ mix test
Compiling 1 file (.ex)
..

Finished in 0.05 seconds
2 tests, 0 failures

Randomized with seed 811304
```

In addition to `assert/1`, you may use `refute/1`, which expects the condition you are testing to be `false` in order for a test to pass. Both `assert/1` and `refute/1` automatically generate an appropriate message. There is also a two-argument version of each function that lets you specify the message to produce if the assertion or refutation fails.

If you are using floating-point operations, you may not be able to count on an exact result. In that case, you can use the `assert_in_delta/4` function. Its four arguments are the expected value, the value you actually received, the delta, and a message. If the expected and received values are within *delta* of each other, the test passes. Otherwise, the test fails and ExUnit prints your message. Here is a test to see if a fall velocity from a distance of 1 meter on Earth is close to 4.4 meters per second. You could add the test to the current *drop_test.exs* file, or you can (as we have) create a new file named *drop2_test.exs* in the *test* directory:

```
defmodule Drop2Test do
  use ExUnit.Case, async: true
  test "Earth calculation correct" do
    calculated = Drop.fall_velocity(:earth, 1)
    assert_in_delta calculated, 4.4, 0.05,
      "Result of #{calculated} is not within 0.05 of 4.4"
  end
end
```

If you want to see the failure message, add a new test to require the calculation to be more precise, and save it (this version is in the file *ch11/ex4-testing/test/drop3_test.exs*):

```
defmodule Drop3Test do
  use ExUnit.Case, async: true
  test "Earth calculation correct" do
    calculated = Drop.fall_velocity(:earth, 1)
    assert_in_delta calculated, 4.4, 0.0001,
      "Result of #{calculated} is not within 0.0001 of 4.4"
  end
end
```

This is the result:

```
$ mix test
..

  1) test Earth calculation correct (Drop3Test)
     test/drop3_test.exs:4
     Result of 4.427188724235731 is not within 0.0001 of 4.4
     stacktrace:
       test/drop3_test.exs:6: (test)

  .

Finished in 0.08 seconds
```

```
4 tests, 1 failure

Randomized with seed 477713
```

You can also test that parts of your code will correctly raise exceptions. The following two tests will check that an incorrect planemo and a negative distance actually cause errors. In each test, you wrap the code you want to test in an anonymous function. You can find these additional tests in the file *ch11/ex4-testing/test/drop4_test.exs*:

```
defmodule Drop4Test do
  use ExUnit.Case, async: true
  test "Unknown planemo causes error" do
    assert_raise CaseClauseError, fn ->
      Drop.fall_velocity(:planetX, 10)
    end
  end

  test "Negative distance causes error" do
    assert_raise ArithmeticError, fn ->
      Drop.fall_velocity(:earth, -10)
    end
  end
end
```

Setting Up Tests

You can also specify code to be run before and after each test, as well as before any tests start and after all tests finish. For example, you might want to make a connection to a server before you do any tests, and then disconnect when the tests finish.

To specify code to be run before any of the tests, you use the `setup_all` callback. This callback should return :ok and, optionally, a keyword list that is added to the testing *context*, which is an Elixir Map you may access from your tests. Consider this code, which you will find in *ch11/ex5-setup*:

```
setup_all do
  IO.puts "Beginning all tests"

  on_exit fn ->
    IO.puts "Exit from all tests"
  end

  {:ok, [connection: :fake_PID]}

end
```

This code adds a :connection keyword to the context for the tests; the on_exit specifies code to be run after all the tests finish.

Code to be run before and after each individual test is specified via `setup`. This code accesses the context:

```
setup context do
  IO.puts "About to start a test. Connection is #{Map.get(context,
    :connection)}"

  on_exit fn ->
    IO.puts "Individual test complete."
  end

  :ok
end
```

Finally, you may access the context within an individual test, as shown here:

```
test "Zero distance gives zero velocity", context do
  IO.puts "In zero distance test. Connection is #{Map.get(context,
    :connection)}"
  assert Drop.fall_velocity(:earth,0) == 0
end
```

Here is the result of running the tests:

```
$ mix test
Beginning all tests
About to start a test. Connection is fake_PID
In zero distance test, connection is fake_PID
Individual test complete.
.About to start a test. Connection is fake_PID
Test two
Individual test complete.
.Exit from all tests


Finished in 0.08 seconds
2 tests, 0 failures

Randomized with seed 519579
```

Embedding Tests in Documentation

There is one other way to do tests: by embedding them in the documentation for your functions and modules. These are referred to as *doctests*. In this case, your test script looks like this:

```
defmodule DropTest do
  use ExUnit.Case, async: true
  doctest Drop
end
```

Following doctest is the name of the module you want to test. doctest will look through the module's documentation for lines that look like commands and output from IEx. These lines begin with iex> or iex(n)> where n is a number; the following line is the expected output. Blank lines indicate the beginning of a new test. The following code shows an example, which you may find in *ch11/ex6-doctest*:

```
defmodule Drop do

  @doc """
  Calculates speed of a falling object on a given planemo
  (planetary mass object)

    iex(1)> Drop.fall_velocity(:earth, 10)
    14.0

    iex(2)> Drop.fall_velocity(:mars, 20)
    12.181953866272849

    iex> Drop.fall_velocity(:jupiter, 10)
    ** (CaseClauseError) no case clause matching: :jupiter
  """
  def fall_velocity(planemo, distance) do
    gravity = case planemo do
      :earth -> 9.8
      :moon -> 1.6
      :mars -> 3.71
    end
    :math.sqrt(2 * gravity * distance)
  end
end
```

Elixir's testing facilities also allow you to test whether messages have been received or not, write functions to be shared among tests, and much more. The full details are available in the Elixir documentation (*http://elixir-lang.org/docs.html*).

## CHAPTER 12

Storing Structured Data

Despite Elixir's general preference for avoiding side effects, storing and sharing data is a fundamental side effect needed for a wide variety of projects.

Because Elixir works well with Erlang, you can use Erlang Term Storage (ETS) to help you store and manipulate your data, and the Mnesia database provides additional features for reliable distributed storage.

Records: Structured Data Before Structs

As you saw in "From Maps to Structs" on page 84, Elixir's structs allow you to use names to connect with data rather than order (as with tuples). Structs, however, are based on maps, which are new to Erlang and Elixir. Before maps existed, Erlang had to solve the problem of keeping structured data, and that solution was the concept of records. As with structs, you can read, write, and pattern match data in a record without having to worry about the details of where in a tuple a field lurks or whether someone's added a new field.

Records are not especially loved in Erlang, and are supported but not encouraged in Elixir. The record definition requirement creates headaches. However, records are common in Erlang APIs and run efficiently, so they are still worth understanding. At the very least you'll have a better sense of what people are arguing about in discussions of Elixir and Erlang data structures.

 There are still tuples underneath records, and occasionally Elixir will expose them to you. Do not attempt to use the tuple representation directly, or you will add all the potential problems of using tuples to the slight extra syntax of using records.

Setting Up Records

Using records requires telling Elixir about them with a special declaration. Instead of defmodule, you use a defrecord declaration:

    defrecord Planemo, name: :nil, gravity: 0, diameter: 0, distance_from_sun: 0

That defines a record type named Planemo, containing fields named name, gravity, diameter, and distance_from_sun with their default values. This declaration creates records for different towers for dropping objects:

    defrecord Tower, location: "", height: 20, planemo: :earth, name: ""

Unlike defstruct declarations, you'll often want to share record declarations across multiple modules and (for the examples in this chapter at least) even use them in the shell. To share record declarations reliably, just put the record declarations in their own file, ending with the extension *.ex*. You may want to put each record declaration in a separate file or all of them in a single file, depending on your needs. To get started, to see how these behave, you can put both of the declarations into a single file, *records.ex*, shown in Example 12-1. (You can find it in *ch12/ex1-records*.)

Example 12-1. A records.ex file containing two rather unrelated record declarations

```
defmodule Planemo do
  require Record
  Record.defrecord :planemo, [name: :nil, gravity: 0, diameter: 0,
  distance_from_sun: 0]
end

defmodule Tower do
  require Record
  Record.defrecord :tower, Tower,
    [location: "", height: 20, planemo: :earth, name: ""]
end
```

Record.defrecord constructs a set of macros to create and access a record. The first item after Record.defrecord is the record name. The second item is optional; it is the *tag*. If you don't provide a tag, Elixir uses the record name. In this case, we have provided a tag for Tower records, but not for Planemo records. The name and optional tag are followed by a list that gives pairs of key names and default values. Elixir automatically builds functions into the module that let you create new records, access record values, and update record values. Because records are defined in their own modules, all you need to do to make a record available to your program is to be sure that it has been compiled and is in the same directory as your other modules. You can use the elixirc program from the command line to compile defrecord declarations, or you can have Mix compile them when starting with iex -S mix.

The shell now understands records with the names Planemo and Tower, but you must require them in order to use them in a program or in the shell.

 You can also declare records directly in the shell by typing a module definition that contains the defrecord declaration, but if you're doing anything more than just poking around, it's easier to have them in an external file.

Creating and Reading Records

You can now create variables that contain new records. You create a new record by using the record name function:

```
iex(1)> require Tower
Tower
iex(2)> tower1 = Tower.tower()
{Tower, "", 20, :earth, ""}
iex(3)> tower2 = Tower.tower(location: "Grand Canyon")
{Tower, "Grand Canyon", 20, :earth, ""}
iex(4)> tower3 = Tower.tower(location: "NYC", height: 241,
...(4)> name: "Woolworth Building")
{Tower, "NYC", 241, :earth, "Woolworth Building"}
iex(5)> tower4 = Tower.tower location: "Rupes Altat 241", height: 500,
...(5)> planemo: :moon, name: "Piccolini View"
{Tower, "Rupes Altat 241", 500, :moon, "Piccolini View"}
iex(6)> tower5 = Tower.tower planemo: :mars, height: 500,
...(6)> name: "Daga Vallis", location: "Valles Marineris"
{Tower, "Valles Marineris", 500, :mars, "Daga Vallis"}
```

These towers (or at least drop sites) demonstrate a variety of ways to use the record syntax to create variables as well as interactions with the default values:

- Line 2 just creates tower1 with the default values. You can add real values later.
- Line 3 creates a tower with a location, but otherwise relies on the default values.
- Line 4 overrides the default values for location, height, and name, but leaves the planemo alone.
- Line 5 replaces all of the default values with new values. Note also that, as is usual with Elixir, you do not need to put the arguments to new inside parentheses.
- Line 6 replaces all of the default values, and also demonstrates that *it doesn't matter in what order you list the name-value pairs*. Elixir will sort it out.

You can read record entries with two different approaches. You can use a "fully qualified name" using a syntax that puts the record name before the dot (.); this may look familiar from other languages. For example, to find out which planemo tower5 is on, you could write:

```
iex(7)> Tower.tower(tower5, :planemo)
:mars
```

Or you can make your life easier by doing an import so that you no longer need to
fully qualify the name:

```
iex(8)> import Tower
nil
iex(9)> tower(tower5, :height)
500
```

If you want to change a value in a record, you can do so. In the following example,
the righthand side actually returns an entirely new record and rebinds that new
record to tower5, overwriting its old value:

```
iex(10)> tower5
{Tower, "Valles Marineris", 500, :mars, "Daga Vallis"}
iex(11)> tower5 = tower(tower5, height: 512)
{Tower, "Valles Marineris", 512, :mars, "Daga Vallis"}
```

Using Records in Functions

You can pattern match against records submitted as arguments. The simplest way to
do this is to just match against the type of the record, as shown in Example 12-2,
which is in *ch12/ex2-records*.

Example 12-2. A method that pattern matches a complete record

```
defmodule RecordDrop do
  require Planemo
  require Tower

  def fall_velocity(t = Tower.tower()) do
    fall_velocity(Tower.tower(t, :planemo), Tower.tower(t, :height))
  end

  def fall_velocity(:earth, distance) when distance >= 0 do
    :math.sqrt(2 * 9.8 * distance)
  end

  def fall_velocity(:moon, distance) when distance >= 0 do
    :math.sqrt(2 * 1.6 * distance)
  end

  def fall_velocity(:mars, distance) when distance >= 0 do
    :math.sqrt(2 * 3.71 * distance)
  end

end
```

This uses a pattern match that will match only Tower records, and puts the matched record into a variable t. Then, like its predecessor in Example 3-8, it passes the individual arguments to fall_velocity/2 for calculations, this time using the record syntax:

```
iex(12)> r(RecordDrop)
warning: redefining module RecordDrop (current version loaded from
  _build/dev/lib/record_drop/ebin/Elixir.RecordDrop.beam)
  lib/record_drop.ex:1

{:reloaded, RecordDrop, [RecordDrop]}
iex(13)> RecordDrop.fall_velocity(tower5)
60.909769331364245
iex(14)> RecordDrop.fall_velocity(tower1)
19.79898987322333
```

The RecordDrop.fall_velocity/1 function shown in Example 12-3 pulls out the planemo field and binds it to the variable planemo. It pulls out the height field and binds it to distance. Then it returns the velocity of an object dropped from that distance, just like earlier examples throughout this book.

You can also extract the specific fields from the record in the pattern match, as shown in Example 12-3, which is in *ch12/ex3-records*.

Example 12-3. A method that pattern matches components of a record

```
defmodule RecordDrop do
  require Tower
  def fall_velocity(Tower.tower(planemo: planemo, height: distance)) do
    fall_velocity(planemo, distance)
  end

  def fall_velocity(:earth, distance) when distance >= 0 do
    :math.sqrt(2 * 9.8 * distance)
  end

  def fall_velocity(:moon, distance) when distance >= 0 do
    :math.sqrt(2 * 1.6 * distance)
  end

  def fall_velocity(:mars, distance) when distance >= 0 do
    :math.sqrt(2 * 3.71 * distance)
  end
end
```

You can take each of the records created and feed them into this function, and it will tell you the velocity resulting from a drop from the top of that tower to the bottom.

Finally, you can pattern match against both the fields and the records as a whole. Example 12-4, in *ch12/ex4-records*, demonstrates using this mixed approach to create a more detailed response than just the fall velocity.

Example 12-4. A method that pattern matches the whole record as well as components of a record

```
defmodule RecordDrop do
  require Tower
  import Tower
  def fall_velocity(t = tower(planemo: planemo, height: distance)) do
    IO.puts("From #{tower(t, :name)}'s elevation" <>
      "of #{distance} meters on #{planemo},")
    IO.puts("the object will reach #{fall_velocity(planemo, distance)} m/s")
    IO.puts("before crashing in #{tower(t, :location)}")
  end

  def fall_velocity(:earth, distance) when distance >= 0 do
    :math.sqrt(2 * 9.8 * distance)
  end

  def fall_velocity(:moon, distance) when distance >= 0 do
    :math.sqrt(2 * 1.6 * distance)
  end

  def fall_velocity(:mars, distance) when distance >= 0 do
    :math.sqrt(2 * 3.71 * distance)
  end
end
```

 As noted previously, you can have a variable with the same name as a field (in this case, planemo).

If you pass a Tower record to RecordDrop.fall_velocity/1, it will match against individual fields it needs to do the calculation and match the whole record into t so that it can produce a more interesting, if not necessarily grammatically correct, report:

```
iex(15)> RecordDrop.fall_velocity(tower5)
From Daga Vallis's elevation of 500 meters on mars,
the object will reach 60.909769333136424520399 m/s
before crashing in Valles Marineris
:ok
iex(16)> RecordDrop.fall_velocity(tower3)
From Woolworth Building's elevation of 241 meters on earth,
the object will reach 68.72845116834803036454 m/s
```

```
before crashing in NYC
:ok
```

Storing Data in Erlang Term Storage

Erlang Term Storage (ETS) is a simple but powerful in-memory collection store. It holds tuples, and since records are tuples underneath, they're a natural fit. ETS and its disk-based cousin DETS provide a (perhaps too) simple solution for many data management problems. ETS is not exactly a database, but it does similar work and is useful by itself as well as underneath the Mnesia database, which you'll see in the next section.

Every entry in an ETS tables is a tuple (or corresponding record), and one piece of the tuple is designated the key. ETS offers a few different structural choices depending on how you want to handle that key. ETS can hold four kinds of collections:

Sets (:set)
  Can contain only one entry with a given key. This is the default.

Ordered sets (:ordered_set)
  Same as sets, but also maintain a traversal order based on the keys. Great for anything you want to keep in alphabetic or numeric order.

Bags (:bag)
  Let you store more than one entry with a given key. However, if you have multiple entries that have completely identical values, they get combined into a single entry.

Duplicate bags (:duplicate_bag)
  Not only let you store more than one entry with a given key, but also let you store multiple entries with completely identical values.

By default, ETS tables are sets, but you can specify one of the other options when you create a table. The examples here will be sets because they are simpler to figure out, but the same techniques apply to all four table varieties.

 There is no requirement in ETS that all of your entries look at all similar. When you're starting out, however, it's much simpler to use the same kind of record, or at least tuples with the same structure. You can also use any kind of value for the key, including complex tuple structures and lists, but again, it's best not to get too fancy at the beginning.

All of the examples in the following section will use the Planemo record type defined in "Records: Structured Data Before Structs" on page 145, and the data in Table 12-1.

Table 12-1. Planemos for gravitational exploration

Planemo	Gravity (m/s²)	Diameter (km)	Distance from Sun (10⁶ km)
mercury	3.7	4878	57.9
venus	8.9	12104	108.2
earth	9.8	12756	149.6
moon	1.6	3475	149.6
mars	3.7	6787	227.9
ceres	0.27	950	413.7
jupiter	23.1	142796	778.3
saturn	9.0	120660	1427.0
uranus	8.7	51118	2871.0
neptune	11.0	30200	4497.1
pluto	0.6	2300	5913.0
haumea	0.44	1150	6484.0
makemake	0.5	1500	6850.0
eris	0.8	2400	10210.0

Although the name is *Erlang* Term Storage, you can still use ETS from Elixir. Just as you can use Erlang's `math` module to calculate square roots by saying `:math.sqrt(3)`, you can use ETS functions by preceding them with `:ets`.

Creating and Populating a Table

The `:ets.new/2` function lets you create a table. The first argument is a name for the table, and the second argument is a list of options. There are lots and lots of options, including the identifiers for the table types described in the previous section, but the two most important for getting started are `:named_table` and the tuple starting with `:keypos`.

Every table has a name, but only some can be reached using that name. If you don't specify `:named_table`, the name is there but visible only inside the database. You'll have to use the value returned by `:ets.new/2` to reference the table. If you do specify `:named_table`, processes can reach the table as long as they know the name, without needing access to that return value.

Even with a named table, you still have some control over which processes can read and write the table through the `:private`, `:protected`, and `:public` options.

The other important option, especially for ETS tables containing records, is the :keypos tuple. By default, ETS treats the first value in a tuple as the key. The tuple representation underneath records (which you shouldn't really touch) always uses the first value in a tuple to identify the kind of record, so that approach works very badly as a key for records. Using the :keypos tuple lets you specify which record value should be the key.

Remember, the record format for a Planemo looks like the following:

```
defmodule Planemo do
  require Record
  Record.defrecord :planemo, [name: :nil, gravity: 0, diameter: 0,
  distance_from_sun: 0]
end
```

Because this table is mostly used for calculations based on a given planemo, it makes sense to use the :name as a key. An appropriate declaration for setting up the ETS table might look like the following:

```
planemo_table = :ets.new(:planemos,[ :named_table, {:keypos,
  Planemo.planemo(:name) + 1} ])
```

That gives the table the name :planemos and uses the :named_table option to make that table visible to other processes that know the name. Because of the default access level of :protected, this process can write to that table but other processes can only read it. This declaration also tells ETS to use the :name field as the key.

 ETS expects the :keypos to be a number that gives the position of the key field in the underlying tuple, with the first entry numbered as one. The call to the planemo function returns the index of the field in the underlying Elixir tuple, with the first entry numbered as zero. That's why the preceding code had to add one.

Because it doesn't specify otherwise, the table will be treated as a :set, where each key maps to only one instance of record, and ETS doesn't keep the list sorted by key.

Once you have the table set up, as shown in Example 12-5, you use the :ets.info/1 function to check out its details. (You can find this in *ch12/ex5-ets*.)

Example 12-5. Setting up a simple ETS table and reporting on what's there

```
defmodule PlanemoStorage do
  require Planemo

  def setup do
    planemo_table = :ets.new(:planemos,[:named_table,
      {:keypos, Planemo.planemo(:name) + 1}])
    :ets.info planemo_table
```

```
    end
end
```

If you compile and run this, you'll get a report of an empty ETS table with more properties than you probably want to know about at the moment:

```
$ iex -S mix
Erlang/OTP 19 [erts-8.0] [source] [64-bit] [smp:4:4] [async-threads:10]
  [hipe] [kernel-poll:false]

Compiling 2 files (.ex)
Generated planemo_storage app
Interactive Elixir (1.3.1) - press Ctrl+C to exit (type h() ENTER for help)
iex(1)> PlanemoStorage.setup
[read_concurrency: false, write_concurrency: false, compressed: false,
 memory: 299, owner: #PID<0.57.0>, heir: :none, name: :planemos, size: 0,
 node: :nonode@nohost, named_table: true, type: :set, keypos: 2,
 protection: :protected]
```

Most of this is either more information than you need or unsurprising, but it is good to see the name (:planemos), size (0—empty!), and keypos (not 1, the default, but 2, the location of the name in the tuple underneath the record). It is, as the defaults specify, set up as a :protected :set.

You can set up only one ETS table with the same name. If you call the function Plane moStorage.setup/0 twice, you'll get an error:

```
iex(2)> PlanemoStorage.setup
** (ArgumentError) argument error
    (stdlib) :ets.new(:planemos, [:named_table, {:keypos, 2}])
            planemo_storage.ex:5: PlanemoStorage.setup/0
```

To avoid this, at least in these early tests, you'll want to use the :ets.delete/1 command to delete the table. Give the table name—in this case, :planemos—as the argument. If you think you're likely to call your initialization code repeatedly after you figure out the basics, you can also test :ets.info/1 for :undefined to make sure the table doesn't already exist, or put a try...catch construct around the :ets.new/2 call.

A more exciting ETS table, of course, will include content. The next step is to use :ets.insert/2 to add content to the table. The first argument is the table, referenced either by its name (if you set the named_table option) or by the variable that captured the return value of :ets.new/2. In Example 12-6, which is in *ch12/ex6-ets*, the first call uses the name, to show that it works, and the rest use the variable. The second argument is a record representing one of the rows from Table 12-1.

Example 12-6. Populating a simple ETS table and reporting on what's there

```
defmodule PlanemoStorage do
  require Planemo

  def setup do
    planemo_table = :ets.new(:planemos,[:named_table,
      {:keypos, Planemo.planemo(:name) + 1}])
    :ets.insert :planemos, Planemo.planemo(name: :mercury, gravity: 3.7,
      diameter: 4878, distance_from_sun: 57.9)
    :ets.insert :planemos, Planemo.planemo(name: :venus, gravity: 8.9,
      diameter: 12104, distance_from_sun: 108.2)
    :ets.insert :planemos, Planemo.planemo(name: :earth, gravity: 9.8,
      diameter: 12756, distance_from_sun: 149.6)
    :ets.insert :planemos, Planemo.planemo(name: :moon, gravity: 1.6,
      diameter: 3475, distance_from_sun: 149.6)
    :ets.insert :planemos, Planemo.planemo(name: :mars, gravity: 3.7,
      diameter: 6787, distance_from_sun: 227.9)
    :ets.insert :planemos, Planemo.planemo(name: :ceres, gravity: 0.27,
      diameter: 950, distance_from_sun: 413.7)
    :ets.insert :planemos, Planemo.planemo(name: :jupiter, gravity: 23.1,
      diameter: 142796, distance_from_sun: 778.3)
    :ets.insert :planemos, Planemo.planemo(name: :saturn, gravity: 9.0,
      diameter: 120660, distance_from_sun: 1427.0)
    :ets.insert :planemos, Planemo.planemo(name: :uranus, gravity: 8.7,
      diameter: 51118, distance_from_sun: 2871.0)
    :ets.insert :planemos, Planemo.planemo(name: :neptune, gravity: 11.0,
      diameter: 30200, distance_from_sun: 4497.1)
    :ets.insert :planemos, Planemo.planemo(name: :pluto, gravity: 0.6,
      diameter: 2300, distance_from_sun: 5913.0)
    :ets.insert :planemos, Planemo.planemo(name: :haumea, gravity: 0.44,
      diameter: 1150, distance_from_sun: 6484.0)
    :ets.insert :planemos, Planemo.planemo(name: :makemake, gravity: 0.5,
      diameter: 1500, distance_from_sun: 6850.0)
    :ets.insert :planemos, Planemo.planemo(name: :eris, gravity: 0.8,
      diameter: 2400, distance_from_sun: 10210.0)

    :ets.info planemo_table
  end
end
```

Again, the last call is to `:ets.info/1`, which now reports that the table has 14 items:

```
iex(2)> r(PlanemoStorage)
warning: redefining module PlanemoStorage (current version loaded from
  Elixir.PlanemoStorage.beam)
  lib/planemo_storage.ex:1

{:reloaded, PlanemoStorage, [PlanemoStorage]}
iex(3)> :ets.delete(:planemos)
true
iex(4)> PlanemoStorage.setup
[read_concurrency: false, write_concurrency: false, compressed: false,
```

```
      memory: 495, owner: #PID<0.57.0>, heir: :none, name: :planemos, size: 14,
      node: :nonode@nohost, named_table: true, type: :set, keypos: 2,
      protection: :protected]
```

If you want to see what's in that table, you can do it from the shell by using
the :ets.tab2list/1 function, which will return a list of records, broken into separate lines for ease of reading:

```
iex(5)> :ets.tab2list :planemos
[{:planemo, :neptune, 11.0, 30200, 4497.1},
 {:planemo, :jupiter, 23.1, 142796, 778.3},
 {:planemo, :haumea, 0.44, 1150, 6484.0}, {:planemo, :pluto, 0.6, 2300, 5913.0},
 {:planemo, :mercury, 3.7, 4878, 57.9}, {:planemo, :earth, 9.8, 12756, 149.6},
 {:planemo, :makemake, 0.5, 1500, 6850.0}, {:planemo, :moon, 1.6, 3475, 149.6},
 {:planemo, :mars, 3.7, 6787, 227.9}, {:planemo, :saturn, 9.0, 120660, 1427.0},
 {:planemo, :uranus, 8.7, 51118, 2871.0}, {:planemo, :ceres, 0.27, 950, 413.7},
 {:planemo, :venus, 8.9, 12104, 108.2}, {:planemo, :eris, 0.8, 2400, 10210.0}]
```

If you'd rather keep track of the table in a separate window, Erlang's Observer table
visualizer shows the same information in a slightly more readable form. You can start
it from the shell with :observer.start(), and click the Table Viewer tab. You will see
something that looks like Figure 12-1. Double-click the planemos table, and you'll see
a more detailed report on its contents like the one shown in Figure 12-2.

The visualizer doesn't know about your record declarations; it only knows the field
numbers. The Edit menu lets you poll the table to be sure you have its latest contents,
and set a polling interval if you want it to refresh automatically. If you declare tables
public, you can even edit their contents in the table viewer.

> If you want to see a table of all the current ETS tables, try issu-
> ing :ets.i() in the shell. You'll see the tables you've created (prob-
> ably) near the bottom.

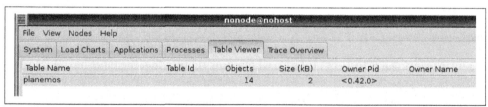

Figure 12-1. Opening the table visualizer

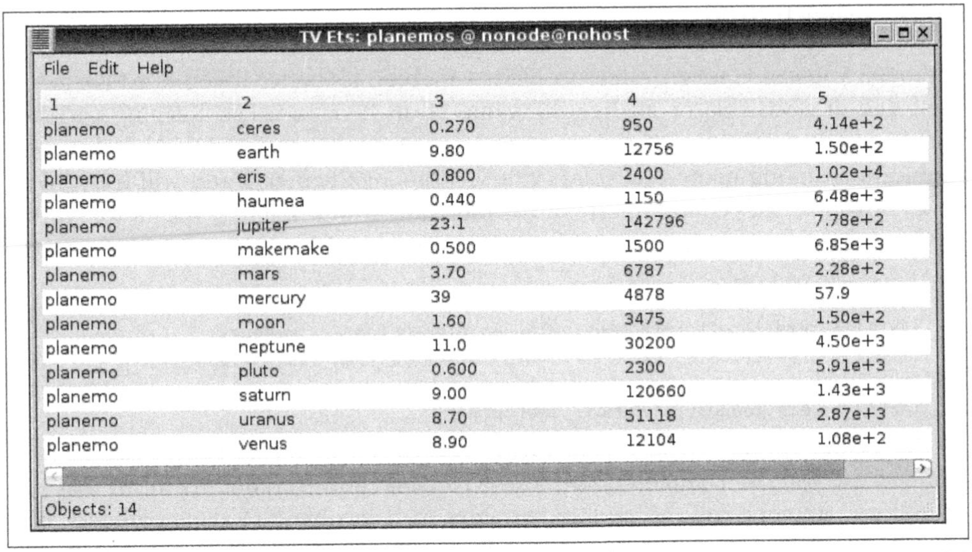

File Edit Help

1	2	3	4	5
planemo	ceres	0.270	950	4.14e+2
planemo	earth	9.80	12756	1.50e+2
planemo	eris	0.800	2400	1.02e+4
planemo	haumea	0.440	1150	6.48e+3
planemo	jupiter	23.1	142796	7.78e+2
planemo	makemake	0.500	1500	6.85e+3
planemo	mars	3.70	6787	2.28e+2
planemo	mercury	39	4878	57.9
planemo	moon	1.60	3475	1.50e+2
planemo	neptune	11.0	30200	4.50e+3
planemo	pluto	0.600	2300	5.91e+3
planemo	saturn	9.00	120660	1.43e+3
planemo	uranus	8.70	51118	2.87e+3
planemo	venus	8.90	12104	1.08e+2

Objects: 14

Figure 12-2. Reviewing the planemos table in the visualizer

Simple Queries

The easiest way to look up records in your ETS table is with the `:ets.lookup/2` function and the key. You can test this easily from the shell:

```
iex(6)> :ets.lookup(:planemos, :eris)
[{:planemo, :eris, 0.8, 2400, 10210.0}]
```

The return value is always a list. This is true despite Elixir's knowing that this ETS table has the `:set` type, so only one value can match the key, and despite there being only one value. In situations like this where you know that there will only be one returned value, the `hd/1` function will get you the head of a list quickly. Since there is only one item, the head is just that item:

```
iex(7)> hd(:ets.lookup(:planemos, :eris))
{:planemo, :eris, 0.8, 2400, 10210.0}
```

The square brackets are gone, which means that you can now extract, say, the gravity of a planemo:

```
iex(8)> result = hd(:ets.lookup(:planemos, :eris))
{:planemo, :eris, 0.8, 2400, 10210.0}
iex(9)> require Planemo
Planemo
iex(10)> Planemo.planemo(result, :gravity)
0.8
```

Overwriting Values

Although you can reassign values to Elixir variables, it's better if you don't overwrite the value of a variable or change the value of an item in a list. Keeping variables "single-assignment" makes it easier to write more reliable programs that involve communication among many processes (you saw this in Chapter 9 and will learn more about how processes communicate in Chapter 13). However, ETS is meant for storing values that might need to be reassigned. If you want to change the value of gravity on :mercury, you can:

```
iex(11)> :ets.insert(:planemos, Planemo.planemo(name: :mercury,
...(11)> gravity: 3.9, diameter: 4878, distance_from_sun: 57.9))
true
iex(12)> :ets.lookup(:planemos, :mercury)
[{:planemo, :mercury, 3.9, 4878, 57.9}]
```

Just because you *can* change values in an ETS table, however, doesn't mean that you should rewrite your code to replace variables with flexible ETS table contents. Nor should you make all your tables public so that various processes can read and write whatever they like to the tables (making this a different form of shared memory).

Ask yourself when making changes is going to be useful, and when it might introduce tricky bugs. You probably won't have to change the gravity of Mercury, but it certainly could make sense to change a shipping address. If you have doubts, lean toward caution.

ETS Tables and Processes

Now that you can extract gravitational constants for planemos, you can expand the Drop module to calculate drops in many more locations. Example 12-7 combines the Drop module from Example 9-6 with the ETS table built in Example 12-6 to create a more powerful drop calculator. (You can find this in *ch12/ex7-ets-calculator*.)

Example 12-7. Calculating drop velocities using an ETS table of planemo properties

```
defmodule Drop do
  require Planemo
  def drop do
    setup
    handle_drops
  end

  def handle_drops do
    receive do
      {from, planemo, distance} ->
        send(from, {planemo, distance, fall_velocity(planemo, distance)})
        handle_drops
    end
```

```
end

def fall_velocity(planemo, distance) when distance >= 0 do
  p = hd(:ets.lookup(:planemos, planemo))
  :math.sqrt(2 * Planemo.planemo(p, :gravity) * distance)
end

def setup do
  :ets.new(:planemos, [:named_table,
    {:keypos, Planemo.planemo(:name) + 1}])
  info = [
    {:mercury, 3.7, 4878, 57.9},
    {:venus, 8.9, 12104, 108.2},
    {:earth, 9.8, 12756, 149.6},
    {:moon, 1.6, 3475, 149.6},
    {:mars, 3.7, 6787, 227.9},
    {:ceres, 0.27, 950, 413.7},
    {:jupiter, 23.1, 142796, 778.3},
    {:saturn, 9.0, 120660, 1427.0},
    {:uranus, 8.7, 51118, 2871.0},
    {:neptune, 11.0, 30200, 4497.1},
    {:pluto, 0.6, 2300, 5913.0},
    {:haumea, 0.44, 1150, 6484.0},
    {:makemake, 0.5, 1500, 6850.0},
    {:eris, 0.8, 2400, 10210.0}]
  insert_into_table(info)
end

def insert_into_table([]) do  # stop recursion
  :undefined
end

def insert_into_table([{name, gravity, diameter, distance} | tail]) do
  :ets.insert(:planemos, Planemo.new(name: name, gravity: gravity,
    diameter: diameter, distance_from_sun: distance))
  insert_into_table(tail)
end
end
```

The drop/0 function changes a little to call the initialization separately and avoid setting up the table on every call. This moves the message handling to a separate function, handle_drops/0. The fall_velocity/2 function also changes, as it now looks up planemo names in the ETS table and gets the gravitational constant from that table rather than hardcoding those contents into the function. (While it would certainly be possible to pass the planemo_table variable from the previous example as an argument to the recursive message handler, it's simpler to just use it as a named table.)

The `setup` function has also changed dramatically. Rather than doing a series of `:ets.insert` calls, it creates a list of tuples with the planemo information and then calls `insert_into_table/1` recursively to insert each entry.

 If this process crashes and needs to be restarted, restarting it will trigger the `setup/0` function, which currently doesn't check to see if the ETS table exists. That could cause an error, except that ETS tables vanish when the processes that created them die. ETS offers an `heir` option and an `:ets.give_away/3` function if you want to avoid that behavior, but for now it works well.

If you combine this module with the `MphDrop` module from Example 9-7, you'll be able to calculate drop velocities on all of these planemos. Since messages are passed asynchronously, the tuple may appear in the middle of the output:

```
iex(1)> c("drop.ex")
[Drop]
iex(2)> c("mph_drop.ex")
[MphDrop]
iex(3)> pid1 = spawn(MphDrop, :mph_drop, [])
#PID<0.47.0>
iex(4)> send(pid1, {:earth, 20})
On earth, a fall of 20 meters yields a velocity of 44.289078952755766 mph.
{:earth,20}
iex(5)> send(pid1, {:eris, 20})
On eris, a fall of 20 meters yields a velocity of 12.65402255793022 mph.
{:eris,20}
iex(6)> send(pid1, {:makemake, 20})
On makemake, a fall of 20 meters yields a velocity of 10.003883211552367 mph.
{:makemake,20}
```

That's a lot more variety than its `:earth`, `:moon`, and `:mars` predecessors!

Next Steps

While many applications just need a fast key-value store, ETS tables are far more flexible than the examples so far demonstrate. You can use Erlang's match specifications and `:ets.fun2ms` to create more complex queries with `:ets.match` and `:ets.select`. You can delete rows (as well as tables) with `:ets.delete`.

The `:ets.first`, `:ets.next`, and `:ets.last` functions let you traverse tables recursively.

Perhaps most important, you can also explore DETS, the Disk-Based Erlang Term Storage, which offers similar features but with tables stored on disk. It's slower, with a 2 GB limit, but the data doesn't vanish when the controlling process stops.

You can dig deeper into ETS and DETS, but if your needs are more complex, and especially if you need to split data across multiple nodes, you should probably explore the Mnesia database.

Storing Records in Mnesia

Mnesia is a database management system (DBMS) that comes with Erlang, and, by extension, one that you can use with Elixir. It uses ETS and DETS underneath, but provides many more features than those components.

You should consider shifting from ETS (and DETS) tables to the Mnesia database if:

- You need to store and access data across a set of nodes, not just a single node.
- You don't want to have to think about whether you're going to store data in memory or on a disk or both.
- You need to be able to roll back transactions if something goes wrong.
- You'd like a more approachable syntax for finding and joining data.
- Management prefers the sound of "database" to the sound of "tables."

You may even find that you use ETS for some aspects of a project and Mnesia for others.

 That isn't "amnesia," the forgetting, but "mnesia," the Greek word for memory.

Starting Up Mnesia

If you want to store data on disk, you need to give Mnesia some information. Before you turn Mnesia on, you need to create a database, which you do using the function :mnesia.create_schema/1. For now, because you'll be getting started using only the local node, that will look like the following:

```
iex(1)> :mnesia.create_schema([node()])
:ok
```

By default, when you call :mnesia.create_schema/1, Mnesia will store schema data in the directory where you are when you start it. If you look in the directory where you started Elixir, you'll see a new directory with a name like *Mnesia.nonode@nohost*. Initially, it holds a *FALLBACK.BUP* file. The node/0 function just returns the identifier of the node you're on, which is fine when you're getting started.

If you start Mnesia without calling :mnesia.create_schema/1, Mnesia will keep its schema in memory, and it will vanish if and when Mnesia stops.

Unlike ETS and DETS, which are always available, you need to turn Mnesia on:

```
iex(2)> :mnesia.start()
:ok
```

This will create a *schema.DAT* file in the *Mnesia.nonode@nohost* directory. There's also a :mnesia.stop/0 function if you want to stop it.

If you run Mnesia on a computer that goes to sleep, you may get odd messages like Mnesia(nonode@nohost): ** WARNING ** Mnesia is overloaded: {dump_log, time_threshold} when it wakes up. Don't worry; it's a side effect of waking up, and your data should still be safe. You probably shouldn't run production systems on devices that go to sleep, of course.

Creating Tables

Like ETS, Mnesia's basic concept of a table is a collection of records. It also offers :set, :orderered_set, and :bag options, just like those in ETS, but doesn't offer :duplicate_bag.

Mnesia wants to know more about your data than ETS, too. ETS pretty much takes data in tuples of any shape, counting only on there being a key it can use. The rest is up to you to interpret. Mnesia wants to know more about what you store, and takes a list of field names. The easy way to handle this is to define records and consistently use the field names from the records as Mnesia field names. There's even an easy way to pass the record names to Mnesia, using record_info/2.

The planemos table can work just as easily in Mnesia as in ETS, and some aspects of dealing with it will be easier. Example 12-8, which is in *ch12/ex8-mnesia*, shows how to set up the table in Mnesia. The setup/0 method creates a schema, then starts Mnesia, and then creates a table based on the Planemo record type. Once the table is created, it writes the values from Table 12-1 to it.

Example 12-8. Setting up a Mnesia table of planemo properties

```
defmodule Drop do
  require Planemo

  def drop do
    setup
```

```
    handle_drops
end

def handle_drops do
  receive do
    {from, planemo, distance} ->
      send(from, {planemo, distance, fall_velocity(planemo, distance)})
      handle_drops
  end
end

def fall_velocity(planemo, distance) when distance >= 0 do
  {:atomic, [p | _]} = :mnesia.transaction(fn() ->
    :mnesia.read(PlanemoTable, planemo) end)
  :math.sqrt(2 * Planemo.planemo(p, :gravity) * distance)
end

def setup do
  :mnesia.create_schema([node()])
  :mnesia.start()
  :mnesia.create_table(PlanemoTable, [{:attributes,
    [:name, :gravity, :diameter, :distance_from_sun]},
    {:record_name, :planemo}])

  f = fn ->
  :mnesia.write(PlanemoTable, Planemo.planemo(name: :mercury, gravity: 3.7,
    diameter: 4878, distance_from_sun: 57.9), :write)
  :mnesia.write(PlanemoTable, Planemo.planemo(name: :venus, gravity: 8.9,
    diameter: 12104, distance_from_sun: 108.2), :write)
  :mnesia.write(PlanemoTable, Planemo.planemo(name: :earth, gravity: 9.8,
    diameter: 12756, distance_from_sun: 149.6), :write)
  :mnesia.write(PlanemoTable, Planemo.planemo(name: :moon, gravity: 1.6,
    diameter: 3475, distance_from_sun: 149.6), :write)
  :mnesia.write(PlanemoTable, Planemo.planemo(name: :mars, gravity: 3.7,
    diameter: 6787, distance_from_sun: 227.9), :write)
  :mnesia.write(PlanemoTable, Planemo.planemo(name: :ceres, gravity: 0.27,
    diameter: 950, distance_from_sun: 413.7), :write)
  :mnesia.write(PlanemoTable, Planemo.planemo(name: :jupiter, gravity: 23.1,
    diameter: 142796, distance_from_sun: 778.3), :write)
  :mnesia.write(PlanemoTable, Planemo.planemo(name: :saturn, gravity: 9.0,
    diameter: 120660, distance_from_sun: 1427.0), :write)
  :mnesia.write(PlanemoTable, Planemo.planemo(name: :uranus, gravity: 8.7,
    diameter: 51118, distance_from_sun: 2871.0), :write)
  :mnesia.write(PlanemoTable, Planemo.planemo(name: :neptune, gravity: 11.0,
    diameter: 30200, distance_from_sun: 4497.1), :write)
  :mnesia.write(PlanemoTable, Planemo.planemo(name: :pluto, gravity: 0.6,
    diameter: 2300, distance_from_sun: 5913.0), :write)
  :mnesia.write(PlanemoTable, Planemo.planemo(name: :haumea, gravity: 0.44,
    diameter: 1150, distance_from_sun: 6484.0), :write)
  :mnesia.write(PlanemoTable, Planemo.planemo(name: :makemake, gravity: 0.5,
    diameter: 1500, distance_from_sun: 6850.0), :write)
  :mnesia.write(PlanemoTable, Planemo.planemo(name: :eris, gravity: 0.8,
```

```
        diameter: 2400, distance_from_sun: 10210.0), :write)
    end

    :mnesia.transaction(f)
  end
end
```

In the setup, the `:mnesia.create_table` call gives the attributes for the table explicitly because, as of this writing, there is no easy way to extract all the field names for a record. Ordinarily, Mnesia presumes that the table name is the same as the name of the first field of the record, but in this case, the table is `PlanemoTable` and the record starts with `:planemo`. You give the record name explicitly with this code: `{:record_name, :planemo}`.

The `:mnesia_write` calls take three parameters: the table name, the record, and the type of lock to use on the database (in this case, `:write`).

Apart from the setup, the key thing to note is that all of the writes are contained in a `fn` that is then passed to `:mnesia.transaction` to be executed as a transaction. Mnesia will restart the transaction if there is other activity blocking it, so the code may get executed repeatedly before the transaction happens. Because of this, you should not include any calls that create side effects in the function you will be passing to `:mnesia.transaction`, and don't try to catch exceptions on Mnesia functions within a transaction. If your function calls `:mnesia.abort/1` (probably because some condition for executing it wasn't met), the transaction will be rolled back, returning a tuple beginning with `:aborted` instead of `:atomic`.

You may also want to explore the more flexible `:mnesia.activity/2` when you need to mix more kinds of tasks in a transaction.

Your interactions with Mnesia should be contained in transactions, especially when your database is shared across multiple nodes. The main `:mnesia.write`, `:mnesia.read`, and `:mnesia.delete` methods work only within transactions, period. There are `dirty_` methods, but every time you use them, especially to write data to the database, you're taking a risk.

Just as in ETS, you can overwrite values by writing a new value with the same key as a previous entry.

If you want to check on how this function worked out, try the `:mnesia.table_info` function, which can tell you more than you want to know. The following listing is abbreviated to focus on key results:

```
iex(1)> c("drop.ex")
[Drop]
iex(2)> Drop.setup
{:atomic,:ok}
iex(3)> :mnesia.table_info(PlanemoTable, :all)
[access_mode: :read_write,
 active_replicas: [:"nonode@nohost"],
 all_nodes: [:"nonode@nohost"],
 arity: 5,
 attributes: [:name,:gravity,:diameter,:distance_from_sun],
 ...
 ram_copies: [:"nonode@nohost"],
 record_name: :planemo,
 record_validation: {:planemo,5,:set},
 type: :set,
 size: 14,
 ...]
```

You can see which nodes are involved in the table (nonode@nohost is the default for the current node). `arity` in this case is the count of fields in the record, and `attributes` tells you what their names are. `ram_copies` plus the name of the current node tells you that this table is stored in memory locally. It is, as in the ETS example, of type `:set`, and there are 14 records.

 By default, Mnesia will store your table in RAM only (`ram_copies`) on the current node. This is speedy, but it means the data vanishes if the node crashes. If you specify `disc_copies` (note the spelling), Mnesia will keep a copy of the database on disk, but still use RAM for speed. You can also specify `disc_only_copies`, which will be slow. Unlike with ETS, the table you create will still be around if the *process* that created it crashes, and will likely survive even a node crash so long as it wasn't only in RAM on a single node. By combining these options and (eventually) multiple nodes, you should be able to create fast and resilient systems.

The table is now set up, and you can start to use it. If you're running Observer, you can take a look at the contents of your Mnesia tables as well as your ETS tables. Choose the Table Viewer tab, then, in the View menu, choose Mnesia Tables. The interface is similar to that for ETS tables.

Reading Data

Just like writes, you should wrap `:mnesia.read` calls in a `fn`, which you then pass to `:mnesia.transaction`. You can do that in the shell if you want to explore:

```
iex(4)> :mnesia.transaction(fn()->:mnesia.read(PlanemoTable, :neptune) end)
{:atomic, [{:planemo, :neptune, 11.0, 30200, 4497.1}]}
```

The result arrives as a tuple, which when successful contains `:atomic` plus a list with the data from the table. The table data is packaged as a record, and you can get to its fields easily.

You can rewrite the `fall_velocity/2` function from Example 12-8 to use a Mnesia transaction instead of an ETS call. The ETS version looked like the following:

```
def fall_velocity(planemo, distance) when distance >= 0 do
  p = hd(:ets.lookup(:planemos, planemo))
  :math.sqrt(2 * Planemo.planemo(p, :gravity) * distance)
end
```

Line 2 of the Mnesia version is a bit different:

```
def fall_velocity(planemo, distance) when distance >= 0 do
  {:atomic, [p | _]} = :mnesia.transaction(fn() ->
    :mnesia.read(PlanemoTable, planemo) end)
  :math.sqrt(2 * Planemo.planemo(p, :gravity) * distance)
end
```

Because Mnesia returns a tuple rather than a list, this uses pattern matching to extract the first item in the list contained in the second item of the tuple (and throws away the tail of that list with _). This table is a set, so there will always be only one item there, so we could have as well matched on `{:atomic, [p]}`. Then the data, contained in `p`, can be used for the same calculation as before.

If you compile and run this, you'll see a familiar result:

```
iex(5)> r(Drop)
warning: redefining module Drop (current version loaded from
  _build/dev/lib/mph_drop/ebin/Elixir.Drop.beam)
  lib/drop.ex:1

{:reloaded, Drop, [Drop]}
iex(6)> Drop.fall_velocity(:earth, 20)
19.79898987322333
iex(7)> pid1 = spawn(MphDrop, :mph_drop, [])
#PID<0.115.0>
iex(8)> send(pid1, {:earth, 20})
On earth, a fall of 20 meters yields a velocity of 44.289078952755766 mph.
{:earth, 20}
```

For these purposes, the simple `:mnesia.read` is enough. You can tell Mnesia to build indexes for fields other than the key, and query those with `:mnesia.index_read` as well.

 If you want to delete records, you can run `:mnesia.delete/2`, also inside of a transaction.

## CHAPTER 13

Getting Started with OTP

At this point, it might seem like you have all you need to create process-oriented projects with Elixir. You know how to create useful functions, can work with recursion, know the data structures Elixir offers, and, probably most important, know how to create and manage processes. What more could you need?

Process-oriented programming is great, but the details matter. The basic Elixir tools are powerful but can also lead you into frustrating mazes debugging race conditions that happen only once in a while. Mixing different programming styles can lead to incompatible expectations, and code that worked well in one environment may prove harder to integrate in another.

Ericsson encountered these problems early when developing Erlang (remember, Elixir runs on Erlang's virtual machine), and created a set of libraries that ease them. OTP, the Open Telecom Platform, is useful for pretty much any large-scale project you want to do with Elixir and Erlang, not just telecom work. It's included with Erlang, and though it isn't precisely part of the language, it is definitely part of Erlang culture. The boundaries of where Elixir and Erlang end and OTP begins aren't always clear, but the entry point is definitely behaviors. You'll combine processes built with behaviors and managed by supervisors into an OTP application.

So far, the lifecycle of the processes we've seen has been pretty simple. If needed, they set up other resources or processes to get started. Once running, they listen for messages and process them, collapsing if they fail. Some of them might restart a failed process if needed.

OTP formalizes those activities, and a few more, into a set of behaviors (or behaviours—the original spelling was British). The most common behaviors are `GenServer` (generic server) and `Supervisor`. Through Erlang, you can use the `gen_fsm` (finite state machine) and `gen_event` behaviors. Elixir provides the Mix build tool for creating applications so that you can package your OTP code into a single runnable (and updatable) system.

The behaviors predefine the mechanisms you'll use to create and interact with processes, and the compiler will warn you if you're missing some of them. Your code will handle the callbacks, specifying how to respond to particular kinds of events, and you will need to decide upon a structure for your application.

 If you'd like a video introduction to OTP, though it is Erlang-centric, see Steve Vinoski's "Erlang's Open Telecom Platform (OTP) Framework" (*http://bitly.com/10Cif1r*). You probably already know the first half hour or so of it, but the review is excellent. In a very different style, if you'd like an explanation of why it's worth learning OTP and process-oriented development in general, Francesco Cesarini's slides (*http://bitly.com/10CiqKo*) work even without narration (especially the second half).

Creating Services with GenServer

Much of the work you think of as the core of a program—calculating results, storing information, and preparing replies—will fit neatly into the GenServer behavior. It provides a core set of methods that let you set up a process, respond to requests, end the process gracefully, and even pass state to a new process if this one needs to be upgraded in place.

Table 13-1 shows the functions you need to implement in a service that uses Gen Server. For a simple service, the first two or three are the most important, and you may just use placeholder code for the rest.

Table 13-1. What calls and gets called in GenServer

Function	Triggered by	Does
init/1	GenServer.start_link	Sets up the process
handle_call/3	GenServer.call	Handles synchronous calls
handle_cast/2	GenServer.cast	Handles asynchronous calls
handle_info/2	Random messages	Deals with non-OTP messages
terminate/2	Failure or shutdown signal from supervisor	Cleans up the process
code_change/3	System libraries for code upgrades	Lets you switch out code without losing state

Example 13-1, which you can find in *ch13/ex1-drop*, shows an example that you can use to get started. It mixes a simple calculation from way back in Example 2-1 with a counter like that in Example 9-4.

Example 13-1. A simple gen_server example

```elixir
defmodule DropServer do
  use GenServer

  defmodule State do
    defstruct count: 0
  end

  # This is a convenience method for startup
  def start_link do
    GenServer.start_link(__MODULE__, [], [{:name, __MODULE__}])
  end

  # These are the callbacks that the GenServer behavior will use
  def init([]) do
    {:ok, %State{}}
  end

  def handle_call(request, _from, state) do
    distance = request
    reply = {:ok, fall_velocity(distance)}
    new_state = %State{count: state.count + 1}
    {:reply, reply, new_state}
  end

  def handle_cast(_msg, state) do
    IO.puts("So far, calculated #{state.count} velocities.")
    {:noreply, state}
  end

  def handle_info(_info, state) do
    {:noreply, state}
  end

  def terminate(_reason, _state) do
    {:ok}
  end

  def code_change(_old_version, state, _extra) do
    {:ok, state}
  end

  # internal function
  def fall_velocity(distance) do
    :math.sqrt(2 * 9.8 * distance)
  end

end
```

The module name (DropServer) should be familiar from past examples. The second line specifies that the module is going to be using the GenServer module.

The nested `defmodule` declaration should be familiar; it creates a structure that contains only one field, to keep a count of the number of calls made. Many services will have more fields, including things like database connections, references to other processes, perhaps network information, and metadata specific to this particular service. It is also possible to have services with no state, which would be represented by an empty tuple here. As you'll see later, every single `GenServer` function will reference the state.

The `State` structure declaration is a good example of a declaration you should make inside of a module and not in a separate file. It is possible that you'll want to share state models across different processes that use `GenServer`, but it's easier to see what `State` should contain if the information is right there.

The first function in the sample, `start_link/0`, is *not* one of the required `GenServer` functions. Instead, it calls Elixir's `GenServer.start_link` function to start up the process. When you're just getting started, this is useful for testing. As you move toward production code, you may find it easier to leave `start_link/0` out and use other mechanisms.

The `start_link/0` function uses the built-in `__MODULE__` declaration, which returns the name of the current module:

```
# This is a convenience method for startup
def start_link do
   GenServer.start_link(__MODULE__, [], [{:name, __MODULE__}])
end
```

The first argument is an atom (`__MODULE__`) that will be expanded to the name of the current module, and that name will be used as the name for this process. This is followed by a list of arguments to be passed to the module's initialization procedure and a list of options. Options can specify things like debugging, timeouts, and options for spawning the process. By default, the name of the process is registered with just the local Elixir instance. Because we want it registered with all associated nodes, we have put the tuple `{:name, __MODULE__}` in the options list.

You may also see a form of `GenServer.start_link` with `:via` as an atom in an option tuple. This lets you set up custom process registries, of which `gproc` (*https://github.com/uwiger/gproc*) is the best known.

All of the remaining functions are part of the `GenServer` behavior. `init/1` creates a new state structure instance whose `count` field is 0—no velocities have yet been calculated. The two functions that do most of the work here are `handle_call/3` and `handle_cast/2`. For this demonstration, `handle_call/3` expects to receive a distance in meters and returns a velocity for a fall from that height on Earth, while `handle_cast/2` is a trigger to report the number of velocities calculated.

`handle_call/3` makes synchronous communications between Erlang processes simple:

```
def handle_call(request, _from, state) do
  distance = request
  reply = {:ok, fall_velocity(distance)}
  new_state = %State{count: state.count + 1}
  {:reply, reply, new_state}
end
```

This extracts the `distance` from the `request`, which isn't necessary except that we wanted to leave the variable names for the function almost the same as they were in the template. (`handle_call(distance, _from, state)` would have been fine.) Your `request` is more likely to be a tuple or a list rather than a bare value, but this works for simple calls.

The function then creates a reply based on sending that `distance` to the simple `fall_velocity/1` function at the end of the module. Next, it creates a `new_state` containing an incremented count. Then the atom `:reply`, the `reply` tuple containing the velocity, and the `new_state` containing the updated count get passed back.

Because the calculation is really simple, treating the drop as a simple synchronous call is perfectly acceptable. For more complex situations where you can't predict how long a response might take, you may want to consider sending a `:noreply` response and using the `_from` argument to send a response later. (There is also a `:stop` response available that will trigger the `:terminate/2` method and halt the process.)

 By default, OTP will time out any synchronous calls that take longer than five seconds to calculate. You can override this by making your call using `GenServer.call/3` to specify a timeout (in milliseconds) explicitly, or by using the atom `:infinity`.

The `handle_cast/2` function supports asynchronous communications. It isn't supposed to return anything directly, though it does report `:noreply` (or `:stop`) and updated state. In this case, it takes a very weak approach (but one that serves well for a demonstration), calling `IO.puts/1` to report on the number of calls:

```
def handle_cast(_msg, state) do
  IO.puts("So far, calculated #{state.count} velocities.")
  {:noreply, state}
end
```

The state doesn't change, because asking for the number of times the process has calculated a fall velocity is not the same thing as actually calculating a fall velocity.

Until you have good reason to change them, you can leave the handle_info/2, terminate/2, and code_change/3 functions alone.

Making a GenServer process run and calling it looks a little different than starting the processes you saw in Chapter 9:

```
iex(1)> DropServer.start_link()
{:ok,#PID<0.46.0>}
iex(2)> GenServer.call(DropServer, 20)
{:ok,19.79898987322333}
iex(3)> GenServer.call(DropServer, 40)
{:ok,28.0}
iex(4)> GenServer.call(DropServer, 60)
{:ok,34.292856398964496}
iex(5)> GenServer.cast(DropServer, {})
So far, calculated 3 velocities.
:ok
```

The call to DropServer.start_link() sets up the process and makes it available. Then, you're free to use GenServer.call or GenServer.cast to send it messages and get responses.

 While you can capture the pid, you don't have to keep it around to use the process. Because start_link returns a tuple, if you want to capture the pid you can do something like {:ok, pid} = DropServer.start_link().

Because of the way OTP calls GenServer functions, there's an additional bonus—or perhaps a hazard—in that you can update code on the fly. For example, we tweaked the fall_velocity/1 function to lighten Earth's gravity a little, using 9.1 as a constant instead of 9.8. Recompiling the code and asking for a velocity now returns a different answer:

```
iex(6)> r(DropServer)
warning: redefining module DropServer (current version loaded from
  _build/dev/lib/drop_server/ebin/Elixir.DropServer.beam)
  lib/drop_server.ex:1

warning: redefining module DropServer.State (current version loaded from
  _build/dev/lib/drop_server/ebin/Elixir.DropServer.State.beam)
  lib/drop_server.ex:4

{:reloaded, DropServer, [DropServer.State, DropServer]}
iex(7)> GenServer.call(DropServer, 60)
{:ok,33.04542328371661}
```

This can be very convenient during the development phase, but be careful doing anything like this on a production machine. OTP has other mechanisms for updating code on the fly. There is also a built-in limitation to this approach: init gets called only when start_link sets up the service. It does not get called if you recompile the code. If your new code requires any changes to the structure of its state, your code will break the next time it's called.

A Simple Supervisor

When you started the DropServer module from the shell, you effectively made the shell the supervisor for the module—though the shell doesn't really do any supervision. You can break the module easily:

```
iex(8)> GenServer.call(DropServer, -60)
** (EXIT from #PID<0.141.0>) an exception was raised:
    ** (ArithmeticError) bad argument in arithmetic expression
        (stdlib) :math.sqrt(-1176.0)
        (drop_server) lib/drop_server.ex:44: DropServer.fall_velocity/1
        (drop_server) lib/drop_server.ex:20: DropServer.handle_call/3
        (stdlib) gen_server.erl:615: :gen_server.try_handle_call/4
        (stdlib) gen_server.erl:647: :gen_server.handle_msg/5
        (stdlib) proc_lib.erl:247: :proc_lib.init_p_do_apply/3

Interactive Elixir (1.3.1) - press Ctrl+C to exit (type h() ENTER for help)
iex(1)>
10:50:58.899 [error] GenServer DropServer terminating
** (ArithmeticError) bad argument in arithmetic expression
    (stdlib) :math.sqrt(-1176.0)
    (drop_server) lib/drop_server.ex:44: DropServer.fall_velocity/1
    (drop_server) lib/drop_server.ex:20: DropServer.handle_call/3
    (stdlib) gen_server.erl:615: :gen_server.try_handle_call/4
    (stdlib) gen_server.erl:647: :gen_server.handle_msg/5
    (stdlib) proc_lib.erl:247: :proc_lib.init_p_do_apply/3
Last message: -60
State: %DropServer.State{count: 5}
```

The error message is nicely complete, even telling you the last message and the state, but when you go to call the service again, you can't, because the IEx shell has restarted. You can restart it with DropServer.start_link/0 again, but you're not always going to be watching your processes personally.

Instead, you want something that can watch over your processes for you and make sure they restart (or not) as appropriate. OTP formalizes the process management you saw in Example 9-10 with its Supervisor behavior.

A basic supervisor needs to support only one callback function, init/1, and can also have a start_link function to fire it up. The return value of that init/1 function tells OTP which child processes your supervisor manages and how you want to handle their failures. A supervisor for the Drop module might look like Example 13-2, which is in *ch13/ex2-drop-sup.*

Example 13-2. A simple supervisor

```
defmodule DropSup do
  use Supervisor

  # convenience method for startup

  def start_link do
    Supervisor.start_link(__MODULE__, [], [{:name, __MODULE__}])
  end

  # supervisor callback

  def init([]) do
    child = [worker(DropServer, [], [])]
    supervise(child, [{:strategy, :one_for_one}, {:max_restarts, 1},
      {:max_seconds, 5}])
  end

  # internal functions (none here)
end
```

The init/1 function's job is to specify the process or processes that the supervisor is to keep track of, and specify how it should handle failure.

The worker/3 function specifies a module that the supervisor should start, its argument list, and any options to be given to the worker's start_link function. In this example, there is only one child process to supervise, and the options are given as a list of key-value tuples.

> You can also specify the options as a keyword list, which you would write this way:
> ```
> supervise(child, [strategy: :one_for_one, max_restarts: 1,
> max_seconds: 5])
> ```

The supervise/2 function takes the list of child processes as its first argument and a list of options as its second argument.

The :strategy of :one_for_one tells OTP that it should create a new child process every time a process that is supposed to be :permanent (the default) fails. You can also go with :one_for_all, which terminates and restarts all of the processes the supervisor oversees when one fails, or :rest_for_one, which restarts the process and any processes that began after the failed process had started.

When you're ready to take more direct control of how your processes respond to their environment, you might explore working with the dynamic functions `Supervisor.start/2`, `Supervisor.terminate_child/2`, `Supervisor.restart_child/2`, and `Supervisor. delete_child/2`, as well as the restart strategy `:simple_one_for_one`.

The next two values define how often the worker processes can crash before terminating the supervisor itself. In this case, it's one restart every five seconds. Customizing these values lets you handle a variety of conditions but probably won't affect you much initially. (Setting `:max_restarts` to 0 means that the supervisor will just terminate if a worker has an error.)

The `supervise` function takes those arguments and creates a data structure that OTP will use. By default, this is a `:permanent` service, so the supervisor should always restart a child when it fails. You can specify a `:restart` option when defining the worker if you want to change this to a different value. By default, the supervisor waits five seconds before shutting down the worker completely; you can change this with the `:shutdown` option when defining the worker. More complex OTP applications can contain trees of supervisors managing other supervisors, which themselves manage other supervisors or workers. To create a child process that is a supervisor, you use the `supervisor/3` function, whose arguments are the same as those of `worker/3`.

OTP wants to know the dependencies so that it can help you upgrade software in place. It's all part of the magic of keeping systems running without ever bringing them to a full stop.

Now that you have a supervisor process, you can set up the `DropServer` by just calling the supervisor. However, running a supervisor from the shell using the `start_link/0` function call creates its own set of problems; the shell is itself a supervisor and will terminate processes that report errors. After a long error report, you'll find that both your worker and the supervisor have vanished.

In practice this means that you need a way to test supervised OTP processes (that aren't yet part of an application) directly from the shell. This method explicitly breaks the bond between the shell and the supervisor process by catching the pid of the supervisor (line 1) and then using the `Process.unlink/1` function to remove the link (line 2). Then you can call the process as usual with `GenServer.call/2` and get answers. If you get an error (line 5), it'll be OK. The supervisor will restart the worker, and you can make new calls successfully. The calls to `Process.whereis(Drop Server)` on lines 3 and 6 demonstrate that the supervisor has restarted `DropServer` with a new pid:

```
iex(1)> {:ok, pid} = DropSup.start_link()
{:ok,#PID<0.44.0>}
iex(2)> Process.unlink(pid)
true
iex(3)> Process.whereis(DropServer)
#PID<0.45.0>
iex(4)> GenServer.call(DropServer, 60)
{:ok,34.292856398964496}
iex(5)> GenServer.call(DropServer, -60)
** (exit) exited in: GenServer.call(DropServer, -60, 5000)
    ** (EXIT) an exception was raised:
        ** (ArithmeticError) bad argument in arithmetic expression
            (stdlib) :math.sqrt(-1176.0)
            (drop_sup) lib/drop_server.ex:44: DropServer.fall_velocity/1
            (drop_sup) lib/drop_server.ex:20: DropServer.handle_call/3
            (stdlib) gen_server.erl:615: :gen_server.try_handle_call/4
            (stdlib) gen_server.erl:647: :gen_server.handle_msg/5
            (stdlib) proc_lib.erl:247: :proc_lib.init_p_do_apply/3

11:05:00.438 [error] GenServer DropServer terminating
** (ArithmeticError) bad argument in arithmetic expression
    (stdlib) :math.sqrt(-1176.0)
    (drop_sup) lib/drop_server.ex:44: DropServer.fall_velocity/1
    (drop_sup) lib/drop_server.ex:20: DropServer.handle_call/3
    (stdlib) gen_server.erl:615: :gen_server.try_handle_call/4
    (stdlib) gen_server.erl:647: :gen_server.handle_msg/5
    (stdlib) proc_lib.erl:247: :proc_lib.init_p_do_apply/3
Last message: -60
State: %DropServer.State{count: 1}
    (elixir) lib/gen_server.ex:604: GenServer.call/3
iex(5)> GenServer.call(DropServer, 60)
{:ok,34.292856398964496}
iex(6)> Process.whereis(DropServer)
#PID<0.46.0>
```

You can also open the Process Manager in Observer and whack
away at worker processes through the Kill option on the Trace
menu, and watch them reappear.

This works, but it is only the tiniest taste of what supervisors can do. They can create
child processes dynamically and manage their lifecycle in greater detail.

Packaging an Application with Mix

In this section, you will use Mix to create an application for the drop supervisor and
server that you have written.

Reiterating what we did in "Firing It Up" on page 2, create a directory to hold your application by typing mix new *name*, as in the following example:

```
$ mix new drop_app
* creating README.md
* creating .gitignore
* creating mix.exs
* creating config
* creating config/config.exs
* creating lib
* creating lib/drop_app.ex
* creating test
* creating test/test_helper.exs
* creating test/drop_app_test.exs

Your Mix project was created successfully.
You can use "mix" to compile it, test it, and more:

    cd drop_app
    mix test

Run "mix help" for more commands.
```

Mix creates a set of files and directories for you. Change directory to the *drop_app* directory that Mix created. Then open up the *mix.exs* file in your favorite text editor. We haven't talked about this file before because we never needed to make changes to it, but now we *will* need to modify it. So take a look:

```
defmodule DropApp.Mixfile do
  use Mix.Project

  def project do
    [app: :drop_app,
     version: "0.0.1",
     elixir: "~> 1.3",
     build_embedded: Mix.env == :prod,
     start_permanent: Mix.env == :prod,
     deps: deps]
  end

  # Configuration for the OTP application
  #
  # Type "mix help compile.app" for more information
  def application do
    [applications: [:logger]]
  end

  # Dependencies can be Hex packages:
  #
  #   {:mydep, "~> 0.3.0"}
  #
  # Or git/path repositories:
```

```
#
#    {:mydep, git: "https://github.com/elixir-lang/mydep.git", tag: "0.1.0"}
#
# Type "mix help deps" for more examples and options
defp deps do
  []
end
end
```

The project/0 function lets you name your application, give it a version number, and specify the dependencies for building the project.

The dependencies are returned by the deps/0 function. The commented example says that you need to have the mydep project version 0.3.0 or higher, and it is available via git at the specified URL. In addition to git:, you may specify the location of a dependency as a local file (path:)

In this example, the application doesn't have any dependencies, so you may leave everything exactly as it is.

If you type the command mix compile, Mix will compile your empty project. If you look in your directory, you will see that Mix has created a _build_ directory for the compiled code:

```
$ mix compile
Compiling 1 file (.ex)
Generated drop_app app
$ ls
_build  config  lib  mix.exs  README.md  test
```

An empty application isn't very exciting, so copy the *drop_server.ex* and *drop_sup.ex* files that you wrote into the *lib* folder. Then run iex -S mix. Mix will compile the new files, and you can start using the server straightaway:

```
$ iex -S mix
Erlang/OTP 19 [erts-8.0] [source] [64-bit] [smp:4:4] [async-threads:10]
  [hipe] [kernel-poll:false]

Compiling 2 files (.ex)
Generated drop_app app
Interactive Elixir (1.3.1) - press Ctrl+C to exit (type h() ENTER for help)
iex(1)> {:ok, pid} = DropServer.start_link()
{:ok,#PID<0.60.0>}
```

The last steps you need to do are to write the application code itself and then tell Mix where everything is.

Inside *mix.exs*, change the application/0 function to look like this:

```
def application do
  [ applications: [:logger],
    registered: [:drop_app],
    mod: {DropApp, []} ]
end
```

The :registered key is a list of all the names that your application registers (in this case, just :drop_app), and :mod is a tuple that gives the name of the module to be run when the application starts up and a list of any arguments to be passed to that module. :applications lists any applications that your application depends on at runtime.

Here is the code that we have added to the DropApp module, which is in a file named *drop_app.ex* in the *ch13/ex3-drop-app/drop_app/lib* directory:

```
defmodule DropApp do
  use Application

  def start(_type, _args) do
    IO.puts("Starting the app...") # show that app is really starting
    DropSup.start_link()
  end
end
```

The start/2 function is required. The first argument tells how you want the virtual machine that Elixir runs on to handle application crashes. The second argument gives the arguments that you defined in the :mod key. The start/2 function should return a tuple of the form {:ok, *pid*}, which is exactly what DropSup.start_link/0 does.

If you type mix compile at the command prompt, Mix will generate the file *_build/dev/lib/drop_app/ebin/drop_app.app*. (If you look at that file, you will see an Erlang tuple that contains much of the information gleaned from the files you have already created.) You may then run the application from the command line:

```
$ elixir -pa _build/dev/lib/drop_app/ebin --app drop_app
Starting the app...
```

There is much, much more to learn. OTP deserves a book, or several, all on its own. Hopefully this chapter provides you with enough information to try some things out and understand those books. However, the gap between what this chapter can reasonably present and what you need to know to write solid OTP-based programs is, to say the least, vast.

## CHAPTER 14

Using Macros to Extend Elixir

You have now learned enough Elixir to write interesting and fairly powerful programs. Sometimes, though, you need to extend the language itself in order to make your code easier to read or to implement some new functionality. Elixir's macro feature lets you do this.

Functions Versus Macros

On the surface, macros look a lot like functions, except that they begin with `defmacro` instead of `def`. However, macros work very differently than functions. The best way to explain the difference is to show you Example 14-1, which is in the directory *ch14/ ex1-difference.*

Example 14-1. Showing the difference between function and macro calls

```
defmodule Difference do

  defmacro m_test(x) do
    IO.puts("#{inspect(x)}")
    x
  end

  def f_test(x) do
    IO.puts("#{inspect(x)}")
    x
  end

end
```

In order to use a macro, you must `require` the module that it's in. Type the following in the shell:

```
iex(1)> require Difference
Difference
iex(2)> Difference.f_test(1 + 3)
4
4
iex(3)> Difference.m_test(1 + 3)
{:+, [line: 3], [1, 3]}
4
```

Line 2 gives you exactly what you'd expect—Elixir evaluates 1 + 3 and passes it on to the f_test function, which prints the number 4 and returns the number 4 as its result.

Line 3 may be something of a surprise. Instead of an evaluated expression, the argument is a tuple that is the internal representation of the code before it is executed. The macro returns the tuple (in Elixir terms, the macro has been *expanded*), and then that tuple is passed on to Elixir to be evaluated.

> The first item in the tuple is the operator, the second item is a list of metadata about the operation, and the third item is a list of the operands.

A Simple Macro

Because defmacro gets the code before Elixir has had a chance to evaluate it, a macro has the power to transform the code before sending it on to Elixir for evaluation. Example 14-2 is a macro that creates code to double whatever its argument is. (This is something that could much more easily be accomplished with a function, but we need to start with something easy.) It works by manually creating the tuple that Elixir will recognize as a multiplication operation. You can find it in *ch14/ex2-double*.

Example 14-2. A manually created macro

```
defmodule Double do

  defmacro double x do
    {:*, [], [2, x]}
  end

end
```

After recompiling, you can try this out in the shell:

```
iex(1)> require Double
Double
iex(2)> Double.double(3)
```

```
6
iex(3)> Double.double(3 * 7)
42
```

That works, but there must be an easier way. It would be nice if you could say, "Turn this Elixir code into internal format" so that Elixir would create the tuples for you. In fact, you *can* do this by using quote, which takes any Elixir expression and converts it to internal format:

```
iex(4)> quote do: 1 + 3
{:+, [context: Elixir, import: Kernel], [1, 3]}
iex(5)> x = 20
20
iex(6)> quote do: 3 * x + 20
{:+, [context: Elixir, import: Kernel],
 [{:*, [context: Elixir, import: Kernel], [3, {:x, [], Elixir}]}, 20]}
```

As you see, quote takes normal Elixir code and converts it to the internal format that macros accept as input and return as their expanded result. You might be tempted to rewrite the macro from the previous example as follows:

```
defmodule Double do

  defmacro double(x) do
    quote do: 2 * x
  end

end
```

But if you try this code, it won't work. The reason is that you are saying, "Turn 2 * x into its tuple form," but x already *is* in tuple form, and you need a way to tell Elixir to leave it alone. Example 14-3 uses the unquote/1 function do exactly that. (You may find this example in *ch14/ex3-double.*)

Example 14-3. Using quote to create a macro

```
defmodule Double do

  defmacro double(x) do
    quote do
      2 * unquote(x)
    end
  end

end
```

This says, "Turn 2 * x into internal form, but don't bother converting x; it doesn't need quoting":

```
iex(7)> r(Double)
warning: redefining module Double (current version loaded from
  _build/dev/lib/double/ebin/Elixir.Double.beam)
  /Users/elixir/code/ch14/ex3-double/lib/double.ex:1

{:reloaded, Double, [Double]}

double.ex:1: redefining module Double
[Double]
iex(8)> require Double
Double
iex(9)> Double.double(3 * 5)
30
```

 The most common mistake people make when writing macros is to forget to unquote arguments. Remember that all of a macro's arguments are already in internal format.

To summarize: quote means "Turn everything in the do block into internal tuple format"; unquote means "Do not turn this into internal format." (The terms quote and unquote come from the Lisp programming language.)

 If you quote an atom, number, list, string, or tuple with two elements, you will get back the same item and not an internal-format tuple.

Creating New Logic

Macros also let you add new commands to the language. For example, if Elixir didn't already have an unless construct (which works as the opposite of if), you could add it to the language by writing the macro shown in Example 14-4, which is in *ch14/ex4-unless*.

Example 14-4. Creating a macro to implement the unless construct

```
defmodule Logic do

  defmacro unless(condition, options) do
    quote do
      if(!unquote(condition), unquote(options))
    end
  end

end
```

This macro takes a `condition` and `options` (in their internal form) and expands them to the internal code for an equivalent `if` statement with a reversed test for the condition. As in the previous example, the `condition` and `options` must remain in an unquote state, as they are already in internal form. You can test it in the shell after compiling via `iex -S mix`:

```
iex(1)> require(Logic)
Logic
iex(2)> Logic.unless (4 == 5) do
...(2)>    IO.puts("arithmetic still works")
...(2)> end
arithmetic still works
:ok
```

Creating Functions Programatically

Everything in Elixir has an internal representation, even functions. This means that a macro can take data as input and output a customized function as its result.

Example 14-5 is a simple macro, `create_multiplier`, that takes an atom and a multiplication factor as its input. It produces a function whose name is the atom you gave, and that function will multiply *its* input by the factor.

Example 14-5. Using a macro to programmatically create a function

```
defmodule FunctionMaker do
  defmacro create_multiplier(function_name, factor) do
    quote do
      def unquote(function_name)(value) do
        unquote(factor) * value
      end
    end
  end
end
```

You now need another module to invoke the macro:

```
defmodule Multiply do
  require FunctionMaker

  FunctionMaker.create_multiplier(:double, 2)
  FunctionMaker.create_multiplier(:triple, 3)

  def example do
    x = triple(12)
    IO.puts("Twelve times 3 is #{x}")
  end

end
```

Once this is done, you can use the programmatically created functions:

```
iex(1)> Multiply.double(21)
42
iex(2)> Multiply.triple(54)
162
iex(3)> Multiply.example()
Twelve times 3 is 36
:ok
```

The entire example is in *ch14/ex5-programmatic*.

 You can't define a function programmatically outside of a module or inside of a function.

You can even write a single macro that creates many different functions. If, for example, you wanted to have a separate drop/1 function for each planemo, you could have a macro that takes a list of planemos with their gravity constants and creates those functions. Example 14-6 will create functions mercury_drop/1, venus_drop/1, etc. from a keyword list.

Example 14-6. Creating multiple functions with a macro

```
defmodule FunctionMaker do
  defmacro create_functions(planemo_list) do
    Enum.map planemo_list, fn {name, gravity} ->
      quote do
        def unquote(:"#{name}_drop")(distance) do
          :math.sqrt(2 * unquote(gravity) * distance)
        end
      end
    end
  end
end
```

The expression :"#{name}_drop" uses interpolation to append the string "drop" to the planemo's name, and the leading : converts the result to an atom. The whole expression is unquoted, as atoms are already in quoted form.

Again, you need another module to invoke the macro:

```
defmodule Drop do
  require FunctionMaker

  FunctionMaker.create_functions([{:mercury, 3.7}, {:venus, 8.9},
    {:earth, 9.8}, {:moon, 1.6}, {:mars, 3.7},
    {:jupiter, 23.1}, {:saturn, 9.0}, {:uranus, 8.7},
    {:neptune, 11.0}, {:pluto, 0.6}])

end
```

Once compiled, the 10 new functions are available to you:

```
iex(1)> Drop.earth_drop(20)
19.79898987322333
iex(2)> Drop.moon_drop(20)
8.0
```

The entire example is in *ch14/ex6-multidrop*.

When (Not) to Use Macros

What you have seen so far are good examples of sample programs. Everything in this chapter could have been done more easily with simple Elixir functions, though. While you're learning about Elixir, go wild and experiment with macros as much as you like. But when you start writing programs for general use and are tempted to write a macro, first ask yourself, "Could I do this with a function?" If the answer is "Yes" (and it will be, most of the time), then stick with functions. Use macros only when it will make the lives of people who use your code easier.

Why, then, has this chapter made such a big tzimmes about macros, if you aren't encouraged to use them? First, Elixir itself uses macros extensively. For example, when you define a record, Elixir programatically generates the functions that let you access that record's fields. Even def and defmodule are macros!

More important, when you read other people's code, you may find that they have used macros, and the information from this chapter will help you understand what they've written. (It's sort of like learning a foreign language; there are phrases you may never have to say yourself, but you want to be able to understand them when someone says them to you.)

## CHAPTER 15

Using Phoenix

While it's great to use Elixir from the command line, sometimes you'll want to expose your work to the web as well. The Phoenix framework offers an Elixir-based toolkit, somewhat like Ruby on Rails, for building web applications. Phoenix is designed for robustness and scalability, building on macros, OTP, and Erlang's Cowboy server. It wraps those powerful features, though, so you can get started building simple things without mastering those details.

Skeleton Installation

Once you have Elixir itself installed, installing just Phoenix isn't difficult. Installing everything that Phoenix might want, including PostgreSQL and Node.js, is more than this introduction can cover, but you can do (at least sort of) useful things with only Phoenix.

To get started, install Phoenix from Mix (the command line and output have been formatted to fit the page margins here, but you should enter the entire command on a single line):

```
$ mix archive.install
https://github.com/phoenixframework/archives/raw/master/phoenix_new.ez
Are you sure you want to install archive "https://github.com/phoenixframework/
  archives/raw/master/phoenix_new.ez"? [Yn] y
* creating .mix/archives/phoenix_new
```

Once you've installed Phoenix, you can have it build a minimalist application. The --no-brunch directive turns off Phoenix's support for managing assets, which requires you to install Node. --no-ecto turns off the object relational mapping (ORM) that expects you to have installed PostgreSQL:

```
$ mix phoenix.new fall --no-brunch --no-ecto
* creating web/config/config.exs
* creating web/config/dev.exs
...
* creating web/web/views/layout_view.ex
* creating web/web/views/page_view.ex

Fetch and install dependencies? [Yn] y
* running mix deps.get

We are all set! Run your Phoenix application:

$ cd fall
$ mix phoenix.server

You can also run your app inside IEx as:

$ iex -S mix phoenix.server
```

The directory Phoenix created contains a lot of parts, as shown in Figure 15-1.

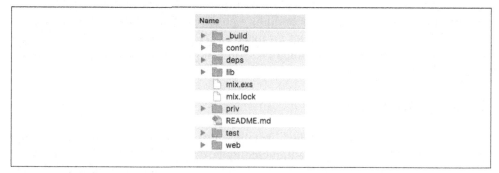

Figure 15-1. Files created by Phoenix

For the rest of this chapter, you'll be working in the *web* directory.

Take Phoenix's advice and change to the *fall* directory, then start Phoenix:

```
$ cd fall
$ iex -S mix phoenix.server
```

 Phoenix may ask to install local copies of more software the first time you run it. Our installation required Rebar, which it installed without a hitch.

The first time you run Phoenix, it will take a while to build before starting. After a lot of notices about files Phoenix is compiling, you'll see:

```
Generated web app
[info] Running Web.Endpoint with Cowboy using http://localhost:4000
```

A basic site will now be running on port 4000 of your machine. When you visit *http://localhost:4000*, you'll see the barely customized welcome page shown in Figure 15-2.

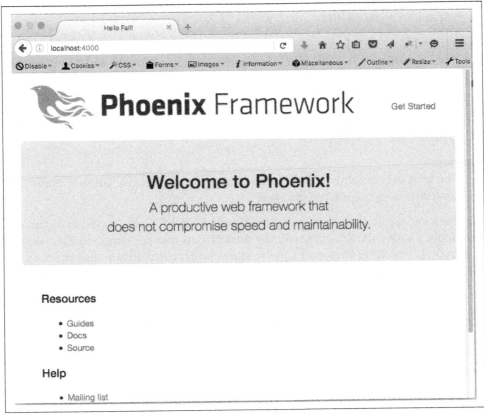

Figure 15-2. Phoenix's welcome page

You can tell it came from your app because the tab title says "Hello Fall!" At the command line where you started Phoenix, you should see something like:

```
[info] GET /
[debug] Processing by Web.PageController.index/2
  Parameters: %{}
  Pipelines: [:browser]
[info] Sent 200 in 2ms
```

Structuring a Basic Phoenix Application

A minimal Phoenix application that does just one thing (beyond the welcome page!) requires you to work in four different places:

Router

The router logic gives Phoenix basic direction on what to do when it receives a request for a given URL.

Controller

The controller is the switchboard for information coming in and going out, the piece that will connect requests for calculations to the calculations.

View

The view takes results from the controller and makes everything ready for final formatting in the template.

Template

The template combines HTML formatting with variables that come to it from the controller using logic from the view.

For this basic application, we're going to skip the M in MVC, the model that manages interactions with data. Phoenix typically uses Ecto to manage data, and Ecto expects PostgreSQL, which requires a potentially more complex installation than the basics of Phoenix.

 If you liked Mnesia, it is possible to use it with Phoenix, though it is far enough off the beaten path that you should probably get familiar with Phoenix first. For more, see AmberBit's "Using mnesia database from Elixir" (*https://www.amberbit.com/elixir-cocktails/ elixir/using-mnesia-database-from-elisir/*).

Presenting a Page

Getting a simple HTML page posted—one that isn't the installation's default page—requires setting up all four of the components just listed. While posting HTML may seem even duller than calculating the velocity of falling objects, establishing that foundation will give you a solid base on which to build more. Even stranger, chasing the errors you get from a not quite complete installation will teach you lessons you'll need for future construction. When something goes wrong, it will be easier to see at which layer the problem occurred.

First, start Phoenix and then try visiting *http://localhost:4000/welcome*. You'll see something like Figure 15-3.

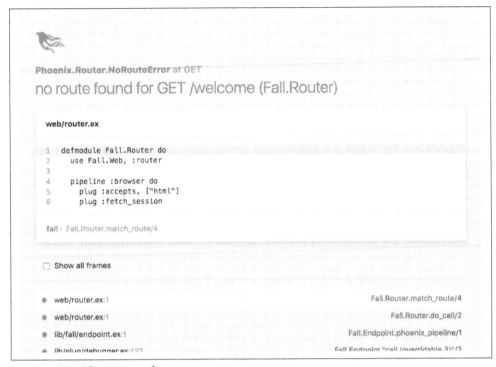

Figure 15-3. Phoenix needs a route

Routing

Phoenix needs explicit instructions about where to send requests for particular URLs. It understood how to show the welcome page because the *web/router.ex* file that comes in a new Phoenix app provided that information:

```
defmodule Fall.Router do
  use Fall.Web, :router

  pipeline :browser do
    plug :accepts, ["html"]
    plug :fetch_session
    plug :fetch_flash
    plug :protect_from_forgery
    plug :put_secure_browser_headers
  end

  pipeline :api do
    plug :accepts, ["json"]
  end
```

```
scope "/", Fall do
  pipe_through :browser # Use the default browser stack
  get "/", PageController, :index
end

# Other scopes may use custom stacks.
# scope "/api", Fall do
#   pipe_through :api
# end
end
```

There's a lot going on in that file. First, it makes clear that the application is called Fall. You'll see Fall.Web a lot here, and one of the common perils of cutting and pasting code from another app is to forget to change all of those references. (Fall.Web gets defined in the *web/web.ex* file, but for now and probably for the most part you should leave that alone.)

The router also defines two pipelines. The first is meant for content to be displayed in a browser, typically HTML, and the second is for JSON-based API content. For now that's all you need to know about those, but you can see the work Phoenix does for you, especially in the browser pipeline.

The place where you'll tell Phoenix to support a new URL for an HTML interface is in the scope function. Phoenix knows to show the Phoenix default page because of get "/", PageController, :index, which kicks off a series of events that will show it. get tells Phoenix it will be handling an HTTP GET request. To create your own URL, you'll add a line right above that line:

```
get "/welcome", FallController, :welcome
```

When the router gets a request for *welcome*, it will pass the information from that call to the welcome function on the FallController. This means that you can advance to the next error, shown in Figure 15-4.

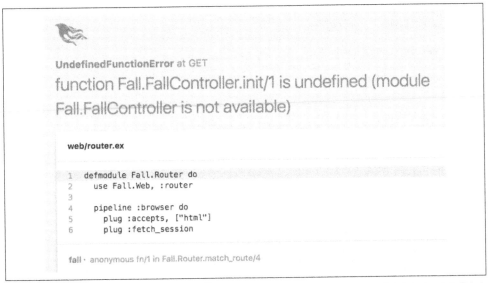

Figure 15-4. Phoenix wants a controller

A Simple Controller

Phoenix expects to find controllers in the *web/controllers* directory. In the beginning, there's only one file there, *page_controller.ex*, which is part of the welcome page. Its form provides a sense of what controllers should look like:

```
defmodule Fall.PageController do
  use Fall.Web, :controller

  def index(conn, _params) do
    render conn, "index.html"
  end
end
```

The controller file as a whole is a module, relying on the Web code for the whole application. The router also relies on it, but the router referenced :router while the controller (unsurprisingly) references :controller.

Each function in the module should take a connection (conn) and parameters, and (perhaps after some processing) call render with that connection and the name of a file to send back.

To create the FallController specified in the earlier change to the routing file, make a *fall_controller.ex* file in *web/controllers*, and give it a welcome function:

```
defmodule Fall.FallController do
  use Fall.Web, :controller

def welcome(conn, params) do

  render conn, "welcome.html"

end

end
```

Then reload *http://localhost:4000/welcome*. The next error will ask for a view, as shown in Figure 15-5.

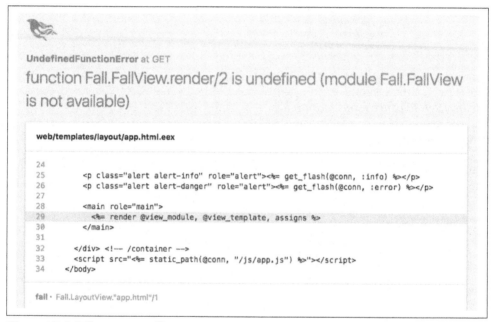

Figure 15-5. When a controller points to a nonexistent view

A Simple View

Creating the view requires building two parts. The first, the view code in *web/views/fall.ex*, starts out as an extremely simple pass-through:

```
defmodule Fall.FallView do
  use Fall.Web, :view
end
```

You're almost there, but the error message isn't much more encouraging, as you can see in Figure 15-6.

Figure 15-6. When a controller points to a nonexistent template

The final piece you need is a template. The controller code said to render *wel-come.html*, so you need to create a template for that in */web/templates/fall/welcome.html.eex*. EEx, Embedded Elixir, is a part of Elixir that lets you create string templates that Elixir can process efficiently. In this case, Phoenix uses EEx to generate HTML, which will then go to the browser for display. Your templates don't need to create a whole page: Phoenix already has templates that wrap your content, making it easy to keep applications looking consistent. That means your opening template can be as simple as:

```
<h1>Falling starts now!</h1>
```

This produces the welcome in Figure 15-7—you might not even have to reload, as Phoenix in development mode retries failed code periodically.

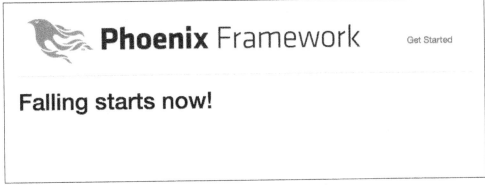

Figure 15-7. A complete set of parts finally produces a result

You may not want the Phoenix Framework logo stamped on all of your work. To remove it, explore *web/templates/layout/app.html.eex*, and remove the `header` element.

 You can have Phoenix generate basic controller and view code with `mix phoenix.gen.html`, but it will also want to generate a model, which won't work in this simple example.

Calculating

Now that you have a page, it's time to do something with the data that it sends the server. This means learning to build a simple form, and dealing with the minor challenge that picking parameters out of an HTTP request is a bit trickier than receiving parameters in a function call.

Phoenix expects that long chain of files because it helps keep code organized as applications grow complex, but most of the changes you need to make to build a simple application are confined to the controller and the template, with an occasional visit to *router.ex*. Until you start building complex applications that need to reuse code across multiple interfaces, you shouldn't need to make a lot of changes to the other files.

To get started, ask visitors some questions on that welcome page. This example uses the same fall velocity calculations as many previous examples, so you can focus on the form and the controller rather than the calculations. Phoenix supports a core set of functions that safely create HTML markup from data you provide.

Put the following in */web/templates/fall/welcome.html.eex*:

```
<h1>Falling starts now!</h1>

<%= form_for @conn, fall_path(@conn, :faller), [as: :calculation],
fn f -> %>
  <%= select f, :planemo, @choices %>
  <%= text_input f, :distance %>
  <%= submit "Calculate" %>
<% end %>
```

The h1 stays the same—it's just a headline—but `form_for` and its contents are all new. Elixir code surrounded by <%= and %> will produce results that turn up in the result HTML. (If it's surrounded by <% and %>, without the =, the Elixir will run but won't modify the HTML.) In this case, `form_for` is the core function, producing an HTML `form` element, and each of the lines in that function also produces some HTML (part of that form).

HTML forms need a few things to work. They need controls inside them to collect user input. In this case a selector and text input will tell our velocity calculator the information it needs. A submit button provides a way for the user to tell the form that the data is ready to be sent.

But where? How should that data be presented? In Phoenix, the form_for function handles all that. The first arguments about where the request came from and where the form response should go. @conn is the connection information that led to the form being presented, passed along through the whole chain. For now, this form will send its data to another page, which doesn't yet exist, connected to the :faller controller method. fall_path provides the information needed to send the data from the form in the browser back to your Phoenix server, and is the piece that will break when you load your page after making these changes.

The [as: :calculation] piece is required because this form isn't working with an underlying model. as: tells form_for how to present the collected information when it's sent back, as you'll see when the controller processes it. fn f creates a hook that the other pieces of the form use to access the information applying to the whole form.

Both the select and text_input functions take that f as their first argument. Their second argument is the name of the field that the controller will use to extract it when the form is submitted. select takes a third argument, @choices. (The @ makes it an *assign*, a variable that comes through from the controller.) That will provide the items in the select field, but it has to be provided by the controller, which doesn't exist yet.

Right now, of course, the template fails before it gets to the missing @choices assign, as shown in Figure 15-8.

ArgumentError at GET

No helper clause for Fall.Router.Helpers.fall_path/2 defined for action :faller. The following fall_path actions are defined under your router:

* :welcome

Figure 15-8. Broken again, pointing to a route that doesn't exist yet to a page that doesn't exist yet

Adding the new page will require adding a new entry to the routing file, as well as creating a new set of controller, view, and template files. Open up *web/router.ex*, and find the scope method. Add get "/fall", FallController, :faller just after the route for /welcome:

```
scope "/", Fall do
    pipe_through :browser # Use the default browser stack

    get "/welcome", FallController, :welcome
    get "/fall", FallController, :faller
    get "/", PageController, :index
end
```

That helps—but now that it has the route, Phoenix fails on the missing assign, as seen in Figure 15-9.

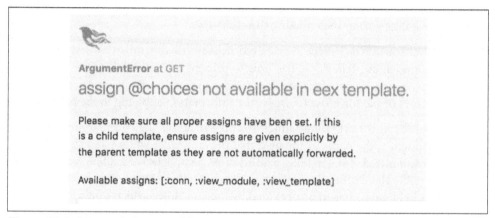

Figure 15-9. Just a missing variable now

Adding @choices requires one new line of code and an addition to the render call:

```
def welcome(conn, params) do
  choices = ["Earth": 1, "Moon": 2, "Mars": 3]
  render conn, "welcome.html", choices: choices
end
```

The choices probably look familar from earlier examples, and now Phoenix has all it needs to create the form in Figure 15-10.

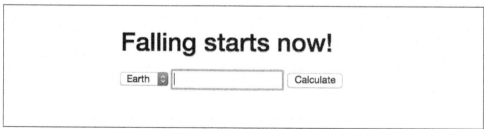

Figure 15-10. Form, presented

Excellent! A quick look at the form Phoenix generated provides some sense of what
form_for and its companions did:

```
<form accept-charset="UTF-8" action="/fall" method="post">
<input name="_csrf_token" type="hidden"
value="bnAhLkknegAwUXENPw48ByQ5FTYmJgAAZDjE0C+mY4+KNyuOOWwCHA==">
<input name="_utf8" type="hidden" value="✓">

<select id="calculation_planemo" name="calculation[planemo]">
  <option value="1">Earth</option>
  <option value="2">Moon</option>
  <option value="3">Mars</option>
 </select>

<input id="calculation_distance" name="calculation[distance]"
type="text">

<input type="submit" value="Calculate">
</form>
```

form_for created a lot by default and a little specific to your form. The action came
from the routing addition. The information about the UTF-8 charset (and the hidden
field for it), the method (POST), and the extra hidden CRSF prevention token all
came by default. The select is built out of content you provided, combining the
name from the as: argument with the names of the forms. This will make it easier to
pick out the form data later.

Now, pick a planemo, enter a distance, and hit Calculate. Figure 15-11 shows the not
so excellent result.

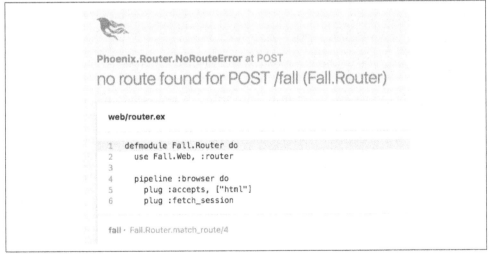

Figure 15-11. No place to go

Because form_for defaulted to the HTTP POST method, and the route added only handled GET, Phoenix is confused (though you could say it created the situation). Fix this by adding a POST route to *web/router.ex*:

```
scope "/", Fall do
    pipe_through :browser # Use the default browser stack

  get "/welcome", FallController, :welcome
  get "/fall", FallController, :faller
  post "/fall", FallController, :faller
  get "/", PageController, :index
  end
```

Now the route works, but Figure 15-12 demonstrates that it's time to build the path for the response.

Figure 15-12. Needing a function to answer the request

That's the last error message you should see for a while. Fortunately, creating a new set of pieces for the response will be easier, with most of the challenge in the controller. In the existing */web/controllers/fall_controller.ex* file, add a new function:

```
def faller(conn, params) do
  choices = ["Earth": 1, "Moon": 2, "Mars": 3]
  speed = 0
  render conn, "faller.html", speed: speed, choices: choices
end
```

Yes, that simply throws away the form data, but it also lets you build a template and make sure that all the connections are working before diving into the details of parameter handling.

In */web/templates/faller* ., create a new file called *faller.html.eex*. Make its contents look like *welcome.html.eex*, with a key change—a @speed reference in the headline:

```
<h1>Speed at impact was <%= @speed %> m/s.</h1>

<p>Fall again?</p>

<%= form_for @conn, fall_path(@conn, :faller), [as: :calculation],
fn f -> %>
  <%= select f, :planemo, @choices %>
```

```
    <%= text_input f, :distance %>
    <%= submit "Calculate" %>
  <% end %>
```

Technically you could skip the form for trying again if you wanted to, but Figure 15-13 shows what Phoenix created.

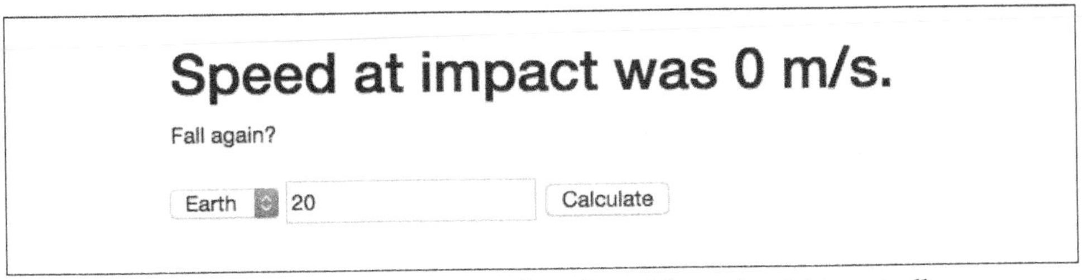

Speed at impact was 0 m/s.

Fall again?

| Earth ⬍ | 20 | | Calculate |

Figure 15-13. The speed may be zero, but data flowed from the right controller

To move into calculating and returning a real speed, you need to extract the parameters received from the form. In the terminal window where you ran Phoenix, you'll see something like:

```
[info] POST /fall
[debug] Processing by Fall.FallController.faller/2
  Parameters: %{"_csrf_token" => "bnAhLkknegAwUXENPw48ByQ5FTYmJgA
AZDjE0C+mY4+KNyuOOWwCHA==", "_utf8" => "✓", "calculation" =>
%{"distance" => "20", "planemo" => "1"}}
  Pipelines: [:browser]
[info] Sent 200 in 664µs
```

The `distance` and `planemo` parameters are there as maps, wrapped—as `form_for` said —in the `calculation` parameter. You have a few choices for how to get those parameters. `Map.get` can extract them for you. However, pattern matching seems more Elixir-like, and makes it easy to build controllers that smoothly handle things like requests that come without parameters. (Elixir lets things crash and doesn't worry. Web users are a little more particular.)

To grab the parameters, open up the */web/controllers/fall_controller.ex* file. Add another `faller` function that pattern matches instead of just accepting `params`, and some familiar `fall_velocity` functions to handle the calculations:

```
def faller(conn, %{"calculation" => %{"planemo" => planemo,
"distance" => distance}}) do
  calc_planemo = String.to_integer(planemo)
  calc_distance = String.to_integer(distance)
  speed = fall_velocity(calc_planemo, calc_distance)
  choices = ["Earth": 1, "Moon": 2, "Mars": 3]
  render conn, "faller.html", speed: speed, choices: choices
end

def fall_velocity(1, distance) do
```

```
    :math.sqrt(2 * 9.8 * distance)
  end

  def fall_velocity(2, distance) do
    :math.sqrt(2 * 1.6 * distance)
  end

  def fall_velocity(3, distance) do
    :math.sqrt(2 * 3.71 * distance)
  end
```

The pattern match at the start that replaces the `params` mention, `%{"calculation" => %{"planemo" => planemo, "distance" => distance}}`, matches the `calcula tion` map that should come from a normal form submission. It also breaks that down further, into `planemo` and `distance`.

The next two lines deal with another challenge in handling parameters from web forms: everything arrives as a string. The `String.to_integer/1` function handles the conversion, and you should expect to do explicit conversions on parameters routinely. Eventually you may want to create your own validation, to prevent errors caused by nonnumeric data, but this will get things started.

The calculations are familiar, and the results in Figure 15-14 should be too.

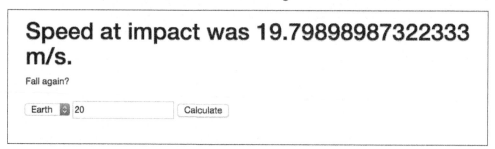

Speed at impact was 19.79898987322333 m/s.

Fall again?

Earth ⇕ | 20 | | Calculate |

Figure 15-14. Reporting the correct speed

Obviously, you're going to want to do more. Generating JSON and working with data both go well beyond the scope of this book. However, if you can make these parts work, you're ready to move further. The online documentation for Phoenix is generally good, and *Programming Phoenix* (Pragmatic Programmers) can take you deeper.

Sharing the Gospel of Elixir

While this concludes your introduction to Elixir, be aware that Elixir is a young language with a growing ecosystem, and there are many more features available for you to learn.

It may seem easy to argue for Elixir. The broad shift from single computers to networked and distributed systems of multiprocessor-based computing gives the Elixir/ Erlang environment a tremendous advantage over practically every other environment out there. More and more of the computing world is starting to face exactly the challenges that Elixir and Erlang were built to address. Veterans of those challenges may find themselves breathing a sigh of relief because they can stop pondering toolsets that tried too hard to carry single-system approaches into a multisystem world.

At the same time, though, we'd encourage you to consider a bit of wisdom from Joe Armstrong (*http://bit.ly/erlang-ques*): "New technologies have their best chance a) immediately after a disaster or b) at the start of a new project."

While it is possible you're reading this because a project you're working on has had a disaster (or you suspect it will have one soon), it's easiest to apply Elixir to new projects, preferably projects where the inevitable beginner's mistakes won't create new disasters.

Find projects that look like fun to you and that you can share within your organization or with the world. There's no better way to show off the power of a programming language and environment than to build great things with it!

An Elixir Parts Catalog

Like every language, Elixir has drawers full of parts that are fun to peruse, and there are many more available through Erlang.

These are a few of the more common ones, all represented using Elixir calling conventions. If you want (much, much) more, see the Erlang User Guide (*http://bit.ly/ erlang-docs*).

Shell Commands

You can use most Elixir functions from the shell, but the commands shown in Table A-1 are ones that are exclusive to the shell.

Table A-1. Elixir shell commands

Command	Action
c(*file*)	Compiles the specified Erlang file
c(*file,path*)	Compiles the specified file and puts object code in the directory specified by path
ls()	Lists files at the current location
ls(*path*)	Lists files at the specified path
cd(*directory*)	Changes to the specified directory
pwd()	Gets the present working directory
clear()	Clears the screen
h()	Prints list of available helpers
h(*item*)	Prints help for the specified item
l(*module*)	Loads the given module's code, purging the current version
m()	Lists all loaded modules
r(*module*)	Recompiles and reloads the given module's source file

Command	Action
v()	Prints a list of all commands and returned values for this session
v(*n*)	Retrieves the *n*th output value from the shell session
flush()	Flushes all messages sent to the shell

Reserved Words

There are a few Elixir terms you can't use outside of their intended context.

The Elixir compiler will wonder what you're trying to do if you use certain keywords as function names (see a list of these words in Table A-2). It will try to treat your functions as if they were code, and you can get very strange errors.

Table A-2. Reserved words that require careful use

after	and	catch	do	else	end	false	fn
in	nil	not	or	rescue	true	when	

The answer is simple: use something else.

There are also a few atoms commonly used in return values (see Table A-3). While these aren't reserved words, it's probably best to use them only in the circumstances where they're normally expected.

Table A-3. Commonly used return-value atoms

Atom	Means
:ok	Normal exit to a method. Does *not* mean that whatever you asked for succeeded.
:error	Something went wrong. Typically accompanied by a larger explanation.
:undefined	A value hasn't been assigned yet. Common in record instances.
:reply	A reply is included with some kind of return value.
:noreply	No return value is included. A response of some sort may come, however, from other communication.
:stop	Used in OTP to signal that a server should stop. Triggers the terminate function.
:ignore	Returned by an OTP supervisor process that can't start a child.

Operators

Table A-4. Logical (Boolean) operators

Operator	Operator	Description
and	&&	Logical and
or	||	Logical or
not	!	Unary logical not

The logical not operator has the highest precedence. and, &&, or, and || are short-circuit operators. If they don't need to process all the possibilities in their arguments, they stop at the first one that gives them a definite answer.

Operators in the first column require their argument(s) to be Boolean. Operators in the second column will accept any expression, with any value that is not false or nil treated as true. Because of short-circuiting, the && and || operators will return whichever value "decided" the ultimate true or false value. For example, nil || 5 returns 5, and nil && 5 returns nil.

Table A-5. Term-comparison operators

Operator	Description
==	Equal to
!=	Not equal to
<=	Less than or equal to
<	Less than
>=	Greater than or equal to
>	Greater than
===	Exactly equal to
!==	Exactly not equal to

You can compare elements of different types in Elixir. The relationship of types from "least" to "greatest" is:

```
number < atom < reference < fn < port < pid < tuple < list < bit string
```

Within number, you can compare integers and floats except with the more specific === and !== operators, both of which will return false when you compare numbers of different types.

You can also compare tuples even when they contain different numbers of values. Elixir will go through the tuples from left to right and evaluate on the first value that returns a clear answer.

Table A-6. Arithmetic operators

Operator	Description
+	Unary + (positive)
-	Unary – (negative)
+	Addition
-	Subtraction
*	Multiplication

Operator	Description
/	Floating-point division

To calculate integer division and integer remainder, use the `div` and `rem` functions. Thus, `div(17, 3)` yields 5, and `rem(17, 3)` yields 2.

Table A-7. Binary operators

Function	Operator	Description
bnot	~	Unary bitwise not
band	&&&	Bitwise and
bor	|||	Bitwise or
bxor	^	Arithmetic bitwise xor
bsl	<<<	Arithmetic bitshift left
bsr	>>>	Bitshift right

If you wish to use these operators and functions, your code must use `Bitwise`.

Table A-8. Operator precedence, from highest to lowest

Operator	Associativity
Unary + - ! ^ not ~~~	Not associative
=~ |>	Right
++ -- **	Right
<>	Right
* /	Left
+ -	Left
&&& |||	Left
..	Left
in	Left
< > <= >= == === != !==	Left
and	Left
or	Left
&&	Left
||	Left
<-	Right
=	Right
		Right
//	Right

Operator	Associativity
when	Right
::	Right
,	Left
->	Right
do	Left
@	Not associative

The highest-priority operator in an expression is evaluated first. Elixir evaluates operators with the same priority by following associative paths. (Left-associative operators go left to right, and right-associative operators go right to left.)

Guard Components

Elixir allows only a limited subset of functions and other features in guard expressions, going well beyond a "no side effects" rule to keep a simple subset of possibilities. The list of allowed components includes the following:

- `true`
- Other constants (regarded as `false`)
- Term comparisons (Table A-5)
- Arithmetic expressions (Tables A-6 and A-7)
- Boolean expressions and these logical operators: `and` and `or`
- The following functions: `hd/1`, `is_atom/1`, `is_binary/1`, `is_bitstring/1`, `is_boolean/1`, `is_float/1`, `is_function/1`, `is_function/2`, `is_integer/1`, `is_list/1`, `is_number/1`, `is_pid/1`, `is_port/1`, `is_record/1`, `is_record/2`, `is_reference/1`, `is_term/2`, `is_tuple/1`

Common Functions

Table A-9. Mathematical functions

Function	Use
`:math.pi/0`	The constant pi
`:math.sin/1`	Sine
`:math.cos/1`	Cosine
`:math.tan/1`	Tangent
`:math.asin/1`	Inverse sine (arcsine)

Function	Use
`:math.acos/1`	Inverse cosine (arcosine)
`:math.atan/1`	Inverse tangent (arctangent)
`:math.atan2/2`	Arctangent that understands quadrants
`:math.sinh/1`	Hyperbolic sine
`:math.cosh/1`	Hyperbolic cosine
`:math.tanh/1`	Hyperbolic tangent
`:math.asinh/1`	Hyperbolic arcsine
`:math.acosh/1`	Hyperbolic arccosine
`:math.atanh/1`	Hyperbolic arctangent
`:math.exp/1`	Exponential function
`:math.log/1`	Natural logarithm (base e)
`:math.log10/1`	Logarithm (base 10)
`:math.pow/2`	First argument to the second argument power
`:math.sqrt/1`	Square root
`:math.erf/1`	Error function
`:math.erfc/1`	Complementary error function

Arguments for all trigonometric functions are expressed in radians. To convert degrees to radians, divide by 180 and multiply by pi.

 The `erf/1` and `erfc/1` functions may not be implemented in Windows. The Erlang documentation (*http://bit.ly/2gP7A0Z*) also warns more broadly that "Not all functions are implemented on all platforms," but these come directly from the C-language libraries.

Table A-10. Approachable higher-order functions for processing collections and lists (take an enumerable and a function as arguments)

Function	Returns	Use
`Enum.each/2`	`:ok`	Performs the side effects specified in the function
`Enum.map/2`	New list	Applies the function to the list values
`Enum.filter/2`	Subset	Creates a list containing the items for which the function returns `true`
`Enum.all?/2`	Boolean	Returns `true` if the function is `true` for all values, otherwise `false`
`Enum.any?/2`	Boolean	Returns `true` if the function is `true` for any values, otherwise `false`
`Enum.take_while/2`	Subset	Collects the head of the list until the function is `true`
`Enum.drop_while/2`	Subset	Deletes the head of the list until the function is `true`
`List.foldl/3`	Accumulator	Passes the function a list value and an accumulator, moving forward through the list

Function	Returns	Use
`List.foldr/3`	Accumulator	Passes the function a list value and an accumulator, moving backward through the list
`Enum.partition/2`	Tuple of two lists	Splits the list based on the function

Chapter 8 describes these in greater detail.

Table A-11. Escape sequences for strings

Sequence	Produces
`\"`	Double quote
`\'`	Single quote
`\\`	Backslash
`\b`	Backspace
`\d`	Delete
`\e`	Escape
`\f`	Form feed
`\n`	Newline
`\r`	Carriage return
`\s`	Space
`\t`	Tab
`\v`	Vertical tab
`\x`XY	Character in hex
`\x{`X`...}`	Characters in hex, where X... is one or more hexadecimal characters
`^a...\^z` or `^A...\^Z`	Ctrl-A to Ctrl-Z

Table A-12. String sigils

Sigil	Meaning
`%c %C`	Returns a list of characters
`%r %R`	Returns a regular expression
`%s %S`	Returns a binary string
`%w %W`	Returns a list of words

Sigils created with lowercase letters will use escaping and interpolation as usual; those created with uppercase letters will be created exactly as written, with no escaping or interpolation.

Datatypes for Documentation and Analysis

Table A-13. Basic datatypes for @spec and ExDoc

atom()	binary()	float()	fun()	integer()	list()	tuple()
union()	node()	number()	String.t()	char()	byte()	[] (nil)
any()	none()	pid()	port()	reference()		

The type `String.t()` is used for Elixir binaries; the type `string()` is used for what Erlang calls strings but which are char lists in Elixir. For more on Erlang types, see the User's Guide (*http://erlang.org/doc/reference_manual/typespec.html*).

Generating Documentation with ExDoc

In Chapter 2, you learned how to add documentation to your programs. The ExDoc tool takes that documentation and produces nicely formatted reference documentation in web page format. ExDoc works in conjunction with Mix, a tool for creating, compiling, and testing projects. You can find out more about Mix in Chapter 13.

Using ExDoc with Mix

The easiest way to create documentation is to create a project using the Mix tool, using a command of the form:

```
mix new project_name
```

Here is what it looks like when creating the documentation for the code in Example 2-4:

```
$ mix new combined
* creating README.md
* creating .gitignore
* creating mix.exs
* creating lib
* creating lib/combined.ex
* creating test
* creating test/test_helper.exs
* creating test/combined_test.exs

Your mix project was created successfully.
You can use "mix" to compile it, test it, and more:

    cd combined
    mix test

Run "mix help" for more commands.
```

Change to the *combined* directory and put all of your source files (for this example, *combined.ex*, *drop.ex*, and *convert.ex*) into the *lib* directory. The *combined.ex* file you wrote before will replace the one that Mix created for you in the *lib* directory.

Now edit the file *mix.exs* so that the deps function reads as follows:

```
def deps do
  [{:ex_doc, github: "elixir-lang/ex_doc}]
end
```

Typing mix deps.get will install ExDoc in a directory named *deps*. If you have not yet installed Hex (Elixir's package manager), Mix will prompt you to do so. You can now compile all the Elixir files in one go using mix compile:

```
$ mix compile
==> ex_doc
Compiled lib/ex_doc/cli.ex
Compiled lib/ex_doc.ex
Compiled lib/ex_doc/markdown/cmark.ex
Compiled lib/ex_doc/markdown/earmark.ex
Compiled lib/ex_doc/markdown.ex
Compiled lib/ex_doc/markdown/hoedown.ex
Compiled lib/ex_doc/markdown/pandoc.ex
Compiled lib/mix/tasks/docs.ex
Compiled lib/ex_doc/formatter/html.ex
Compiled lib/ex_doc/retriever.ex
Compiled lib/ex_doc/formatter/html/templates.ex
Compiled lib/ex_doc/formatter/html/autolink.ex
Generated ex_doc app
==> combined
Compiled lib/convert.ex
Compiled lib/combined.ex
Compiled lib/drop.ex
Generated combined app
Consolidated List.Chars
Consolidated IEx.Info
Consolidated String.Chars
Consolidated Collectable
Consolidated Enumerable
Consolidated Inspect
```

You can then generate the documentation with mix docs. If you have a Markdown processor installed, it should all be smooth sailing. If you don't (one of the authors didn't on his Linux system), you might get an error message like this:

```
** (RuntimeError) Could not find a markdown processor to be used on ex_doc.
You can either:

1. Add {:markdown, github: "devinus/markdown"} to your mix.exs deps
2. Ensure pandoc (http://johnmacfarlane.net/pandoc) is available in your system
```

In our case, the first option seemed simpler, so we changed the function deps in *mix.exs* to:

```
defp deps do
  [ {:ex_doc, github: "elixir-lang/ex_doc"},
    {:markdown, github: "devinus/markdown"}]
end
```

We then did another mix deps.get:

```
* Getting markdown (git://github.com/devinus/markdown.git)
Cloning into '/Users/code/ex6-docs/combined/deps/markdown'...
remote: Reusing existing pack: 83, done.
remote: Total 83 (delta 0), reused 0 (delta 0)
Receiving objects: 100% (83/83), 12.52 KiB | 0 bytes/s, done.
Resolving deltas: 100% (34/34), done.
Checking connectivity... done.
* Getting hoedown (git://github.com/hoedown/hoedown.git)
Cloning into '/Users/code/ex6-docs/combined/deps/hoedown'...
remote: Counting objects: 1869, done.
remote: Compressing objects: 100% (805/805), done.
remote: Total 1869 (delta 1050), reused 1869 (delta 1050)
Receiving objects: 100% (1869/1869), 504.60 KiB | 481.00 KiB/s, done.
Resolving deltas: 100% (1050/1050), done.
Checking connectivity... done.
```

Then we redid the mix docs (which caused the Markdown processor to be compiled with the C compiler), recompiled the Elixir files, and finally created the documents. The following is the output without the compiler messages:

```
Compiled lib/markdown.ex
Generated markdown.app
==> combined
Compiled lib/convert.ex
Compiled lib/combined.ex
Compiled lib/drop.ex
Generated combined.app
%{green}Docs successfully generated.
%{green}View them at "doc/index.html".
```

Sure enough, listing the directory will now show a *doc* directory that contains an *index.html* file. The result will look like Figure B-1.

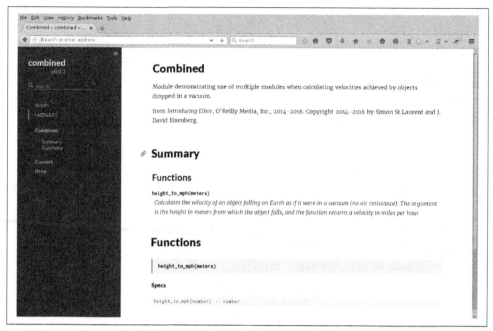

Figure B-1. Example of web page produced by ExDoc

Index

Symbols

! (exclamation point), 130
" (double quotes), 55
""" (three double quotes), 58
(hashtag) sign, 22
#{} operator, 56
$PATH variable, 3
%> notation, 200
%{} operator, 83
& (capture operator), 13, 17, 94
&1 notation, 94
' (single quotes), 59
* (multiplication) operator, 5
+ (addition) operator, 5
++ operator, 59, 68
- (subtraction) operator, 5
-> operator, 14, 40
-export directive, 19
-import directive, 19
/ (backslash) operator, 5
: (colon), 130
:dbg module (Erlang), 130
:debug logging level, 129
:error logging level, 129, 210
:ets.delete function, 160
:ets.delete/1 function, 154
:ets.first function, 160
:ets.fun2ms function, 160
:ets.give_away/3 function, 160
:ets.i() function, 156
:ets.info/1 function, 153
:ets.insert function, 160
:ets.insert/2 function, 154
:ets.last function, 160

:ets.lookup/2 function, 157
:ets.match function, 160
:ets.new/2 function, 152, 154
:ets.next function, 160
:ets.select function, 160
:ets.tab2list/1 function, 156
:ignore response, 210
:infinity atom, 173
:info logging level, 128
:keypos tuple, 153
:noop (no operation), 15
:noreply response, 173, 210
:observer.start() function, 156
:ok response, 15, 50, 210
:one_for_all function, 176
:one_for_one option, 176
:protected access level, 153
:reply response, 210
:stop response, 173, 210
:terminate/2 method, 173
:undefined response, 210
:warn logging level, 129
; (semicolon), 10
<%= notation, 200
<< notation, 130
<= comparison operator, 50
<> operator, 56, 59
== comparison operator, 50, 57
=== comparison operator, 50, 57
>= comparison operator, 50
? (question marks), 99
@doc tag, 23
@opaque, 138
@spec, 136

packaging an application with, 178-181
using ExDoc with, 217-219
working with modules, 13
Mnesia
  benefits of, 161
  creating tables, 162-165
  overload error message, 162
  reading data, 166
  starting up, 161
  using with Phoenix framework, 194
modules (see also functions)
  defining, 13-16
  documenting, 25-26
  importing functions from, 20
  passing functions from, 95
  spawning processes from, 105-108
  splitting code across, 17
multiplication (*) operator, 5

N

name-value pairs
  from lists to maps
    creating maps, 83
    maps vs. lists, 83
    reading maps, 84
    updating maps, 84
  from maps to structs
    adding behavior to structs, 89
    adding to existing protocols, 90
    creating/reading structs, 85
    maps vs. structs, 84
    pattern matching against structs, 86
    setting up structs, 85
    using structs in functions, 86-88
  hash dictionaries, 82
  keyword lists, 79
  lists of tuples with multiple keys, 81
  vs. tuples and lists, 79
negative numbers, 7
newlines
  IO.puts function and, 47
  separating pieces of functions with, 12, 56
  strings containing, 58
nil value, 43
"no match..." error, 70
no operation (:noop), 15
:noreply response, 173, 210

O

Observer tool (Erlang), 114, 156
:ok response, 15, 50, 210
:one_for_all option, 176
:one_for_one option, 176
only argument, 20
Open Telecom Platform (OTP), x
  benefits of, 169
  creating services with GenServer, 170-175
  Supervisor module, 175-178
  video introduction to, 170
operators
  arithmetic, 211
  atomic Booleans, 29
  binary, 212
  logical (Boolean), 210
  operator precedence, 212
  term comparison, 211
ordered sets, 151

P

parentheses, 6
Pascal's triangle, 74
pattern matching
  against records submitted as arguments, 148
  against structs, 86
  against structures submitted as arguments, 86
  inside of functions using case construct, 39
  with atoms, 27
  with tuples, 36
Persistent Lookup Table (PLT), 133
Phoenix framework
  basic application structuring, 194
  benefits of, 191
  calculating data, 200-206
  online documentation, 206
  page presentation
    routing, 195
    simple controller for, 197
    simple view for, 198
  resources for learning, 206
  skeleton installation, 191-193
  starting, 194
pid (process identifier), 103, 111
pipe (|>) operator, 19, 65
pipe forward (see |> (pipe) operator)
predicates, 99
"pretty printing", 91

About the Authors

Simon St.Laurent is a Content Manager at LinkedIn Learning, focusing primarily on the client side of the web. He is a past co-chair of the Fluent and OSCON conferences. He's authored or co-authored books including *Introducing Elixir*, *Introducing Erlang*, *Learning Rails 3*, *XML Pocket Reference*, 3rd edition, *XML: A Primer*, and *Cookies*.

You can find more of his writing on technology, Quakerism, and the Town of Dryden at *simonstl.com*.

J. David Eisenberg is a programmer and instructor living in San Jose, CA. David has a talent for teaching and explaining. He has developed courses for HTML and CSS, JavaScript, XML, and Perl. He also teaches computer and information technology courses at Evergreen Valley College in San Jose and has developed online courses providing introductory tutorials for Korean, Modern Greek, and Russian. David has been developing education software since 1975, when he worked with the Modern Foreign Language project at the University of Illinois to develop computer-assisted instruction on the PLATO system. He is coauthor of *SVG Essentials* (O'Reilly). When not programming, David enjoys digital photography, caring for a feral cat colony at work, and riding his bicycle.

Colophon

The animal on the cover of *Introducing Elixir* is a four-horned antelope (*Tetracerus quadricornis*), found in India and Nepal. Also called *chousingha*, these antelope are the smallest of Asian bovids, standing at 22 to 25 inches at the shoulder and weighing from 37 to 49 pounds. They have a slender build with thin legs and short tails, and a yellow-brown or reddish coat that fades to white on the underbelly and inner legs. They also have a black stripe of hair that runs down each leg. The antelope's most distinctive features are the four horns seen on males: two between the ears, which grow in at just a few months' age, and two on the forehead, which grow in after 10 to 14 months. The front pair can reach about 2 inches whereas the hind pair can grow nearly 4 inches in length.

Four-horned antelope tend to live near a water supply and in areas with significant vegetation cover, such as from tall grass or heavy undergrowth. They are generally solitary animals, occasionally found in groups of up to four, and they tend to avoid human-inhabited areas. During mating season—May to July—males can become aggressive toward other males. Gestation lasts around eight months and usually results in one or two young, which remain with their mothers for about a year, reaching sexual maturity at two years.

The antelope communicate through alarm calls, which sound like a husky "phronk," and through scent marking (leaving piles of droppings to mark their territory or using large scent glands in front of their eyes to mark vegetation).

Because they live in such a densely populated area of the world, the four-horned antelope's natural habitat is threatened by agricultural development. This species is listed as Vulnerable by the International Union for Conservation of Nature (IUCN) because of habitat loss. They have also become a target for trophy hunters who seek their unusual horned skull. There are estimated to be only around 10,000 individuals of this species left in the wild; many are being protected in animal conservatories. The four-horned antelope is protected under the Indian Wildlife Protection Act.

Many of the animals on O'Reilly covers are endangered; all of them are important to the world. To learn more about how you can help, go to *animals.oreilly.com*.

The cover image is from *Wood's Animate Creation*. The cover fonts are URW Typewriter and Guardian Sans. The text font is Adobe Minion Pro; the heading font is Adobe Myriad Condensed; and the code font is Dalton Maag's Ubuntu Mono.